The Carefree Cook

Also by Rick Rodgers

Best Barbecues Ever with Irena Chalmers (Longmeadow, 1990)

Best-Ever Brownies with Joan Steuer (Contemporary, 1990)

The Turkey Cookbook (HarperCollins, 1990)

365 Ways to Cook Hamburger and Other Ground Meats (HarperCollins, 1991)

Best-Ever Chocolate Desserts (Contemporary, 1992)

The Slow Cooker Ready and Waiting Cookbook (Morrow, 1992)

Mr. Pasta's Healthy Pasta Cookbook (Morrow, 1994)

Mississippi Memories with The Delta Queen Steamboat Co. (Morrow, 1994)

*The Perfect Parties Series: Picnics and Tailgate Parties; Bridal and Baby Showers;
    Romantic Dinners and Breakfasts; Birthday Celebrations* (Warner, 1996)

On Rice: 60 Toppings That Make the Meal (Chronicle Books, 1997)

50 Best Stuffings and Dressings (Broadway Books, 1997)

Fondue: Fabulous Food to Dip, Dunk, Savor and Swirl (Morrow, 1998)

Simply Shrimp (Chronicle Books, 1998)

Thanksgiving 101 (Broadway Books, 1998)

Fried and True (Chronicle Books, 1999)

Christmas 101 (Broadway Books, 1999)

Pressure Cooking for Everyone (Chronicle Books, 2000)

Williams-Sonoma: Chicken with Chuck Williams (Time-Life, 2001)

Barbecues 101 (Broadway Books, 2001)

*Kaffeehaus: Exquisite Desserts from the Classic Cafés of Vienna, Budapest, and
    Prague* (Clarkson Potter, 2002)

Dip It! (Morrow, 2002)

The Carefree Cook

RICK RODGERS

Broadway Books

New York

PRINTED IN THE UNITED STATES OF AMERICA

BROADWAY BOOKS and its logo, a letter B bisected on the diagonal, are trademarks of Random House, Inc.

Visit our website at www.broadwaybooks.com

Book design by Ph.D., www.phdla.com

Photography by William Meppem

Library of Congress Cataloging-in-Publication Data

Rodgers, Rick, 1953–

    The carefree cook / Rick Rodgers.

        p.   cm.

    1. Cookery. I. Title

TX714.R617 2003

641.5—dc21

                                        2002043882

    ISBN 0-7679-1463-5

First edition published 2003

10 9 8 7 6 5 4 3 2 1

Acknowledgments

As I write this, I feel like I'm gathering snapshots of friends and family for a scrapbook. I know I am very lucky to have such a roster of loyal friends and colleagues whose names and faces crop up so often in my life.

You would not be reading this book if not for Broadway Books' continued belief in my cooking and teaching. It's not often that a food writer is at a loss for words, but as I try to express my gratitude to Broadway's unique group of talented people, I have reached one of those rare obstacles. Publisher Steve Rubin championed this book from the very first day and a mere "thank you" is hardly adequate for a man who gave me a new perspective on my work. My deepest appreciation, as always, to editor Jennifer Josephy, Executive Director of Marketing Jackie Everly-Warren, publicist Jenny Danquist, and editorial assistant Laura Marshall, as well as art director John Fontana and the book's designers, Ph.D.

In my kitchen, nothing would get done without the help of Diane Kniss and Steve Evasew, both wonderful cooks and irreplaceable friends. Diane is the sister I would have chosen for myself, and Steve has saved me more than once from culinary disaster. Also, thanks to David Bonom for his expertise. Long may we chop!

We had a terrific crew for the food photography: photographer William Meppem, food stylist William Smith, and prop stylist Joe Maer. And the back cover photo gang was equally professional and fun to be with: photographer Brian Doben, producer Nancy Corbett, stylist Elisa Flowers, food stylist Jennifer Cohen, and special thanks to my "personal shopper" for the shoot, Solange Amar. I am now addicted to new eye frames.

Susan Ginsburg, the agent of every writer's dreams, and her charming assistants, Annie Leuenberger and Rachel Spector, are incredibly adept at making the business side of my job as carefree as my cooking.

The cooking schools where I teach supply a constant source of taste-testers and inspiration. Thanks to Arlene Ward at Adventures in Cooking, Doraece Dullaghan and the

various cooking school staffs at Sur La Table across the country, Cathy Cocharan-Lewis at Central Markets, Chan Patterson at the Viking Culinary Centers, Pamela Keith, formerly of Draeger's, Phyllis Vacarelli at Let's Get Cooking, Bob Nemerovski at Ramekins, and Sue Sell at Cook 'n' Tell. But we can't do it without the students, who, unfortunately, can't be named individually.

A special word of appreciation to my friends at *Bon Appétit*, food editor Kristine Kidd and editor in chief Barbara Fairchild, who have allowed me to share my recipes with a new audience via that fine magazine.

And finally, I raise my glass to the three people I would rather cook for than anyone else in the world, my partner Patrick Fisher and my parents Dick and Eleanor Rodgers.

Contents

Introduction Recently my buddy Tom Douglas, one of America's top chefs and the owner of some of Seattle's most popular eateries, came to town. We got together with a few other food professionals for a potluck dinner. As if to challenge the image projected by many food writers, who must want you to think that they constantly wallow in four-star splendor (the kind of chefs who surely put truffle oil on their cereal in the morning), our menu would have surprised most cookbook readers. ¶ Tom made pasta with shellfish in a spicy sausage sauce, somewhat similar to the roasted clams on page 184. My contribution was the braised short ribs on page 104. Another friend simply tossed broccoli rabe with garlic oil and roasted it in a very hot oven for a few minutes until it was tender. Dessert was a simple chocolate cake that someone else had brought from home.

No one shaved truffles on anything, rubbed gold foil on dessert, or baked bread with a sourdough starter that took two weeks to nurture. And this group consisted of chefs, food writers, and cookbook editors.

The utter simplicity and fabulous flavors of our repast prompted a discussion on the vast difference between restaurant cooking and home cooking. In a restaurant, complicated garnishes and multiple sauces can be used in a dish because there are a lot of people working in the kitchen. At home, most people are thrilled to have some-one who is willing to help with the dishes! We also noted how many examples of rus-tic cooking have found their way onto chic menus—short ribs or macaroni and cheese, anyone?

Some very passionate home cooks want to learn professional techniques and recipes, even if they take days of preparation and mountains of pots. And you can learn valuable information from a chef's cookbook, even if you don't have the energy to re-create the food. But most cookbook readers are still struggling with the basics. They want to cook delicious meals, but they think they don't have the time, or they have run out of ideas.

The Carefree Cook is about how to get fantastic flavors in your everyday cook-ing with a minimum of effort. It is *not* about cooking with less than five ingredients, or getting dinner on the table in fifteen minutes. Nonetheless, wherever feasible, I have kept the ingredients lists short, and very few recipes have more than five steps. The many dishes that can be cooked in under thirty minutes have been designated with a note at the top of the recipe.

I have nothing against fast and easy cooking, but the habits of my many cook-ing students show that "slow food" also has a place in the kitchen of the busiest home cook. If a recipe requires only a few initial steps and then cooks without any additional effort for a couple of hours, it is a wise investment of time for the return of a deeply fla-vorful meal. Slow food is best for weekend cooking, when we usually have more time to spend in the kitchen, happily chopping, tasting, and simmering our way to a satisfy-ing and tasty conclusion. There is no quick way to caramelize onions or roast garlic, nor any substitute for their complex, delicious flavors, so why pretend that there is?

I have learned new ways to think about a dish, looking ahead to recycle it as another meal—I prefer the term "bonus recipe" to "leftovers." No matter what you call it, it saves incalculable time and effort to make a large batch of a terrific stew on Sunday, then turn some of the leftovers into a tasty pasta sauce for Monday and freeze the remaining portion for another meal.

While I've provided plenty of recipes that can and should be served to company, I've concentrated on "weeknight" food, not dishes for entertaining. On the other hand, soups and salads make fine first courses at a dinner party, and these have their own chapters. Because there are few better ways to brighten a day than a great homemade dessert, I include the easiest and best recipes for sweets that I have collected over the years.

The Carefree Cook is also about learning. As a cooking teacher, I know that the more you understand ingredients and techniques, the better your food will be. So you will find tips, tricks, and other information throughout the book that will help you in the kitchen. And I have written detailed recipes to be sure that your version of a dish turns out as well as mine. I don't want you to cook with a stopwatch by your side, because there are many variables that change a recipe—the exact heat of your stovetop flame, for example. But I resisted writing "short" recipes just to give the reader the impression that every recipe can be made in the blink of an eye.

One of the reasons I am a carefree cook is because I have confidence in the kitchen. There are many ways to gain such confidence. The best way is practice, learning from your cooking experiences. And, frankly, lack of basic cooking skills gets in the way of carefree cooking. No recipe will be carefree if it takes you five minutes to chop an onion. For this reason, I have included a knife skills primer on page 12. Another way to become confident in the kitchen is to read cookbooks and cooking magazines, to pick up tips that you can apply to your regular cooking routine. Professional savvy can be applied to the most humble meal. In fact, the old adage "Knowledge is power" is especially true in the kitchen. Some television shows dispense cooking knowledge while providing entertainment, but learning the difference between the two is becoming increasingly difficult.

And, finally, this book is about sharing. I am often asked how I come up with so many recipe ideas for my cookbooks. It's all about being observant (I never go to a restaurant without coming across a new recipe concept that I can't wait to get home and try) and being willing to learn from others. I have been very, very lucky in my career to cook next to some of the best cooks and bakers in the food business. Many of my readers don't realize that I also consult for other cookbook writers, testing recipes and generally helping them get their cooking out of their heads and down on paper. This aspect of my professional life has been extremely rewarding, and I have learned a lot from these clients. So if you see me mentioning the names of some of your favorite cooks, don't think I am name-dropping—it's more like sharing a recipe, technique, or idea that I "swapped" with that person.

The more you cook, the more confident you become as a cook. That confidence will translate into a new freedom, one that allows you also to become a *carefree* cook. I hope that you will flip through this book and find many appetizing recipes that make you want to run into the kitchen and start cooking immediately. But even more important, I hope that these recipes will make you exclaim, "Hey, I can do that!"

The Secrets of a Carefree Cook

When I cook with friends in my kitchen, it's a very casual affair. Occasionally I pull out the stops for an elegant dinner with all the crystal and fine china, but usually my guests sit on stools at the counter and we all chat while I toss dinner together. I always get some kind of a remark like, "You make it look so easy!" With the right tools and ingredients (and attitude), it *is* easy . . . and fun.

I have to smile with gentle exasperation when I think of the many times I have cooked in an ill-equipped kitchen: kitchens with one scratched nonstick skillet that is barely large enough to hold two chops; an oven with two settings, "off" and "incinerate"; and ancient, flavorless dried herbs that seem to be from the owner's high school days. The people these kitchens belong to tend to say, "I love cooking, but my food never turns out right." No wonder.

In my years as a professional cook (I don't call myself a chef, because I believe that name should be reserved for those talented and stalwart individuals who face the challenges of running a restaurant—an experience I have already had in my life and don't feel the urge to repeat), I have observed a few important tricks that usually result in better cooking.

Use the best pots and pans you can afford   I never had any complaints about my old set of pots and pans, a well-known mid-priced cookware brand that I bought for my first apartment kitchen, but gradually, piece by piece, I upgraded to a top-of-the-line brand, and my cooking changed dramatically. The heavy aluminum core in these pans distributed the heat beautifully, so my food was less prone to scorching, and the stainless-steel interior was easy to clean.

Every cook should have a heavy 12-inch skillet, which is quite large but will easily hold four chops or a whole chicken. This large surface area is important, because when food is crowded in a pan, it gives off too much steam and won't brown well—and caramelized surfaces mean great flavor. I like a stainless-steel interior because it encourages the best browning. Well-equipped kitchens have both regular and nonstick skillets, because a nonstick pan is very helpful for certain foods.

A good knife is worth Its weight in gold   One of the reasons some people become frustrated with cooking is because they are using dull or flimsy knives. In fact, you need at least three knives to be well equipped: a chef's knife, a paring knife, and a medium-length knife. The right knife is very personal—it must fit your hand and have the proper weight to use without tiring. Get knives that can be sharpened (serrated knives are perfect for slicing bread but they do other, less obvious jobs as well), and keep them sharp. See "A Primer on Knife Skills" on page 12, for more tips.

Be adventurous with your groceries   As a cooking teacher, I travel all over the country, and I am amazed at the availability of international foods in grocery stores. Ingredients that used to require a trip to a special ethnic grocer can now be found at the corner store—mascarpone cheese, Kalamata olives, and hoisin sauce, to name just a few. Cooks in more rural areas may have to search a little, but the added variety in your cooking will be worth the effort. And with shopping on the Internet becoming the norm, there is really no excuse for good cooks not to expand their horizons with new flavors. You will not find a listing of mail-order sources in this book, because there isn't one ingredient that I didn't buy in my suburban New Jersey supermarket, and I do not want to send the message that exotic groceries are the norm in my recipes. If you are stuck for a grocery item that you want to try, a simple Web search will yield dozens of sources.

On the other hand, many of my students get annoyed when they buy an ingredient that they rarely use again (although many ethnic condiments and spices are downright cheap). Keeping this in mind, I've used any less familiar groceries in more than one recipe in this book, and the individual ingredients sidebars include ideas for adding them to everyday cooking.

I make it a rule in my cooking classes never to cook with an ingredient that I cannot get in the school's neighborhood. I find it amusing and also a little sad when I hear a student say, "We can't get that here," and I then inform them that I bought the ingredient nearby at a store they have never been in. So get to know the ethnic grocers in your area, and give them a try. You never know what you will come across.

Use your freezer wisely   Remember, frozen food does not last forever. There are few things that freeze well for over six months. If a frozen food is reaching that time limit, cook it and use the freezer space for something else.

Be relentless about keeping your freezer stocked with things that you will really use. In my life, that means quarts of homemade soups and pasta sauce; pints of homemade beef stock (see page 11 for a discussion of homemade beef stock versus canned broth); bags of frozen corn, petite peas, and lima beans (these ingredients can be quickly thawed in a bowl of hot water, drained, and added to many dishes for additional color and flavor); and pancetta and chorizo to provide international seasoning in my cooking.

Use "Seasoning Secrets"   In a few cases, I make my own condiments and herb blends to add zest to everyday meals. Just a spoonful or two of pesto or olivada mixed with sautéed vegetables, or stirred into mashed potatoes or couscous, or spread under chicken skin before roasting changes a mundane dish into something special. Most of these condiment blends are available at supermarkets or gourmet shops, but I prefer homemade versions because I can control the final result, adding more garlic or less red pepper, for example, as I wish. Herb blends are also easy to buy, but if the ingredients are already in my spice cabinet, why not make my own to save money? None of these are hard or time-consuming to make, yet they provide weeks (months, in the case of the herb blends) of flavor.

Cajun Seasoning (page 36)
Italian Herb Seasoning (page 100)
Olivada (page 137)
Five-Spice Powder (page 147)

Herbes de Provence (page 165)

Porcini Powder (page 179)

Year-Round Salsa (page 236)

Sun-Dried Tomato Pesto (page 251)

Pesto (page 268)

Think ahead   There are only two of us in my household, but I never make just two servings of a dish. Look ahead for ways that leftovers can be served at future meals to save time and effort.

A large chicken roasted tonight means chicken salad for tomorrow's lunch or a chicken casserole for the next night's supper. The extra servings from virtually any meat stew with vegetables can be simmered with crushed tomatoes to make a pasta sauce. My Viennese Pot Roast (page 108) provides a main course, leftovers for sandwiches, *and* homemade beef stock. Grilled salmon today becomes salmon cakes tomorrow.

Season your food with authority   One of the most glaring differences between restaurant chefs and home cooks is the way they season. While restaurant food can sometimes be oversalted, most home cooks are guilty of underseasoning. Sometimes the difference between a bland dish and a vibrant one is a sprinkle of salt. Although I am not taking medical concerns into account here, at least the salt that one puts on one's food is a visible amount. Most health professionals agree that the hidden salt in processed foods is seriously affecting the American diet. However, if you are on a low-sodium diet, I am not suggesting indiscriminate salting.

For the recipes in this book, I used iodized table salt because it is the salt found in most homes. There are many different salts, including expensive imported salts, and they all have their individual attributes. They each have a unique taste with various degrees of saltiness, and their various crystallizations make for different volume measurements. For example, because kosher salt crystals are larger than iodized salt, kosher salt measures differently, and will be less salty than the same volume of iodized salt, which has finer crystals. If I used 1 teaspoon kosher salt in my testing, but you used 1 teaspoon iodized salt, your dish could be ruined by oversalting. One can always add more salt to a dish to taste, but oversalted food is very difficult to correct.

Actually, I have about six different kinds of salt in my kitchen. Iodized salt dissolves well in batters and doughs (although some professional bakers say they can taste the iodine and won't use it). I use crunchy French fleur de sel more as a garnish for simply prepared vegetables where its flavor can shine, and coarse sea salt goes into the cooking water for my pasta and vegetable water and tops some of my home-baked breads. Plain salt (without iodine or other additives), sometimes called pickling salt, is used in preserves, because it won't cloud the pickling liquid. I like coarse kosher salt for seasoning meat because I can see the distribution more readily than with fine salt. Tasted individually, each salt has its own flavor and texture profile, but in cooked foods, the differences are subtle. Could I survive in a kitchen with just iodized salt? You betcha.

As for that other component of the seasoning team, pepper, suffice it to say that everything you've heard about freshly ground pepper is true. It does make a huge difference. But be sure to get an efficient pepper mill. I teach in plenty of schools where the mills are pretty but badly designed—they are hard to hold and dispense such a minute amount of pepper that the cook has to stand over the food cranking away like a mad organ grinder. Most kitchenware shops have pepper mills filled with peppercorns on display for testing—so choose one that *works.*

In recipes where the food can be tasted to assess the seasoning, I say "Salt to taste." However, when the salt seasons a raw food that makes it difficult to judge the correct amount, I give a measured volume. This means that the food will be seasoned to *my* taste—every cookbook writer assumes that home cooks will make some adjustments for what works best for them.

When seasoning with salt and pepper together, first mix the measured amounts in a small bowl. This combined salt-and-pepper is much easier to sprinkle evenly over the food, especially when working with small amounts, such as 1/8 teaspoon pepper.

Million-Dollar Flavors

The pantries and refrigerators of good cooks look different from those of uninspired home cooks. The shelves are lined with bottles of "secret ingredients," the bold-tasting foods that automatically punch up the flavors of everyday foods. I admit that some of these foods may have some enemies—we all know anchovy haters. The trick is to use them in quantities that don't call attention to their presence. Here are a few of my favorites.

Anchovies These salty little fish are finding more friends. The most commonly available anchovies are fillets in oil, canned or in jars. After using a few, cover the remaining fillets with olive or vegetable oil, cover tightly with plastic wrap (or the jar's lid), and refrigerate to store for a week or so. Some Mediterranean delicatessens carry large anchovy fillets packed in salt, but because they are a somewhat esoteric ingredient, I won't say any more than that they are excellent and worth searching out if you like anchovies. Anchovy paste is available in tubes at many supermarkets and Italian grocers, works well as a substitute for chopped anchovies, and is convenient to store.

Blue cheese There are many blue cheeses with distinctive flavors. For most cooking, use a supermarket Danish blue cheese or Roquefort—they aren't overly salty and they crumble well. A bit of blue cheese added to dishes with Cheddar or Swiss will boost the cheese profile without making the dish taste overwhelmingly like "blue cheese."

Capers The buds of a Mediterranean bush (the smallest and most prized are labeled "nonpareil"), they are typically pickled and bottled in brine. Remove them from their brine and rinse before using. They can be tricky to get out of the bottle, so if you lose some of the brine, replace it with water and a splash of vinegar. It is interesting to note that capers are never served fresh—their flavor can only develop with preserving.

Crystallized ginger A couple of tablespoons of chopped crystallized ginger will add flair to many fruit desserts. The plump cubes have better flavor than the thin slices. Crystallized ginger is available at many natural food stores and Asian markets in bulk.

Mustard Dijon mustard is the most versatile in this family of condiments, but look for a brand that isn't too hot. Herb-flavored or sweet mustards can spark up sandwiches and many other dishes.

Olives Mediterranean olives have more flavor than the canned California brands. Vinegar-preserved black Kalamata olives are now available pitted at many supermarkets, a real timesaver. If you have to pit olives, don't bother with an olive pitter, a gadget that requires too much fumbling. Simply place an olive on a work surface and lay a chef's knife or cleaver across it, with the wide flat side of the blade parallel to the work surface. Give the blade a whack with your fist to smash the olive. Pick out and discard the pit. Don't worry that the olive is smashed—olives are usually coarsely chopped before using. Get into a rhythm, and you can whip through a mound of olives in no time.

Olive oil   For my everyday cooking, I use a moderately priced extra-virgin olive oil, such as Bertolli or Colavita. Some cooks recommend regular (formerly called pure) olive oil for sautéing; I prefer the richer flavor of the extra-virgin oil, and the heat does not adversely affect the flavor. In Tuscany, I have seen cooks deep-fry with unfiltered extra-virgin olive oil (something that would be prohibitively expensive here), which disproves the myth that one shouldn't expose olive oil to high temperatures. Occasionally, for special meals, I will drizzle an estate-bottled olive oil over simply cooked foods as a condiment. Store olive oil in a cool, dark place.

Pork products   A little bit of pork goes a long way in adding flavor to savory dishes. There are two preserved pork products that I always have on hand. *Pancetta* is an unsmoked bacon easily found at Italian grocers, if not your local supermarket. Buy it in 1-pound chunks and keep it frozen. When you need a slice or two for a recipe, a serrated knife will saw through the frozen slab. You can substitute regular bacon, but it will add a smoky and sometimes sweet flavor that may not go with every dish. If you wish (although I admit I often skip it) to remove some of these flavors, place the sliced bacon in a small saucepan of cold water and bring to a simmer over low heat. Drain and rinse before using.

Chorizo, a spicy sausage popular in Mexican and Spanish cuisines, is most useful when processed into smoked semi-hard links. Don't confuse it with bulk chorizo, which hasn't been smoked and is still raw. Store the chorizo in the freezer—the small links defrost quickly at room temperature. If you live in a Portuguese neighborhood, *linguiça*, which is a bit chunkier and has a more distinct vinegar flavor, is a good substitute. Or use Italian pepperoni, which, I admit, isn't all that similar to either chorizo or linguiça, but works very well in a pinch.

Vinegar With the advent of balsamic vinegar, cooks are appreciating the subtleties of this humble ingredient more and more. A simple thing like changing the vinegar in your salad dressing can be eye-opening. Although moderately priced balsamic vinegar can be found at supermarkets, more expensive gourmet-store brands will reveal many new layers of flavor. I am not suggesting that you cook with a twenty-five-year-old artisan brand, but the best balsamics will really enhance a dish. Fruit-infused vinegars, in flavors such as currant, fig, or cherry, will bring new dimensions to your salad dressings. Recently, special wine vinegars, such as sweet late-harvest Riesling, are appearing, and they can add variety to your cooking as well. Rice vinegar has a mild acidity that works well in Asian recipes.

Taking Stock

Most professional chefs advocate the use of homemade stocks, and I will not deny that well-made stocks are great. However, most home cooks don't have the time to make from-scratch stocks, and even I use canned broth for my everyday cooking. (Technically, a stock is made from bones, usually unsalted, and used as an ingredient in a recipe; broth is made with meat and bones and is seasoned so it can be served as a finished soup, if the cook so wishes.) Some supermarkets have frozen chicken and beef stocks that are very good—give them a try.

Canned chicken broth can be a good product, but it varies greatly from brand to brand. Buy well-known brands and you will be happy—I have ruined a dish more than once by using an inexpensive house label or an unfamiliar "all-natural, unsalted" broth. Reduced-sodium broth tastes more like chicken and less like salt, and I always use it.

One $13^{3}/_{4}$-ounce can of chicken broth equals $1^{3}/_{4}$ cups. What should you do if a recipe calls for 2 cups? Simply add $^{1}/_{4}$ cup water to the canned broth to get the 2 cups. The minor dilution won't hurt at all, and some cooks feel that it actually mellows the "canned" flavor.

In my kitchen, I rarely use beef broth. First of all, canned chicken broth is a neutral ingredient that often works with red meat. But the main problem is finding an acceptable canned beef broth. Instead of using beef broth in soups and stews, use meaty cuts with lots of bones and sinew, such as short ribs, which lend lots of flavor to the cooking liquid without the need for canned broth.

But there are times when a homemade beef stock is the only way to go. For the most convenient way to make it, cook the Viennese Pot Roast (page 108), which gives a couple of quarts of leftover beef stock as a bonus—freeze it in 1-pint containers, and you will be happy you did.

Some cooks use canned clam juice as a substitute for fresh fish stock, but I use it sparingly. As it can be quite salty, it's best to get in the habit of diluting it with an equal amount of water.

A Primer on Knife Skills

As a traveling cooking teacher, I cook alongside people all over the country. While there are exceptions, few home cooks really know how to use a knife. One of the most common questions I hear is, "Can I chop the vegetables in the food processor?" When I say no, I am faced with an audience of crestfallen faces. (While the food processor is a fine time-saver for many kitchen chores, it's difficult to process-chop vegetables into evenly shaped pieces, and onions, in particular, give off too much of their juices.)

Many cooks simply never bother to deconstruct the process of chopping an onion or dicing a carrot, and just do the best they can. There have been many technological improvements in the kitchen, but nothing can truly replace a sharp knife and a pair of hands. The best place to learn how to use a chef's knife is a hands-on cooking class, which are offered at a range of venues from kitchenware shops to vocational culinary schools to small community colleges and recreational centers. Actually, I correct myself: the best place is really your own kitchen, as practice makes perfect—but it helps to have some personal guidance. To help novices to the world of chopping and dicing, here is a short primer.

Choose your weapon   I recently cooked at the home of a friend who says he can't cook. After trying to chop vegetables with the only knife in his kitchen (a whiz-bang "never needs sharpening!" wonder that he'd purchased from a television infomercial during a night of insomnia), I understood his frustration. He was sabotaged by his cooking equipment. It boils down to this: if you have bad knives, you will be a bad cook. Period.

As mentioned earlier, a well-equipped kitchen has at least three knives—a chef's knife for chopping and most cutting chores, a paring knife for produce, and a medium-sized thin-bladed utility knife. Almost as necessary are a serrated knife for crusty breads and a long, thin carving knife for holiday roasts. There are many fine brands of knives available at kitchenware shops. Most home cooks prefer stainless-steel knives because they are easy to care for. While high-carbon-steel knives hold their edge well, they stain easily. When buying a knife, always hold it in your hand to assess its weight and balance, which is a purely personal evaluation.

Knives that purport to "never need sharpening" simply cannot be sharpened, though they will dull with use. They should be avoided.

Stay sharp Regardless of the type of knives you have, keep them sharp! A knife should be honed on a sharpening steel every time it is used—the idea is to *keep* the knife sharp, not neglect it to dullness. A sharp knife is actually safer than a dull one, as it is less apt to slip during slicing. Even properly maintained knives should be sent out for a professional sharpening every few months or so. Your local kitchenware shop should be able to recommend a sharpening service: it might be as close as the neighborhood hardware or shoe repair shop. And many farmers' markets have sharpening stalls.

A sharpening steel should be purchased along with your first high-quality knife, but, unfortunately, the steel is often considered an unnecessary expense. Here's a great way to sharpen a knife, even without a steel. Ceramic materials, which are very hard, can be used to sharpen metal knives. Turn a flat-bottomed ceramic coffee cup upside down. Slide the sharp edge of the knife along the bottom of the cup, running the knife from the bottom of the blade toward its top. Turn the knife over and repeat on the other side of the blade. After a few passes on each side, the blade will be noticeably sharper.

Chopping onions and garlic No one has come up with a surefire way to stop the tears caused by chopping onions, but a good sharp chef's knife will make the job go more quickly. (Apply the same method to shallots, which are essentially small onions.)

Start by trimming off the top and bottom of the onion. Make an incision down the side of the onion, and peel off the skin. (Don't be concerned if you remove a layer of onion with the skin, as there are plenty more layers in every onion.) With the onion standing on one end, cut it lengthwise in half.

You can begin the actual chopping procedure at either end, but for the sake of clarity, let's assume a right-handed cook. Place one onion half flat side down on the work surface. Starting at the right end, make two or three parallel horizontal cuts, stopping about 1/4 to 1/2 inch from the opposite end to keep the onion layers together. (The closer these parallel cuts, the finer the chop will be.) Now, again starting at the right end, make three or four vertical parallel cuts into the onion, again stopping just short of the left end. Working from the right toward the left, cut through the onion at 1/2-inch intervals to slice it into evenly chopped pieces. When you reach the end where the layers are still connected, simply chop it up as best you can or discard it.

The same principles, on a smaller scale, can be applied to chopping garlic. I don't have much use for garlic-peeling gadgets. Just place the garlic clove on the work surface, cover it with the widest part of your chef knife's blade (flat side down), and smack the blade with your fist. This smashes the garlic enough so the peel can be removed easily. If the clove is plump and large, it is usually intact enough to make at least one horizontal cut and a couple of vertical cuts before crosscutting it into fine dice.

Chopping carrots and celery   Many recipes, especially soups and sauces, are flavored with carrots and celery, along with the ubiquitous onions. It is important that these vegetables be uniformly chopped so all of the pieces will cook to equal tenderness.

For carrots, trim off the stem end. Cut the carrot lengthwise in half. Cut each half lengthwise into two or three strips (actually, they'll look more like long wedges). Stack them together and cut crosswise at 1/2-inch intervals into 1/2-inch dice.

For celery, trim the tops (for a stronger celery flavor, keep the leaves attached) and bottoms. Cut each rib lengthwise into strips about 1/2 inch wide. Stack the strips and cut crosswise at 1/2-inch intervals into 1/2-inch dice.

In either case, of course, if you want smaller dice, simply cut the carrot or celery into thinner strips and make the crosswise cuts at narrower intervals.

Chopping bell peppers   Start by cutting off the top "lid" and the bottom inch of the pepper. Poke the stem out of the lid and discard, and set the top and bottom pieces aside. Slice the pepper vertically down the side and open it up into a long strip. Cut out the ribs and seeds. (This is the way to prepare bell peppers for roasting, too.)

For 1/2-inch dice, cut the pepper strip into 1/2-inch-wide strips, then cut the top and bottom into $1/2$-inch-wide strips. (Again, the thinner the strips and the shorter the cross cuts, the finer the dice.) Gather the strips into stacks and cut crosswise at $1/2$-inch intervals.

Chopping herbs Rinse fresh herbs and dry well (a salad spinner does a great job).

For basil, pick the leaves from the stems. Always chop the leaves just before using, or the chlorophyll in the leaves will blacken. Roll up the leaves a few at a time and cut crosswise into thin shreds. These fine ribbons make a lovely garnish for many dishes. To chop the basil, cut the strips crosswise as fine as you wish.

For parsley, remove the stems and gather all of the leaves into a pile. Keeping the tip of the knife on the work surface, move the knife across the leaves in a rocking chopping motion. (If you lift the knife off the work surface to chop, the parsley will scatter.)

For fresh herbs with tough stems, such as thyme, sage, and rosemary, run your thumb and forefinger down the stem to remove the leaves. Gather the leaves into a pile and chop as described for parsley.

Soups It is appropriate that this book starts off with soups because there is no other category where the cook gets such a payoff for the time invested. Chop up some vegetables, toss in some meat, and let the pot simmer into a wonderful conglomeration that can be served immediately with salad and bread for a quick meal, or stored for the future. ¶ My freezer is packed with containers of homemade soups. When I think I don't have a thing to eat, it's great to discover that chicken soup in the freezer. It's best to make big batches to be sure that there are those leftovers to squirrel away. (The few soups in this chapter that don't freeze well have smaller yields.)

The soups in this book are purposely "fork-and-knife soups." They are rib-sticking, chunky, hearty affairs that you will most likely eat with a fork and knife as well as a spoon. They are not delicate soups for light first courses at elegant supper parties but soups with backbone to fill you up.

The Carefree Cook's Tips for Soups

Use a large heavy-bottomed pot   Don't try to crowd soup ingredients into a small pot. The ideal utensil is an 8-quart pot with a heavy bottom to discourage scorching. Pots with stainless-steel or enameled interiors are best, because they don't pick up flavors as easily as unlined pots.

Don't rush the cooking   For my meat soups, I usually include tough, bone-in cuts that add lots of flavor to the broth. But they need time to simmer and become tender. Use a moderately low flame so the soup cooks at a steady simmer. A hard boil is bad not only because it leads to burning, but also because it suspends the fat in the broth, resulting in a stable emulsion, and a greasy-tasting soup. (Even if the soup chills and you remove the hardened fat, it will still taste greasy.) Stir the soup occasionally to be sure nothing is sticking.

Be careful when blending pureed soups   Soups can be pureed in a food processor or a blender, or directly in the pot with an immersion blender. Each machine has its own caveats. With a food processor, the pureed soup has a tendency to leak out of the center shaft area. To avoid this, puree in batches to avoid overflow. Transfer the soup solids to the work bowl with a slotted spoon and process, adding just enough of the liquid to keep the soup level from rising above the top of the center tube.

With a blender, the velocity of the blade can create a strong jet of steam that forces the scalding-hot soup up, pushing off the lid. Vent the lid by leaving it slightly ajar, and start the machine on low speed, or pulse, to puree the soup. Better yet, replace the lid with a kitchen towel, as the steam will pass easily through the fabric's weave.

Immersion blenders are great, but they take some getting used to. They are not as fast as food processors or blenders, but most cooks who have one prefer them to the other machines. Just keep the "business end" of the blender immersed in the soup and watch out for splashing.

Stock up on covered containers Unless you are serving a crowd, you will have leftover soup with most of these recipes. Be sure to have a supply of good containers for storage. Because there are lots of leftovers in my life (testing recipes will do that), I purchase cases of 1-pint and 1-quart plastic containers with lids at a local restaurant supply or wholesale club. Although they are designed to be disposable, they can go through the dishwasher to use again a few times. You can buy smaller quantities of containers from your delicatessen or supermarket at a very reasonable price. The 1-pint size is perfect for single servings, and the 1-quart works well for about three bowls. These containers make efficient use of small freezer spaces.

Chinese Beef, Bok Choy, and Noodle Soup Under 30 minutes

As a frequent customer of the noodle shops in New York's Chinatown, I am constantly amazed at how fast they can get a steaming hot bowl of soup on the counter. Of course, the secret is to have everything ready before you get started. If you have the time, freeze the steak for about thirty minutes or so to firm it up—it will be easier to slice. Bean threads, also called cellophane noodles, are made from soybeans. You'll find them in the international section of most supermarkets or at Asian grocers.

Makes 4 servings

2 skeins (about 2 ounces total) bean threads

12 ounces boneless beef sirloin steak, trimmed of
    excess fat

2 tablespoons vegetable oil

1 large shallot, thinly sliced (about 1/3 cup)

2 tablespoons shredded fresh ginger (use the large holes
    on a box grater)

2 garlic cloves, minced

1 medium head bok choy (1 1/4 pounds), root end trimmed
    and leaves cut crosswise into 1/4-inch-wide slices, or
    substitute 3 cups sliced (1/4-inch-wide) napa cabbage

2 cups canned reduced-sodium chicken broth

2 tablespoons dry sherry

2 tablespoons Japanese soy sauce

1 tablespoon light brown sugar

1/2 teaspoon chili paste with garlic or 1/4 teaspoon crushed
    hot red pepper flakes

1. Remove any strings from the skeins of bean threads. Place the bean threads in a small bowl and add enough very hot tap water to cover. Let stand while you prepare the soup.

2. Holding the knife at a 45-degree angle, cut the steak across the grain into thin slices (holding the knife at this angle makes wider slices). Cut the slices into pieces about 3 inches long.

3. Heat 1 tablespoon of the oil in a large saucepan over high heat until very hot. In batches, without crowding, add the beef and cook, stirring occasionally, until it loses its pink color, about 1 1/2 minutes. Transfer to a plate.

4. Add the remaining 1 tablespoon oil to the saucepan. Add the shallot, ginger, and garlic and stir-fry until the shallot softens, about 1 minute. Add the bok choy

and stir-fry until wilted, about 2 minutes. Add the broth, 2 cups water, the sherry, soy sauce, brown sugar, and chili paste and bring to a boil.

5. Meanwhile, drain the bean threads and return to the bowl. Using kitchen scissors, snip through the bean threads a few times to make shorter lengths (this makes them much easier to eat with a soupspoon). Stir the beef and bean threads into the soup. (The soup can be cooled, covered, and refrigerated for up to 2 days, or frozen for up to 3 months.)

6. Ladle the soup into deep soup bowls and serve hot.

Chinatown Shrimp and Spinach Soup

Substitute 12 ounces peeled, deveined medium shrimp for the beef and stir-fry until it turns opaque, about 3 minutes. Substitute 8 cups loosely packed baby spinach (about 7 ounces) for the bok choy.

Soy Sauce

There are countless brands of soy sauce, which is made from a brew of fermented, aged, and distilled soybeans. The problem is that each producer has its own recipe, and the quality varies enormously (I have ruined a recipe by using a soy sauce that was too strong). To confuse matters further, there are three grades: light (not to be confused with low-sodium), medium (also known as thin soy sauce), and dark (with added molasses, and sometimes called superior soy sauce—which is not an indication of quality), as well as mushroom-flavored soy sauce. Asian cooks use each of these differently.

What's a Westerner to do? Supermarket soy sauce is usually a Japanese brand with reliable quality and flavor, so that's what I recommend. Traditional Asian cooks can argue that it is worthwhile to appreciate the differences among the three soy sauce varieties, but for everyday cooking, I am very happy with the supermarket brand.

Korean Beef and Root Vegetable Soup

A few years ago, I was asked to teach cooking classes on American cuisine in Korea during a chilly Seoul winter. This was a fascinating assignment, and not the least interesting aspect was the chance to sample the local food—I had plenty of opportunity to enjoy bowls of hot, steaming, chunky soups like this one.

Makes 8 to 10 servings

1 tablespoon vegetable oil

3 pounds cross-cut beef short ribs (flanken), cut into
1- or 2-rib pieces

1 large onion, chopped

4 garlic cloves, minced

Three 1/8-inch-thick slices fresh ginger

2 whole star anise or 1/2 teaspoon aniseed

3 medium carrots, cut into 1-inch lengths

1 medium orange-fleshed yam, peeled and cut into 1-inch cubes

1 medium turnip, peeled and cut into 1-inch chunks

2 tablespoons Japanese soy sauce

Salt and crushed hot red pepper flakes to taste

1. Heat the oil in a soup kettle over medium-high heat. In batches, without crowding, add the short ribs and cook, turning once, until browned on both sides, about 8 minutes. Transfer to a platter.

2. Pour out all but 2 tablespoons fat from the pot. Reduce the heat to medium, add the onion, and cook, stirring occasionally, until it softens, about 3 minutes. Stir in the garlic, ginger, and star anise. Return the beef to the pot. Add enough cold water, or homemade beef stock if you have it, to cover the beef (about 2 quarts) and stir to scrape up the browned bits on the bottom of the pot. Bring to a boil over high heat, skimming off the foam that rises to the surface. Reduce the heat to low and simmer, uncovered, for 1 1/2 hours.

3. Add the carrots, yam, and turnip. Simmer until the meat is tender, about 45 minutes longer.

4. Stir in the soy sauce. Season the soup with salt and red pepper flakes. (The soup can be cooled, covered, and refrigerated for up to 2 days, or frozen for up to 3 months.)

5. Ladle the soup into bowls and serve hot.

Short Ribs Borscht with Dilled Sour Cream

There are many ways to make beet-red borscht, from light and vegetarian to this beefy version. Truly one of the most rib-sticking of all soups, it only follows that my recipe includes meaty short ribs, whose bones lend so much flavor that water can be substituted for broth as the cooking liquid. There are recipes for cold borscht, but they are never beef-based, as the rendered fat hardens when chilled, giving the soup a gritty feel in your mouth. So save this recipe for cold days—it is guaranteed to warm you up.

Makes 8 to 12 servings

2 tablespoons vegetable oil

3 pounds cross-cut beef short ribs (flanken), cut into 1- or
    2-rib pieces

1 large onion, chopped

2 medium carrots, cut into $1/2$-inch-thick rounds

2 celery ribs, cut into $1/4$-inch-thick slices

2 garlic cloves, chopped

10 ounces mushrooms, thinly sliced

One $14^1/2$-ounce can diced tomatoes in juice, drained

2 teaspoons dried thyme

2 teaspoons caraway seeds, optional

1 bay leaf

2 teaspoons salt

$1/2$ teaspoon freshly ground black pepper

$1/2$ small head green cabbage, cored and chopped (about
    4 cups)

4 medium beets, peeled and cut into $3/4$-inch cubes

$3/4$ cup sour cream

$1/4$ cup chopped fresh dill

1. Heat the oil in a soup kettle over high heat. In batches, add the short ribs and cook, turning occasionally, until well browned, about 8 minutes. Transfer to a plate.

2. Reduce the heat to medium. Add the onion, carrots, celery, and garlic and cook, stirring occasionally, until the onion softens, about 6 minutes. Add the mushrooms, cover, and cook until the mushrooms soften, about 5 minutes.

3. Stir in the tomatoes, thyme, caraway, if using, bay leaf, salt, and pepper. Return the short ribs to the pot and add enough water to cover the ingredients by 1 inch. Bring to a boil over high heat, skimming off any foam that rises to the

(continued)

top of the liquid. Reduce the heat to low, partially cover, and simmer for 1 1/2 hours.

4. Stir the cabbage and beets into the soup. Partially cover and simmer until the beef is very tender, about 1 hour. Remove the bay leaf. (The soup can be cooled, covered, and refrigerated for up to 2 days, or frozen for up to 3 months.)

5. Stir the sour cream and dill together. Serve the soup hot, with a dollop of the dilled sour cream on each serving.

Sherried Black Bean and Chorizo Soup

When I moved to New York, directly out of college, one of the most elegant and popular restaurants was The Coach House in Greenwich Village. It specialized in regional American food served with flair, and they were famous for their smooth, understated black bean soup. Even though my version is spicier and chunkier, whenever I make it, I think of those meals at The Coach House, where I really first learned how to dine "like a grownup."

Makes 8 servings

2 tablespoons extra-virgin olive oil

4 ounces chorizo or other hard, spicy smoked sausage, cut into $1/2$-inch dice

1 large onion, chopped

1 medium green bell pepper, cored, seeds and ribs removed, and cut into $1/2$-inch dice

1 jalapeño, seeded and finely chopped

2 garlic cloves, finely chopped

Three 15- to 19-ounce cans black beans, drained and rinsed

$3^1/2$ cups canned reduced-sodium chicken broth

$1/2$ cup dry sherry

$1/4$ cup chopped fresh cilantro

Salt and freshly ground black pepper to taste

1. Heat the oil in a soup kettle over medium-high heat. Add the chorizo and cook until lightly browned, about 5 minutes. Add the onion, bell pepper, jalapeño, and garlic and reduce the heat to medium. Cover and cook, stirring occasionally, until the onion is tender, about 8 minutes.

2. Add the beans and broth and bring to a simmer. Reduce the heat to low, cover, and simmer until the soup is well flavored, about 30 minutes.

3. Stir the sherry into the soup and cook for 5 minutes. Transfer about 2 cups of the soup to a food processor or blender and puree. Stir back into the soup. Stir in half of the cilantro. Season with salt and pepper. (The soup can be cooled, covered, and refrigerated for up to 2 days, or frozen for up to 3 months.)

4. Serve hot, sprinkling each serving with some of the remaining cilantro.

Tuscan Bean and Escarole Soup

Tuscan cooks prefer the youngest extra-virgin olive oil for this hearty soup, one whose peppery edge has not mellowed with age. Simply use your favorite brand of full-flavored oil, and get ready to enjoy a hearty bowl of bean and vegetable soup.

Makes 8 servings

$1/4$ cup extra-virgin olive oil, plus more for serving

4 ounces sliced ($1/4$-inch-thick) pancetta, chopped

1 large onion, chopped

2 medium carrots, cut into $1/2$-inch dice

2 medium celery ribs with leaves, cut into $1/2$-inch dice

4 garlic cloves, minced

1 teaspoon fennel seeds

1 teaspoon dried sage

$1/2$ teaspoon crushed hot red pepper flakes, plus more to taste

3 cups canned reduced-sodium chicken broth

One 28-ounce can white kidney (cannellini) beans, drained and rinsed

1 large zucchini, cut into $1/4$-inch-thick rounds

One $14 1/2$-ounce can diced tomatoes in juice, drained

1 medium head escarole (9 ounces), trimmed, well washed, and coarsely chopped

Salt to taste

8 slices crusty Italian bread, toasted

Freshly grated Parmesan cheese for serving

1. Heat the oil in a large soup kettle over medium heat. Add the pancetta and cook, stirring occasionally, until it begins to brown, about 3 minutes. Add the onion, carrots, celery, and garlic. Cover and cook, stirring often, until the vegetables are softened, about 10 minutes.

2. Stir in the fennel, sage, and red pepper flakes, then add the broth, beans, zucchini, tomatoes, and enough water to cover the beans by $1/2$ inch, and bring to a boil. A handful at a time, stir in the escarole, letting each batch wilt before adding another. Reduce the heat to medium-low and simmer, uncovered, until the soup is well flavored, about 30 minutes. Season with salt and additional red pepper flakes. (The soup can be cooled, covered, and refrigerated for up to 2 days, or frozen for up to 3 months.)

3. To serve, place a slice of bread in each of eight soup bowls and ladle in the soup. Drizzle each with some olive oil, sprinkle with Parmesan cheese, and serve hot.

Lentil, Sausage, and Macaroni Soup

The first time I made this soup, I was alarmed at how much the recipe made. I shouldn't have worried about how it was going to get eaten—it was so warming and filling that I kept sneaking back into the kitchen for another serving, and I was glad to have leftovers for freezing. Brown supermarket lentils work best here—no need to use fancy imported green lentils.

Makes 10 to 12 servings

2 tablespoons extra-virgin olive oil

1 pound pork or turkey sweet Italian sausage, casing removed

1 large onion, cut into $1/2$-inch dice

2 carrots, cut into $1/2$-inch dice

2 celery ribs with leaves, cut into $1/2$-inch dice

2 garlic cloves, minced

1 pound lentils, rinsed and checked for stones

$3^1/2$ cups canned reduced-sodium chicken broth

2 tablespoons tomato paste

2 teaspoons Italian Herb Seasoning (page 100), or use 1 teaspoon each dried basil and oregano

$3/4$ cup ditalini or other small "soup" pasta

Salt and freshly ground black pepper to taste

Freshly grated Parmesan cheese for serving

1. Heat the oil in a soup kettle over medium-high heat. Add the sausage and cook, stirring occasionally to break it up into bite-sized pieces, until it loses its raw look, about 10 minutes.

2. Add the onion, carrots, celery, and garlic. Cook, stirring often, until the onion softens, about 5 minutes. Add the lentils, chicken broth, tomato paste, and enough cold water to cover the lentils by 1 inch (about 2 quarts). Bring to a boil over high heat, skimming off the foam that rises to the surface. Add the herbs, reduce the heat to medium-low, cover partially, and simmer until the lentils are barely tender, about 45 minutes.

3. Add the ditalini and cook until tender, about 15 minutes. Season with salt and pepper. (The soup can be cooled, covered, and refrigerated for up to 2 days, or frozen for up to 3 months.)

4. Serve hot, in soup bowls, with the cheese passed on the side.

Potato and Roasted Red Pepper Soup with Sausage

My reader Lynne Tyler suggested the idea for this soup, a version of which she had tried in a local restaurant but that needed more oomph. Lots of roasted peppers give my adaptation a warm color and flavor, and a finish of sausage makes it more fitting for a main course. You can use any sausage you like here—kielbasa, spicy beef links, well-cooked Italian sausage, or even cubes of smoked ham.

Makes 6 to 8 servings

2 tablespoons plus 2 teaspoons extra-virgin olive oil

1 medium onion, chopped

1 medium celery rib, chopped

2 garlic cloves, minced

2 medium baking potatoes (14 ounces), peeled and cut into 1-inch cubes

4 cups canned reduced-sodium chicken broth

4 medium red bell peppers, roasted and peeled (see page 83)

1 teaspoon dried oregano

8 ounces smoked sausage, such as kielbasa, cut into ½-inch dice

Salt and freshly ground black pepper to taste

1. Heat 2 tablespoons of the oil in a large soup kettle over medium heat. Add the onion, celery, and garlic, cover, and cook until the onion is golden, about 10 minutes. Stir in the potatoes and broth and bring to a boil. Reduce the heat to low, cover, and simmer until the potatoes are very tender, about 30 minutes. During the last 5 minutes, add the red peppers and oregano.

2. Meanwhile, heat the remaining 2 teaspoons oil in a medium nonstick skillet over medium heat. Add the sausage and cook, stirring occasionally, until browned, about 5 minutes. Keep warm.

3. In batches, puree the soup in a blender or food processor, or use an immersion blender. Season with salt and pepper. (The soup can be cooled, covered, and refrigerated for up to 2 days, or frozen for up to 3 months.)

4. Ladle the soup into bowls and add some of the cooked sausage to each serving. Serve hot.

Fork-and-Knife Chicken Soup

A fine long-simmered chicken soup is one of the reasons why people have stoves. What do you do when you want comforting chicken soup but don't have the time? My quick version combines fresh chicken and vegetables with canned broth to make a very credible soup that is not necessarily guaranteed to cure any colds, but it will make you feel great. Many chickens are now trimmed to a fare-thee-well, and the fat in the tail area is removed during the process. If it is still on the chicken, use it to give wonderful extra flavor to your soup. Otherwise, simply substitute unsalted butter for the rendered chicken fat.

Makes 4 servings

One 3½-pound chicken, rinsed and patted dry

2 tablespoons unsalted butter, optional (see headnote above)

¼ teaspoon salt, plus more to taste

¼ teaspoon freshly ground black pepper, plus more to taste

1 large leek, white and pale green parts only, cut into ½-inch dice and well rinsed, or use 1 large onion, chopped

2 medium carrots, cut into ½-inch dice

2 medium celery ribs, cut into ½-inch dice

One 13¾-ounce can reduced-sodium chicken broth

1 teaspoon chopped fresh thyme or ½ teaspoon dried thyme

1 teaspoon chopped fresh sage or ½ teaspoon dried sage

Chopped fresh parsley for garnish

1. Pull off the pale yellow pads of chicken fat from either side of the tail area, just inside the body cavity, and finely chop the fat. (If the fat has been removed by the butcher, use the optional butter in the next step.) Cut the chicken into 8 pieces: 2 each drumsticks, thighs, breasts, and wings.

2. Cook the fat in a large saucepan over medium heat until it renders a couple of tablespoons of liquid, about 5 minutes. Or melt the butter. In batches, add the chicken, skin side down, and cook until the underside is browned, about 5 minutes. Transfer to a plate. Season the chicken with the salt and pepper.

3. Add the leek, carrots, and celery to the saucepan, cover and cook, stirring often, until the vegetables soften, about 5 minutes. Add the chicken broth, the

thyme, and sage. Return the chicken to the saucepan, with the meaty parts of the breast facing down, and add enough water to barely cover the chicken. Bring to a boil over high heat. Cover tightly, reduce the heat to low, and simmer, occasionally skimming off any foam that rises to the surface of the broth, until the chicken shows no sign of pink when pierced at the bone, 35 to 40 minutes. Season with salt and pepper. (The soup can be cooled, covered, and refrigerated for up to 2 days, or frozen for up to 3 months.)

4. Using a slotted spoon, divide the chicken among four deep soup bowls, 2 pieces per serving. Ladle in the broth and vegetables. Sprinkle with the parsley and serve immediately, with forks, knives, and soupspoons.

Mussel, Potato, and Saffron Chowder Under 30 minutes

Chowder, that hearty concoction of bacon, potatoes, and shellfish, gets an upscale makeover with this recipe. Mussels are a nice change from the classic clams, with leeks, saffron, and wine adding elegance.

Makes 4 to 6 servings

2 teaspoons vegetable oil

4 ounces sliced bacon

1 cup chopped leeks (white part and pale green parts only)

2 large baking potatoes (1 pound), peeled and cut into ¾-inch cubes

¾ cup dry white wine or dry vermouth

1 cup heavy cream

½ teaspoon crumbled saffron threads

2 pounds mussels, scrubbed and debearded, if necessary

Salt and freshly ground black pepper to taste

1. Put the oil in a soup kettle, add the bacon, and cook over medium-high heat, turning the bacon once, until crisp, about 6 minutes. Using a slotted spoon, transfer the bacon to paper towels to drain, leaving the fat in the pot. Coarsely chop the bacon.

2. Add the leeks to the pot, reduce the heat to medium, cover, and cook until the leeks are wilted, about 3 minutes. Stir in the potatoes and 1 cup water, cover, and cook until the potatoes are barely tender, about 20 minutes.

3. Add the wine and bring to a boil over high heat. Stir in the cream, saffron, and 1½ cups water and return to the boil. Add the mussels, cover tightly, and cook, stirring occasionally, until the mussels open, about 6 minutes.

4. Using tongs, transfer an equal number of mussels to each soup bowl, discarding any unopened mussels. Stir the bacon into the chowder and season with salt and pepper. Ladle the soup over the mussels and serve immediately.

Turkey and Beer Gumbo

Gumbo tastes like a Mardi Gras in your mouth. It should have a hearty consistency, the body achieved by at least one, if not two, thickening agents. Traditional recipes use a dark roux, a long-cooked paste of flour and fat, to both thicken and flavor the gumbo, but I prefer toasting the flour alone in a skillet—it's easier and reduces the fat. There are cooks who say that if it doesn't have okra, it isn't gumbo, as the soup's name comes from an African dialect word for the vegetable. Like the flour, the okra isn't extraneous, because its mucilaginous juices thicken the broth. But as no one in my family is an okra fan, I leave it out. However, you still have another chance to thicken this gumbo—with filé powder.

Makes 8 to 10 servings

1 tablespoon vegetable oil

One 2¾-pound turkey breast half (with skin and bones)

1 large onion, chopped

2 medium celery ribs with leaves, cut into ½-inch dice

1 green bell pepper, cored, seeds and ribs removed, and cut into ½-inch dice

2 scallions, white and green parts, chopped

2 garlic cloves, minced

½ cup all-purpose flour

1½ tablespoons Cajun Seasoning (recipe follows), or use store-bought salt-free Cajun/Creole seasoning

3½ cups canned reduced-sodium chicken broth

One 12-ounce bottle lager beer

2 tablespoons Worcestershire sauce

1 bay leaf

About 1 tablespoon gumbo filé powder, optional

Hot red pepper sauce to taste

Cooked rice for serving, optional

1. Heat the oil in a large soup kettle over medium heat. Add the turkey breast, skin side down, and cook until the skin is browned, about 4 minutes. Transfer the turkey to a plate.

2. Add the onion, celery, green pepper, scallions, and garlic to the pot, cover, and cook, stirring often, until the vegetables soften, about 8 minutes.

3. Meanwhile, heat an empty medium skillet over medium heat. Add the flour and cook, stirring occasionally, until the flour is beige and smells toasted, about 5 minutes.

4. Add the toasted flour and Cajun seasoning to the pot and stir well. Return the

turkey breast to the pot. Add the broth, beer, Worcestershire sauce, bay leaf, and enough cold water to barely cover the turkey. Bring to a boil over high heat, skimming off any foam that rises to the surface. Reduce the heat to medium-low, partially cover, and simmer until an instant-read thermometer inserted in the thickest part of the turkey breast reads 170°F, about 1 1/4 hours. Transfer the turkey breast to a carving board and let stand for 10 minutes (keep the soup simmering).

5. Cut the turkey into bite-sized pieces, discarding the skin and bones, and return it to the pot to heat through. Remove the gumbo from the heat. Discard the bay leaf. If you wish, stir in enough of the filé powder to thicken the soup. Season the gumbo with hot pepper sauce. (The soup can be cooled, covered, and refrigerated for up to 2 days, or frozen for up to 3 months, if not using filé powder.)

6. Serve the gumbo hot, adding some of the rice to each serving, if desired.

Filé Powder

An essential ingredient in Cajun cooking, filé powder is ground sassafras leaves. It has the same thickening power as okra, and it gives the broth a similar gelatinous quality. Because of its dark olive color, filé is not a good all-purpose thickener, and is only used for gumbo. If you use filé, don't let the soup boil after adding it—texture will get stringy and ropey. For this reason, it is not a good idea to use filé if you plan to freeze the soup.

Cajun Seasoning

I am never without a jar of this jazzy herb-and-spice blend in my kitchen cabinet. There are a number of commercial brands available (some are quite salty), but I like being able to control the exact (salt-free) combination of ingredients. Make it with a high-quality imported paprika with plenty of flavor—Hungary and Spain are rightfully famous for their paprika. Use Cajun seasoning whenever you have a plain dish that could use a lift, from grilled fish to popcorn.

Makes about ¹/₃ cup

2 tablespoons sweet Hungarian or Spanish paprika

1 tablespoon dried basil

1 tablespoon dried thyme

1 teaspoon garlic powder

1 teaspoon onion powder

¹/₂ teaspoon freshly ground black pepper

¹/₄ teaspoon ground hot red (cayenne) pepper

Mix all of the ingredients in a small bowl. Transfer to a small jar and seal tightly. Store in a cool, dark place for up to 3 months.

Turkey Tortilla Soup

With a crown of crispy tortilla chips topping each bowl, this soup makes quite an impression. While flavor is certainly the primary factor, texture is also important, and each bite holds a new surprise—crunchy chips, broth-softened chips, smooth avocado, firm hominy, and/or chunky turkey. Tortilla soup is usually made with chicken, but I find the meaty flavor of turkey stands up better to the riot of Mexican seasonings.

Makes 8 to 10 servings

1 tablespoon olive oil

One 2¾-pound turkey breast half (with skin and bones)

1 large onion, chopped

2 large celery ribs with leaves, cut into ½-inch dice

1 jalapeño, seeded and minced

2 garlic cloves, minced

1 teaspoon ground cumin

1 teaspoon dried marjoram or oregano

One 13¾-ounce can reduced-sodium chicken broth

One 14½-ounce can diced tomatoes in juice

One 15-ounce can hominy, drained and rinsed

1 medium zucchini, cut into ½-inch dice

¼ cup chopped fresh cilantro

Salt and freshly ground black pepper to taste

2 ripe avocados, pitted, peeled, and cut into ½-inch dice

About 4 cups tortilla chips for serving

Lime wedges for serving

1. Heat the oil in a soup kettle over medium-high heat. Add the turkey, skin side down, and cook until the skin is browned, about 4 minutes. Transfer the turkey to a plate.

2. Add the onion, celery, jalapeño, and garlic to the pot and reduce the heat to medium. Cook, stirring occasionally, until the onion softens, about 5 minutes. Add the cumin and marjoram and stir well. Add the broth and tomatoes, with their juices, scraping up the browned bits in the bottom of the pot. Return the turkey to the pot and add enough cold water to cover by 1 inch. Bring to a boil over high heat, skimming any foam that rises to the surface. Reduce the heat to medium-low, partially cover, and simmer until an instant-read thermometer inserted in the thickest part of the turkey breast reads 170°F, about 1¼ hours.

(continued)

Transfer the turkey breast to a carving board and let stand for 10 to 15 minutes.

3. Meanwhile, add the hominy, zucchini, and cilantro to the soup and simmer until the zucchini is tender, about 15 minutes.

4. Cut the turkey into bite-sized pieces, discarding the skin and bones, and return it to the pot. Season with salt and pepper. (The soup can be cooled, covered, and refrigerated for up to 2 days, or frozen for up to 3 months.)

5. Skim off the fat on the surface of the soup. Serve the soup hot in deep soup bowls, topping each serving with a spoonful of the avocado dice and a handful of chips. Pass the lime wedges on the side.

Portuguese Cod Chowder with Cilantro Oil

I first enjoyed a soup similar to this during a trip to Cape Cod, where many Portuguese-Americans live and cook. The original was cooked until the cod was chunky and falling apart, but I prefer this more attractive version, where a whole cod fillet is served in each bowl topped with a ladle of aromatic broth with vegetables and sausage. If you can't find linguiça, use chorizo, or even pepperoni.

Makes 6 servings

⅓ cup plus 2 tablespoons extra-virgin olive oil, divided

4 ounces linguiça or other hard, spicy smoked sausage, cut into ½-inch dice

3 medium red-skinned potatoes, cut into ½-inch dice

1 large onion, chopped

1 large green bell pepper, cored, seeds and ribs removed, and cut into ½-inch dice

3 garlic cloves, minced

2 cups bottled clam juice or canned reduced-sodium chicken broth

One 14½-ounce can diced tomatoes in juice

Six 6-ounce cod fillets

¼ cup chopped fresh cilantro

¼ teaspoon crushed hot red pepper flakes

Salt to taste

1. Heat 2 tablespoons of the oil in a 12-inch skillet over medium heat. Add the linguiça and cook, stirring until browned, about 6 minutes. Add the potatoes, onion, green pepper, and garlic. Cook, stirring often, until the onion softens, about 5 minutes.

2. Add the clam juice, the tomatoes, with their juices, and 3 cups water and bring to a boil. Cover tightly, reduce the heat to medium-low, and simmer until the potatoes are almost tender, about 15 minutes.

3. Lay the cod fillets in the skillet, cover, and cook until the fish is opaque when flaked in the center with the tip of a knife, about 10 minutes.

4. Meanwhile, process the remaining ⅓ cup oil and the cilantro in a blender. Pour into a small bowl and set aside.

5. Using a slotted spoon, transfer a fillet to each soup bowl. Season the broth with the red pepper and salt. Ladle the broth, with the vegetables and sausage, over the fillets. Drizzle with the cilantro oil and serve immediately.

Salads Salads are among the most versatile dishes in a carefree cook's kitchen. Too often, salad is regarded as a plate of leafy greens with vinaigrette, no more than the prelude to a meal—and when the main course is hearty, that's perfectly appropriate. But salads created with an eye (or palate) to contrasting textures, colors, and flavors can be used as substantial side dishes or even as main courses. ¶ In this chapter, the recipes run the gamut from the elegant (Spinach Salad with Warm Asian Pears and Goat Cheese) to the retro (Hearts of Romaine with Caesar Buttermilk Dressing). You'll also find main-course salads like Crab Louis with Sun-Dried Tomato Dressing and Farfalle and Broccoli Salad with Gorgonzola Dressing. My Pork Souvlaki (page 116) is doubly delicious when balanced atop Chopped Greek Salad with Feta and Olives, and I like to serve simple grilled fish dishes alongside crisp Fennel and Scallion Slaw.

Speaking of slaws, I have become especially fond of these shredded vegetable salads. They used to be time-consuming to make, but thanks to packaged slaw mixes and the food processor, they can now be whipped up in no time at all. So you'll find such choices as Carrot Slaw with Miso Vinaigrette and a more traditional Coleslaw with Apple–Poppy Seed Dressing.

The salads here were designed as self-contained recipes, but many of the dressings are great for other greens or vegetables: Honey-Yogurt Dressing, Chile-Lime Dressing, Miso Vinaigrette, Sun-Dried Tomato Dressing, Olive Vinaigrette, Rick's Red Dressing, Caesar Buttermilk Dressing, Red Wine–Shallot Vinaigrette, and Sherry-Ginger Vinaigrette. Perhaps one of these will become your house dressing.

In other words, when it comes to salad, there's more to life than mesclun with balsamic vinaigrette.

The Carefree Cook's Tips for Salads

For the smoothest vinaigrettes, use a blender One of the hallmarks of a good vinaigrette is a smooth emulsion. The traditional way to make vinaigrette is to slowly whisk the oil into the vinegar—the gradual addition of the oil encourages its suspension in the vinegar, giving a properly viscous result. However, the blade of a blender does a faster job and breaks up the oil into tinier particles that suspend more completely. A food processor, which has a wider container, doesn't work as well.

Use packaged salad greens to save time Every kitchen should have an efficient salad spinner, a tool that reduces the effort of washing salad greens. However, when cooking against the clock, nothing beats the new bagged salad green blends that are already washed and ready to be dressed. I still like choosing the perfect combination of greens for each salad, but when pressed for time, I reach for a bag of mixed greens without guilt.

Taste before tossing When tasting salad dressing to adjust the seasoning, use a leaf of the salad greens as your tasting utensil to get the true effect. If you taste it from a spoon, the dressing will always taste too tart.

Arugula, Grapefruit, and Peanut Salad with Honey-Yogurt Dressing **Under 30 minutes**

The peppery arugula in this sophisticated salad is balanced by sweet grapefruit, tangy yogurt, and crunchy peanuts. It may sound "chef-y," but it really is easy enough for a weeknight meal. The amount of vinegar needed will vary with the relative tanginess of the yogurt, so adjust the dressing accordingly.

Makes 4 servings

$\frac{1}{2}$ cup plain yogurt

2 tablespoons honey

2 tablespoons red wine vinegar, or more to taste

$\frac{1}{4}$ teaspoon freshly ground black pepper

Salt to taste

12 ounces arugula, tough stems discarded, well rinsed, and dried (about 8 cups)

2 grapefruit, sectioned (see sidebar)

$\frac{1}{4}$ cup coarsely chopped peanuts

1. To make the dressing, whisk the yogurt, honey, vinegar, and pepper in a large bowl. Dip in an arugula leaf, and taste the dressing for seasoning. Season with salt, and adjust with additional vinegar, if you wish.

2. Add the arugula and toss to coat. Season with salt.

3. Transfer the arugula to four salad plates. Top with the grapefruit, and sprinkle with the peanuts. Serve immediately.

Sectioning Citrus

A few slices of orange or grapefruit can really enliven a green salad, especially if you find you don't have the customary tomato or cucumber in the vegetable drawer. Seedless citrus can be peeled and cut crosswise into rounds. But for a more elegant look, the citrus can be sectioned to remove the tough membranes and leave you with tender wedges of fruit.

To section citrus (large seedless oranges or grapefruit work best), trim the top and bottom off the fruit so it stands on the work surface. Using a serrated knife, cut off the thick peel where it meets the flesh so you end up with a skinless sphere. Working over a bowl to catch the juice, hold the fruit in one hand and cut between the thin membranes to release the segments, letting them fall into the bowl. Squeeze the juice from the membranes into the bowl. Drain the segments, reserving the juice for the cook's treat (or for the dish you are making, depending on the recipe), and refrigerate the segments until ready to use.

Black Bean Salad
with Avocado and Red Pepper Under 30 minutes

This versatile salad shows up on my table not only as a side dish but also as a filling for warm tortillas and as a salsa for grilled fish. While you can substitute red or pink beans, the black make a striking color contrast with the avocado and red pepper.

Makes 4 servings

Grated zest of 1 lime

1 tablespoon fresh lime juice

1/2 teaspoon sugar

1/2 teaspoon pure ground dried chiles, such as ancho, or regular chili powder

1 garlic clove, crushed through a press

1/3 cup extra-virgin olive oil

One 15- to 19-ounce can black beans, drained and rinsed

1/3 cup finely chopped red onion

1 ripe Hass avocado, pitted, peeled, and cut into 1/2-inch dice

1 vinegar-packed roasted red bell pepper, seeds and ribs removed, cut into 1/2-inch dice

Salt and freshly ground black pepper to taste

1. To make the dressing, pulse the lime zest and juice, sugar, ground chiles, and garlic in a blender to combine. With the blender on, gradually add the oil through the top vent. Transfer to a medium bowl.

2. Add the beans, red onion, avocado, and bell pepper and mix well. Season with salt and pepper. Cover and refrigerate until chilled, about 2 hours, before serving. (The salad can be made up to 2 days ahead. Season with additional lime juice, salt, and pepper before serving.)

Vinegar-Packed Roasted Red Peppers

Freshly roasted red peppers are the first choice for cooking, but for sandwiches and salads, vinegar-packed peppers work well and should be a staple in any well-stocked pantry. They can be purchased from a delicatessen counter or packed in jars. Rinse them well under cold water before using. Refrigerate delicatessen peppers for up to a week, opened peppers in the jar for about 1 month.

Coleslaw with Apple–Poppy Seed Dressing Under 30 minutes

I consider this my all-purpose coleslaw, the one that I serve most often with sandwiches or fried chicken. Using packaged coleslaw mix, this can almost be prepared with your eyes closed. Apple juice concentrate and shredded apples add a delectably sweet orchard flavor to the slaw.

Makes 4 to 6 servings

$1/2$ cup regular or reduced-fat mayonnaise

1 tablespoon thawed apple juice concentrate

1 tablespoon cider vinegar

One 16-ounce bag coleslaw mix (green cabbage and carrots)

2 scallions, white and green parts, finely chopped

1 Granny Smith apple, peeled

1 tablespoon poppy seeds

Salt and freshly ground black pepper to taste

1. Mix the mayonnaise, apple juice concentrate, and vinegar in a medium bowl. Add the coleslaw mix and scallions and combine.

2. Grate the apple directly into the bowl, stopping when you reach the core and turning it to grate the next side. Add the poppy seeds and mix well. Season with salt and pepper, and serve. (The salad can be made up to 1 day ahead, covered, and refrigerated. Season again with salt and pepper before serving.)

Frozen Fruit Juice Concentrates

The supermarket frozen food department offers a wide range of frozen fruit juice concentrates from orange juice to apple juice, with plenty of choices in between. Even though I rarely reconstitute the frozen stuff to drink, my freezer always holds a can each of orange and apple juice to add a burst of fruity flavor to many dishes from salad dressings to desserts. Simply scrape up the needed amount from the surface of the frozen concentrate with a sturdy spoon, and let it stand at room temperature for a few minutes to thaw. Or, if you're in a hurry, microwave the concentrate at very low power just until it melts without heating.

New Jersey Sweet and Tangy Slaw

New Jersey was famous for its network of high-quality diners that dished out satis-fyingly solid food to hungry drivers. One of the most famous was the Claremont Diner, which was in Verona. Locals still regard their slightly sweet coleslaw as the ultimate version. Note that the slaw must be refrigerated for at least 4 hours (overnight is best). Thanks to Arlene Ward for unearthing the recipe.

Makes 8 servings

1 medium head green cabbage (2¼ pounds), cut into wedges to fit the food processor feed tube and cored

1 large cucumber, peeled, halved lengthwise, and seeded

1 large green bell pepper, halved, cored and seeded

1 small onion, cut lengthwise in half

1 large carrot, trimmed

¼ cup vegetable oil

¼ cup distilled white vinegar

¼ cup sugar

1 tablespoon iodized or plain table salt (see Note)

½ teaspoon freshly ground black pepper

1. Using a food processor fitted with the thin slicing blade (not the shredding blade), slice the cabbage. Transfer to a large bowl. Slice the cucumber, green pepper, and onion, and add to the cabbage.

2. Fit the food processor with the shredding blade. Shred the carrot, and transfer to the bowl with the other vegetables. Mix well.

3. Fit the food processor with the steel blade. Add the oil, vinegar, sugar, and salt and process to dissolve the sugar, salt, and black pepper. Pour the dressing over the vegetables and toss well. Cover with plastic wrap and refrigerate until the slaw is chilled and wilted, and has released a generous amount of brined juices, at least 4 hours, preferably overnight.

4. Serve chilled, using a slotted spoon to remove the slaw from the brine. (The slaw will keep, covered, refrigerated, stored in its brine, for up to 3 days.)

Note: While I don't specify the kind of salt used in the other recipes in the book, it's important to use iodized or plain table salt here to ensure the correct seasoning.

Chinese Cabbage and Sesame Slaw   Under 30 minutes

Napa cabbage, also known as Chinese cabbage, has a more delicate texture than traditional green cabbage, and it is easy to cut crosswise into shreds for slaw. This salad is best served immediately, as it wilts if allowed to stand for too long. I serve it often as a side dish to grilled fish and poultry, or almost any Asian-inspired dish.

Makes 6 servings

3 tablespoons rice vinegar

2 tablespoons Japanese soy sauce

1 tablespoon light or dark brown sugar

¼ teaspoon crushed hot red pepper flakes

½ cup vegetable oil

2 tablespoons dark Asian sesame oil

One 1-pound head napa (Chinese) cabbage, cored and cut crosswise into ⅛-inch-wide shreds (about 8 cups)

2 medium carrots, shredded

2 scallions, white and green parts, thinly sliced

Salt to taste

2 teaspoons sesame seeds, preferably toasted (see Note)

1. Pulse the vinegar, soy sauce, sugar, and red pepper flakes in a blender to dissolve the sugar. With the machine running, gradually pour in the vegetable and sesame oils.

2. Mix the cabbage, carrots, and scallions in a large bowl. Add the dressing and mix well. Season with salt. Sprinkle the sesame seeds over the slaw. Serve immediately.

Note: To toast sesame seeds, heat an empty medium skillet over medium heat. Add the sesame seeds and cook, stirring often, until lightly browned, about one minute. Transfer to a plate and cool.

Chinese Cabbage

There are two varieties of Chinese cabbage available in American markets. Napa cabbage has a squat barrel shape—the leaves may be tightly packed or loose. Celery cabbage is taller and the central celerylike ribs are thicker. They are very similar in flavor and interchangeable. However, because napa cabbage is usually smaller, it is more convenient for most recipes.

Carrot Slaw with Miso Vinaigrette   Under 30 minutes

Until I worked with Jeffrey Nathan (host of PBS's New Jewish Cuisine*) on his book* Adventures in Jewish Cooking, *I rarely cooked with miso. But Jeff used to cook in a Japanese restaurant and he gave me some great ideas for using this tasty soybean paste, including adding a bit to a finished pot of chicken soup. Beyond soup, it also makes a terrific salad dressing. Try it on baby spinach, or use in this slaw.*

Makes 4 servings

Miso Vinaigrette

2 tablespoons rice vinegar

1 tablespoon light (white or yellow) miso

1/2 teaspoon Japanese soy sauce

1 small garlic clove

1/2 cup vegetable oil

Carrot Slaw

1 pound carrots, trimmed

1 scallion, white and green parts, finely chopped

Salt and freshly ground black pepper to taste

Sesame seeds, toasted, if desired (see page 49),
       for garnish

1. To make the vinaigrette, pulse the vinegar, miso, soy sauce, and garlic in a blender to combine. With the machine running, pour in the oil through the top vent.

2. In a food processor fitted with the coarse shredding blade, shred the carrots. (It is important not to shred the carrots too fine; if your food processor only has a fine shredding disk, use a V-slicer to julienne the carrots into strips less than 1/8 inch wide.)

3. Toss the carrots, scallion, and vinaigrette in a medium bowl. Season with salt and pepper. Serve immediately, topping each serving with a sprinkle of sesame seeds.

Crab Louis with Sun-Dried Tomato Dressing **Under 30 minutes**

In my hometown, San Francisco, the classic restaurants are judged on the quality of their crab Louis (pronounced "loo-ie," as in Louis XIV) salad. A proper Louis includes crunchy chilled iceberg lettuce, not fancy greens, and is usually served as a main-course salad, but smaller portions make a great appetizer for a company dinner. Serve with sourdough bread and a chilled glass of Chardonnay, and you'll instantly be transported to the City by the Bay.

Makes 4 appetizer or 2 main-course servings

Dressing

1¼ cups mayonnaise

⅓ cup Sun-Dried Tomato Pesto (page 251), or use
　　⅓ cup drained and finely chopped oil-packed
　　sun-dried tomatoes

¼ cup milk, or more as necessary

1½ teaspoons tomato paste (if using chopped tomatoes)

1½ tablespoons finely chopped fresh chives

1½ tablespoons finely chopped fresh parsley

¼ teaspoon Worcestershire sauce

Hot red pepper sauce

Salad

1 pound asparagus spears, trimmed

1 large head iceberg lettuce, torn into bite-size pieces,
　　washed and dried (about 12 cups)

1 pound lump crabmeat, preferably Dungeness crab,
　　picked over for shells and cartilage

1 cup cherry tomatoes

2 large hard-cooked eggs, cut into wedges

Lemon wedges for garnish

1. To make the dressing, mix all of the ingredients in a medium bowl. If necessary, thin to the desired thickness with more milk.

2. Cook the asparagus in a medium saucepan of lightly salted boiling water until crisp-tender, about 5 minutes. Drain and rinse under cold running water.

3. To serve as a main-course salad, spread the lettuce on a large serving platter. For first-course salads, divide the lettuce among four deep plates. Top the salad(s) with a mound of crabmeat, and garnish with the asparagus, cherry tomatoes, eggs, and lemon wedges. Serve immediately, with the dressing passed on the side.

Farfalle and Broccoli Salad with Gorgonzola Dressing

This pasta salad is always popular at cookouts, where I serve it with Mediterranean-inspired grilled foods. But then I noticed that leftovers were equally popular as lunch the next day, and now I make it as a main course whenever the weather is too hot to cook anything more complicated. For a heartier dish, add sliced roast beef from the deli or even chunks of grilled chicken.

Makes 6 to 8 servings

1 bunch broccoli (1 pound)

1 pound farfalle (bow-tie pasta)

3/4 cup mayonnaise

1/2 cup sour cream

2 tablespoons white wine vinegar

8 ounces Gorgonzola or other blue cheese, finely crumbled

3 celery ribs, cut into 1/8-inch-thick slices

3 scallions, white and green parts, chopped

3 tablespoons chopped fresh parsley

Salt and freshly ground black pepper to taste

1. Bring a medium saucepan of lightly salted water to a boil over high heat. Trim the broccoli and cut the tops into bite-size florets. Peel the stalks, then cut them crosswise into 1/4-inch-thick slices. Cook the broccoli stems in the boiling water for 2 minutes. Add the florets and cook until broccoli is crisp-tender, about 3 minutes longer. Drain, rinse under cold water, and let cool.

2. Bring a large pot of lightly salted water to a boil over high heat. Add the pasta and cook until tender, about 10 minutes. Drain, rinse under cold water, and let cool.

3. Whisk the mayonnaise, sour cream, and vinegar in a large bowl. Add half of the cheese and mash it into the mayonnaise mixture with a rubber spatula. Stir in the remaining cheese. Add the pasta, broccoli, celery, scallions, and parsley and mix. Season with salt and pepper. Cover and refrigerate until cold, about 2 hours.

4. Season the salad again with salt and pepper and serve chilled.

Fennel and Scallion Slaw   **Under 30 minutes**

There is something about the crisp texture and fresh taste of fennel that goes especially well with fish and shellfish. This easy slaw can serve as a side dish as well as a salad for simple grilled seafood dishes. For a bolder licorice flavor, add 2 tablespoons minced fennel fronds to the slaw.

Makes 4 servings

Grated zest of 1 lemon

1½ tablespoons fresh lemon juice

⅓ cup extra-virgin olive oil

Salt and freshly ground black pepper to taste

1 medium fennel bulb (1¼ pounds), trimmed

2 scallions, white and green parts, thinly sliced

1. Mix the lemon zest and juice in a medium bowl. Gradually whisk in the oil. Season with salt and pepper.

2. Cut the fennel lengthwise in half and trim out the hard core. Using a food processor fitted with the thin slicing blade, thinly slice the fennel. Transfer to the bowl of dressing and mix in the scallions. Serve immediately, or cover and refrigerate for up to 4 hours.

Chopped Greek Salad with Feta and Olives **Under 30 minutes**

This salad is much more than a chunky alternative to green salad, and it can also be a sandwich filling in a pita bread, a side dish, or a first course. One of my favorite ways to serve it is with the Pork Souvlaki (page 116).

Makes 4 to 6 servings

1 tablespoon red wine vinegar

1 teaspoon dried oregano

1 garlic clove, crushed through a press

1/4 cup extra-virgin olive oil

1 medium green bell pepper, cored, seeds and ribs removed, and cut into 1/2-inch dice

2 kirby cucumbers, scrubbed, halved lengthwise, seeds removed, and cut into 1/2-inch dice (or use 1/2 English cucumber—no need to scrub or discard seeds)

2 large ripe tomatoes, seeded and cut into 1/2-inch dice

2 scallions, white and green parts, coarsely chopped

1/2 cup crumbled feta cheese (see Note)

1/3 cup coarsely chopped pitted Kalamata olives

Salt and freshly ground black pepper to taste

1. Pulse the vinegar, oregano, and garlic in a blender to combine. With the machine running, gradually add the oil through the top vent.

2. Combine the bell pepper, cucumbers, tomatoes, scallions, feta, and olives in a medium bowl. Add the dressing and mix well. Season with salt and pepper. Cover and refrigerate until chilled, about 1 hour.

3. Serve chilled.

Note: Feta cheese, made from sheep's milk, comes from many different countries, and the quality varies greatly from maker to maker. I have bought feta at my local delicatessen blindly but trustingly and upon tasting, found that it was more funky than flavorful. I am a big fan of Bulgarian feta, which has a lovely creaminess and mild tang, and French feta is excellent too. You are more likely to find a good feta at an ethnic food store or cheese shop than a supermarket, of course.

Seeding Tomatoes

The liquidy seed pockets are often removed from tomatoes because if they are left in, their juices will dilute the finished dish. Seeding a tomato is quick and easy. Cut the tomato crosswise in half. Use your finger to poke out the seeds, which are gathered in jellylike globs, then hold the tomato upside down and give it a shake to get rid of strays (a few won't hurt). That's it.

Green Beans and Grape Tomatoes with Olive Vinaigrette   Under 30 minutes

This is another salad with multiple personalities. It works well both as a colorful first course for a company supper and as a side dish to grilled fish or lamb.

Makes 4 to 6 servings

2 tablespoons Olivada (page 137), or use store-bought olive paste

2 tablespoons red wine vinegar

1 garlic clove, crushed through a press

Grated zest of ½ lemon

Pinch of crushed hot red pepper flakes

⅓ cup extra-virgin olive oil

12 ounces green beans, trimmed and cut into 2-inch lengths

1 pint grape tomatoes

Salt and freshly ground black pepper to taste

1. To make the vinaigrette, pulse the olivada, vinegar, garlic, lemon zest, and red pepper in a blender. With the machine running, gradually add the oil through the top vent.

2. Cook the green beans in a large saucepan of salted boiling water just until crisp-tender, about 3 minutes. Drain and rinse under cold water. Transfer the beans to a bowl of very cold water, add a few ice cubes to the water (if you have a lot of ice in the water, it will be difficult to drain and dry the green beans), and let stand to chill for 5 minutes. Discard any unmelted ice cubes. Drain again and spin the green beans dry in a salad spinner.

3. Toss the green beans, tomatoes, and vinaigrette in a large bowl. Season with salt and pepper. Serve immediately.

House Salad with Rick's Red Dressing   Under 30 minutes

Occasionally I have nostalgic pangs for the so-called French dressing that I loved as a kid . . . yep, the thick, red-orange type that is more shaken than poured out of the bottle. My improved homemade version is created in the same fun spirit. (I was so relieved to see a recent newspaper article on fancy chefs using catsup as a secret ingredient, because I've been sneaking it into my cooking for years.) This dressing makes a frequent appearance in my salad bowl, always with the classic combination of iceberg lettuce, tomatoes, cucumbers, and onions.

Makes 4 servings

1/4 cup catsup

2 tablespoons balsamic vinegar

2 tablespoons chopped shallots

1 teaspoon light brown sugar

1 teaspoon Dijon mustard

1 garlic clove, crushed through a press

1/4 teaspoon salt

1/8 teaspoon freshly ground black pepper

2/3 cup regular olive oil

1 head iceberg lettuce, torn into bite-size pieces, washed, and dried

1 ripe large tomato, cut into wedges

1 medium cucumber, peeled and cut into thin rounds

1 small red onion, thinly sliced

1. To make the dressing, pulse the catsup, vinegar, shallots, brown sugar, mustard, garlic, salt, and pepper in a blender to combine. With the machine running, gradually pour in the oil through the top vent.

2. Mix the lettuce, tomato, cucumber, and onion in a large salad bowl. Serve immediately, with the dressing passed on the side.

Potato and Pea Salad with Chive Aïoli

Every summer, I teach a new round of grilling classes, and they always feature a different potato salad. This one, studded with bright green peas and with the snap of fresh celery, got high marks from my students. Serve it with Mediterranean-flavored entrées, such as grilled poultry or salmon.

Makes 4 to 6 servings

2 pounds red-skinned potatoes, scrubbed but not peeled

1 tablespoon white or red wine vinegar

⅔ cup mayonnaise

2 teaspoons Dijon mustard

1 garlic clove, crushed through a press

Pinch of cayenne pepper

3 celery ribs, cut into ⅛-inch-thick slices

¼ cup chopped fresh chives, plus more for garnish

Salt and freshly ground black pepper to taste

1½ cups thawed frozen peas

1. Cook the potatoes in a large saucepan of boiling salted water until tender, about 25 minutes. Drain and let cool.

2. Cut the potatoes in half. Place in a medium bowl and toss while sprinkling with the vinegar.

3. Whisk the mayonnaise, mustard, garlic, and cayenne pepper in a small bowl to make the aïoli. Add to the potatoes, along with the celery and chives, and toss. Season with salt and pepper. Cover and chill well, about 3 hours.

4. Just before serving, add the peas and mix gently. Season the salad again with salt and pepper. Sprinkle with chives and serve chilled.

Potato and Asparagus Salad

Substitute 1 pound asparagus spears, trimmed and cut into 1-inch lengths, for the peas. Cook in a medium saucepan of boiling lightly salted water just until crisp-tender, about 5 minutes. Drain, rinse under cold water, and pat dry with paper towels. Stir into the salad just before serving.

Hearts of Romaine with
Caesar Buttermilk Dressing Under 30 minutes

When I eat out, it's a toss-up between Caesar and Ranch dressings for my green salad. At home, I don't bother with decisions, I make this concoction, which combines the best flavors of both. A crisp, crunchy romaine is the best foil for the creamy dressing.

Makes 4 servings

½ cup mayonnaise

½ cup buttermilk

½ cup freshly grated Parmesan cheese

1 small onion, grated (use the large holes on a box grater; 1 tablespoon grated onion)

1 teaspoon anchovy paste or ½ teaspoon Worcestershire sauce

Freshly ground black pepper to taste

One 18-ounce bag romaine hearts, separated into individual leaves

1 cup store-bought croutons

A large chunk of Parmesan cheese (about 6 ounces—you will not use all the cheese), for making curls

1. To make the dressing, whisk the mayonnaise, buttermilk, Parmesan, onion, and anchovy paste in a small bowl until combined. Season with pepper.

2. Divide the romaine leaves among four large plates. Top each serving with a few tablespoons of the dressing, then with one-quarter of the croutons. Using a vegetable peeler, shave some curls of Parmesan from the cheese over each salad. Serve chilled.

Spinach Salad with
Warm Asian Pears and Goat Cheese Under 30 minutes

Whenever I teach in California, I head for the many farmers' markets in the Bay Area. Asian pears are always one of the prime offerings, but most of us don't have enough recipes for this juicy and aromatic fruit. A brief sauté to caramelize the outside of the pears intensifies their mild flavor. If baby spinach is unavailable, use flat-leafed spinach, with the stems removed. (Curly spinach is fine for cooking, but it is too tough for most salads.) If you wish, top each serving with a tablespoon or two of chopped walnuts.

Makes 4 servings

Red Wine–Shallot Vinaigrette

2 tablespoons red wine vinegar

1 tablespoon minced shallot

1 teaspoon Dijon mustard

½ cup extra-virgin olive oil

Salt and freshly ground black pepper to taste

Salad

2 teaspoons vegetable oil

1 firm but ripe Asian pear, cored and cut into ¼-inch-thick wedges

7 ounces baby spinach (about 8 cups)

2 ounces goat cheese, crumbled

Freshly ground black pepper

1. To make the vinaigrette, pulse the vinegar, shallot, and mustard in a blender to combine. With the machine running, gradually pour in the oil through the top vent. Season with salt and pepper.

2. Heat the oil in a large nonstick skillet over medium-high heat. Add the pear and cook until the undersides are lightly browned, about 2 minutes. Turn and brown the other sides, about 2 minutes. Remove from the heat.

3. Toss the spinach and dressing in a large bowl. Transfer equal amounts of the spinach to four salad plates. Top with the pears, then the cheese. Grind a generous amount of pepper over each salad. Serve immediately.

Stuffed Tomatoes with Grilled Corn Salad

Grilling has become my favorite cooking method for corn, as the direct heat lightly browns the kernels to bring out their sweetness. With the advent of gas grills, outdoor cooking has become an everyday affair for many cooks. I admit that I prefer the flavor a charcoal grill gives, but because the charred husk of grilled corn will always add a smoky flavor no matter what fuel is used, the ease of turning a knob sounds pretty good to me. If you wish, though, you can boil the corn instead: cook the husked ears for 10 minutes in a large pot of boiling water, then drain, cool, and cut off the kernels.

Makes 4 servings

4 medium beefsteak tomatoes (about 7 ounces each)

2 ears unhusked corn

Grated zest of ½ lime

1 tablespoon fresh lime juice

1 small garlic clove, crushed through a press

¼ cup extra-virgin olive oil

1 vinegar-packed roasted red bell pepper, seeds and ribs removed, chopped

1 tablespoon minced fresh cilantro

1 tablespoon minced shallot or red onion

1 teaspoon seeded, minced jalapeño

Salt and freshly ground black pepper to taste

⅓ cup crumbled goat cheese, optional

1. Cut off the top of each tomato to make a lid; discard the lids. Using a melon baller, scoop out the insides of the tomatoes to make tomato shells. Lightly salt the shells, turn upside on paper towels, and let drain for 30 minutes.

2. Build a charcoal fire in an outdoor grill and let burn until the coals are covered with white ash. (Or preheat a gas grill on High.)

3. Place the corn on the grill, cover, and grill, occasionally turning the ears, until the husks are blackened, 15 to 20 minutes. Let the corn cool. Remove the husks and silks from the corn. Cut the kernels from the cobs. (You should have about 1 cup.)

4. Pulse the lime zest, lime juice, and garlic in blender to combine. With the machine running, gradually add the oil through the top vent. Mix the corn, red bell pepper, cilantro, shallot, and jalapeño in a medium bowl. Add the dressing and mix well. Season with salt and pepper.

5. Spoon the corn salad into the tomato shells. Sprinkle with the cheese, if using. Serve chilled or at room temperature.

Canned Beans

Dried beans are great, but they need to be soaked in cold water for at least 4 hours to hydrate, and I never seem to remember this step (lentils are so thin that no soaking is necessary). With a supply of canned beans in my kitchen, I can use them impromptu. Once you find a brand with firm, unbroken beans and a minimum of saltiness, remember the name and become a loyal customer. My two mainstays are white kidney (cannellini) and black beans, with a couple of cans of pinto or pink beans waiting in the wings.

Tuna and Garbanzo Bean Salad Under 30 minutes

This has become my easy summer substitute for <u>salade Niçoise</u>, which I certainly love, but I would rather have a restaurant deal with the separate cooking of the potatoes, green beans, and eggs. Grilled tuna is popular in our house and I always cook extra so I can make this for lunch or dinner the next day. Nonetheless, I give instructions here on how to grill the tuna, just in case you aren't dealing with leftovers.

Makes 6 servings

1 pound tuna steaks, cut about ¾ inch thick

½ teaspoon salt, divided, plus more to taste

¼ teaspoon freshly ground black pepper, divided, plus
    more to taste

¼ cup fresh lemon juice

2 tablespoons minced shallots

1 teaspoon Dijon mustard

¾ cup extra-virgin olive oil

One 15- to 19-ounce can garbanzo beans (chickpeas),
    drained and rinsed

2 large ripe tomatoes, seeded and cut into ½-inch dice

2 tablespoons chopped fresh basil

6 large leaves red-leaf lettuce

1. Build a charcoal fire in an outdoor grill and let burn until the coals are covered with white ash. (For a gas grill, preheat on High.)

2. Lightly oil the grill. Season the tuna with ¼ teaspoon of the salt and ⅛ teaspoon of the pepper. Grill the tuna steaks until the undersides are seared with grill marks, about 3 minutes. Turn the steaks and cook until the second sides are seared, about 3 minutes for medium-rare tuna. Transfer to a cutting board and let cool for 5 minutes. Cut the tuna into ½-inch dice.

3. Whisk the lemon juice, shallots, mustard, and the remaining ¼ teaspoon salt and ⅛ teaspoon pepper in a small bowl. Gradually whisk in the oil.

4. In another bowl, mix the tuna, garbanzo beans, tomatoes, and basil with ½ cup of the dressing. Season with salt and pepper to taste. Cool.

5. Place a lettuce leaf on each plate, and heap the salad on the leaves. Drizzle with the remaining dressing. Serve immediately.

Tomato and Cucumber Salad
with Sherry-Ginger Vinaigrette   Under 30 minutes

This is one of the most refreshing salads around. The zesty ginger is a wonderful accent to the sweet tomatoes and the cool, crunchy cucumbers. At the height of the summer tomato season, make this with a colorful mix of heirloom varieties. While seasonal produce is always preferable, especially when you're talking about tomatoes, this dressing will immeasurably improve winter supermarket tomatoes.

Makes 4 servings

¼ cup shredded fresh ginger (use the large holes on a box grater)

1 tablespoon sherry vinegar or rice vinegar

½ teaspoon sugar

¼ teaspoon salt

¼ teaspoon freshly ground black pepper

⅓ cup vegetable oil

2 large tomatoes, cored and cut into 6 to 8 wedges each

1 large cucumber, peeled, halved lengthwise, seeded, and cut into ⅛-inch-thick half-moons

1 scallion, white and green parts, thinly sliced

1. To make the vinaigrette, squeeze the shredded ginger in your hand over a blender container to extract as much juice as possible—you should have about 1½ tablespoons juice. Discard the ginger. Add the vinegar, sugar, salt, and pepper and pulse to dissolve the sugar. With the machine running, gradually add the oil through the top vent.

2. Combine the tomatoes, cucumber, and scallion in a medium bowl. Add the vinaigrette and mix well. Serve immediately, or refrigerate until ready to serve. (The salad can be made up to 4 hours ahead, covered, and refrigerated, but if you're using ripe summer tomatoes, the salad will be at its best if served right away.)

Sandwiches A sandwich is the food pyramid on a plate. Grains, meat, dairy, and vegetables all make it into most sandwiches. When you come up with an irresistible fruit sandwich, let me know (and I will not count peanut butter and banana). In this chapter, I concentrate on hot sandwiches or those that are substantial enough to provide a meal. You don't need a recipe for a ham and Swiss on rye with mustard.

The proliferation of ethnic breads has changed the sandwich's profile. Is puffy white sandwich bread still anyone's first choice? Today's sandwiches can be made on focaccia, corn or flour tortillas (not to mention herb- or chile-flavored tortillas), crusty artisan sourdough, or tender egg challah, to name just a few options.

Sandwiches may be easy, but they can be quite sophisticated. Consider both ends of the hot beef sandwich spectrum. At one end you have the Bistro Skirt Steak Sandwich, served with a rich brown gravy. On the other, there are juicy Hamburgers with Roast Pepper Catsup. The sliced skirt steak sandwich is special enough to serve to company, but when I want a comforting meal, it's time to grill some burgers. To round out the meal, you need nothing more than a simple salad (Coleslaw with Apple–Poppy Seed Dressing is usually my first suggestion) or Crisp Oven Fries.

One of my first restaurant jobs was at a health-food emporium in San Francisco, where the specialty of the house was avocado on seven-grain bread (see an updated version on page 76). To play up the wholesome handmade experience, we cut the bread by hand. Even after making thousands of this sandwich, it remains one of my favorite lunches, something that speaks volumes to the satisfying culinary experience of a well-made sandwich.

The Carefree Cook's Tips for Sandwiches

Jazz up familiar condiments for new flavors Catsup, mayonnaise, and mustard are the trio of condiments that show up again and again on sandwiches. But it is easy and fun to give them a makeover—the Roast Pepper Catsup (page 82) and Chutney Mayonnaise (page 79) are perfect illustrations. Or stir a spoonful of pesto or olivada (see the homemade versions on page 268 and 137) into mayonnaise or Dijon mustard.

For perfect hot sandwiches, invest in a sandwich grill If you love hot grilled sandwiches, an electric sandwich grill may be just the ticket. Some waffle irons have reversible flat plates that can be used for sandwiches. These presses weight the sandwich for even toasting and preclude the necessity for turning. If you don't feel like investing in a grill, use a heavy skillet (preferably nonstick) and weight down the sandwich with a flat plate. You will have to turn the sandwich when the underside is toasted to toast the second side.

Portobello Croque Monsieur **Under 30 minutes**

Here is a member of the grilled cheese family, with a meaty portobello mushroom as its raison d'être. It is hard to find a more satisfying hot vegetarian sandwich that can be ready in less time. Use a portobello mushroom cap that will fit on the bread without too much overhang.

Makes 1 sandwich

1 portobello mushroom, stem removed

1 teaspoon extra-virgin olive oil

Salt and freshly ground black pepper to taste

2 teaspoons unsalted butter

2 slices firm white sandwich bread

1 tablespoon Pesto (page 268), or use store-bought

1/3 cup (about 1 1/2 ounces) shredded Gruyère cheese

1. Using a dessert spoon, scrape out the black gills from the underside of the mushroom cap. (Removing the gills reduces the amount of black juice the mushroom will exude.)

2. Heat the oil in a medium nonstick skillet over medium heat. Add the mushroom, flat side down, and cook until the underside is browned, about 4 minutes. Turn the mushroom and cook until tender, about 2 minutes. Transfer to a plate and season with salt and pepper.

3. Wipe out the skillet with moist paper towels. Add the butter and melt over medium heat. Place the mushroom cap on one slice of bread, spread with the pesto, and sprinkle with the cheese. Top with the remaining bread and place the sandwich in the skillet. Cook, turning once, until both sides of the sandwich are golden brown, about 5 minutes. Serve hot.

Grilled Chicken Pan Bagnat

In Provence, pan bagnat is a marinated sandwich made from canned tuna and hard-boiled eggs—it is supposed to have a somewhat moist texture. The concept can be easily applied to grilled chicken. To save time, the lemon–olive oil vinaigrette doubles as a marinade. You can serve the sandwich immediately or let it marinate—I usually can't wait.

Makes 4 sandwiches

2 tablespoons fresh lemon juice

1 teaspoon Herbes de Provence (page 165), or use
    store-bought

1 teaspoon anchovy paste

1 garlic clove, crushed through a press

1/2 cup extra-virgin olive oil

Salt and freshly ground black pepper to taste

1 tablespoon nonpareil capers

Four 6-ounce boneless, skinless chicken breasts,
    pounded gently to an even thickness

4 crusty French or Italian rolls, split lengthwise, and some
    of the insides pulled out

2 medium tomatoes, sliced

2 hard-cooked eggs, thinly sliced (optional)

1/2 small red onion, thinly sliced

4 romaine lettuce leaves, torn crosswise in half

1. Make a vinaigrette by whisking the lemon juice, herbs, anchovy paste, and garlic in a medium bowl. Gradually whisk in the oil. Season with salt and pepper. Pour 1/4 cup vinaigrette into a 1-gallon zip-tight plastic bag.

2. Stir the capers into the remaining vinaigrette and set aside. Add the chicken to the bag, seal the bag, and refrigerate for 1 to 2 hours.

3. Build a charcoal fire on one side of an outdoor grill and let burn until the coals are covered with white ash. (Or preheat one burner of a gas grill on High, and leave the other burner off.)

4. Lightly oil the grill. Remove the chicken from the marinade and shake off the excess. Grill over the hot side of the fire until the underside is seared with grill marks, about 2 minutes. Turn and grill to mark the other side, about 2 minutes. Transfer the chicken to the outer perimeter of the grill, being sure it is not directly over the coals (or place it above the turned-off burner). Cover the grill and cook

until the breasts feel firm when pressed in the center, about 10 minutes. (The chicken can also be cooked in a large nonstick skillet over medium heat, turning occasionally, for about 10 minutes.) Transfer the chicken to a cutting board and let stand for 5 minutes.

5. Slice the chicken on the diagonal into thick slices. For each sandwich, place one sliced chicken breast on the bottom half of a roll. Top the chicken with the tomato, hard-boiled egg, and onion, and drizzle with the reserved vinaigrette. Finish each sandwich with a lettuce leaf and the top of the roll. Press firmly and slice crosswise in half. Serve immediately, or wrap each sandwich in aluminum foil and refrigerate for 2 to 4 hours.

Chicken and Pepper Jack Quesadillas Under 30 minutes

A quesadilla is certainly a sandwich. I have tortillas in my refrigerator more often than I have bread in the bread box, so quesadillas make frequent appearances in my kitchen. This is one of my favorite ways to perk up the ubiquitous boneless, skinless chicken breast. It can be a quick lunch or dinner (serve it with the Black Bean Salad with Avocado and Red Pepper on page 46), or even an appetizer, with cold Mexican beers.

Makes 2 quesadillas, 2 to 4 servings

1 teaspoon dried oregano

$^1\!/_2$ teaspoon ground cumin

$^1\!/_4$ teaspoon salt

One 6- to 7-ounce boneless, skinless chicken breast,
    gently pounded to an even thickness

1 teaspoon olive oil

Four 7-inch flour tortillas

$^2\!/_3$ cup shredded pepper Jack cheese

Year-Round Salsa (page 236), or use store-bought salsa,
    for serving

1. Mix the oregano, cumin, and salt in a shallow dish. Sprinkle evenly over the chicken.

2. Heat the oil in a medium nonstick skillet over medium heat. Add the chicken and cook, turning occasionally, until it is browned and feels firm when pressed in the center, about 8 minutes. Transfer the chicken to a cutting board and let stand for 5 minutes. Set the skillet aside.

3. Holding a sharp knife at a 45-degree angle, cut the chicken into $^1\!/_2$-inch-thick slices.

4. Return the skillet to medium heat. Place 1 tortilla in the skillet and cook until the underside is heated, about 30 seconds. Turn the tortilla and top with half of the chicken slices. Sprinkle with $^1\!/_3$ cup of the cheese. Top with a second tortilla. Cook until the underside is beginning to brown, about 1 minute. Turn and cook until the other side is beginning to brown, about 1 minute. Transfer to a plate and cover loosely with aluminum foil to keep warm. Repeat with the remaining tortillas, chicken, and cheese.

5. Cut the quesadillas into wedges. Serve hot, with the salsa.

Chipotle Guacamole and Bacon Sandwich Under 30 minutes

During my college years, I worked at The Haven, a restaurant at the forefront of the natural foods movement in San Francisco. Even though it was the ultimate in "health food chic," it was also home of the avocado and bacon sandwich (well, bacon bits, but that was before San Francisco's "truth in menu" law went into effect). One of my daily responsibilities was to peel and pit three cases of ripe avocados. It is amazing that I can still look at an avocado, but I love this sandwich, which I now find even more appealing with added Mexican flavors and real bacon.

Makes 2 sandwiches

3 slices thick-cut bacon

2 ripe avocados, pitted and peeled

1½ tablespoons mayonnaise

1½ tablespoons Year-Round Salsa (page 236), or use
    store-bought salsa

¼ teaspoon pure ground chipotle chiles or regular chili
    powder, or more to taste

Salt to taste

4 slices whole wheat bread

2 red-leaf lettuce leaves

1. Place the bacon in a large skillet and cook over medium heat, turning once, until crisp and browned, about 6 minutes (starting the bacon in a cold skillet reduces splattering). Transfer the bacon to paper towels to drain and cool, then coarsely chop.

2. Mash the avocados, mayonnaise, salsa, and ground chipotles in a small bowl with a fork until mixed but still chunky. Add more chipotle, if you wish. Season well with salt (avocados are bland, so don't be shy).

3. For each sandwich, spread half of the guacamole on one slice of bread, top with half the chopped bacon and a lettuce leaf, and finish with a second slice of bread. Cut in half and serve.

Grilled Cheddar, Tomato, and Bacon Sandwich Under 30 minutes

This is a grilled cheese sandwich on steroids. If you dig into one of these babies for lunch, I suggest a nice glass of carrot juice for dinner. You might think that a mayonnaise smear on the outside of the sandwich is too much, but it literally gilds the lily, contributing to the most golden brown beauty of a grilled cheese sandwich you will ever lay your eyes on. Thanks to my friend Kelly Volpe for sharing this tip.

Makes 1 sandwich

2 slices thick-cut bacon

1/2 cup (2 ounces) shredded extra-sharp Cheddar cheese

Two 1/2-inch-thick slices cut from crusty bread with a tight crumb, preferably day-old

2 tomato slices, pockets of seeds poked out

Freshly ground black pepper to taste

1 tablespoon mayonnaise

1. Place the bacon in a large skillet and cook over medium heat, turning once, until crisp and browned, about 6 minutes (starting the bacon in a cold skillet reduces splattering). Transfer the bacon to paper towels to drain. Wash and dry the skillet.

2. Scatter half of the cheese over one slice of bread. Top with the tomato slices and season with pepper. Add the bacon, broken to fit the bread. Sprinkle with the remaining cheese. Spread the second bread slice with half of the mayonnaise, and place over the cheese, mayonnaise side up.

3. Heat the empty skillet over medium heat. Add the sandwich, mayonnaise side down, and place a flat plate on top of it to weight it down. Cook for 2 minutes, or until the underside is golden. Remove the plate and spread the top of the sandwich with the remaining mayonnaise. Turn the sandwich, top with the plate, and cook for another 2 minutes, or until the other side is golden.

4. Cut the sandwich in half with a serrated knife and serve hot.

Ground Pork Burgers
with Chutney Mayonnaise Under 30 minutes

Beef isn't the only contender for a burger, and with the right combination of condiments, pork burgers are a fine change of pace. New Yorkers of a certain age will remember a version of this burger from a twenty-four-hour restaurant on the Upper West Side, where it was the perfect late supper after dancing at Studio 54.

Makes 4 servings

Chutney Mayonnaise

1/4 cup mayonnaise

1/4 cup mango chutney, or any chunks of fruit finely
  chopped

1 tablespoon Dijon mustard

Burgers

1 1/3 pounds ground pork

2 tablespoons dried bread crumbs

1 tablespoon Dijon mustard

1/2 teaspoon salt

1/4 teaspoon freshly ground black pepper

Nonstick vegetable oil spray for the skillet

1/2 cup (2 ounces) shredded extra-sharp Cheddar cheese

4 hamburger buns, split and toasted

Red leaf lettuce, sliced tomatoes, and sliced onion for
  serving

1. To make the chutney mayonnaise, mix the mayonnaise, chutney, and mustard in a small bowl.

2. Working as quickly and gently as possible, mix the ground pork, bread crumbs, mustard, salt, and pepper in a medium bowl. Gently form into 4 patties about 4 inches wide.

3. Spray a 12-inch heavy skillet with the oil and heat over medium-high heat. Add the patties and cook until the undersides are browned, about 3 minutes. Turn and brown the other side, about 3 minutes. Cover tightly, reduce the heat to medium, and cook, turning occasionally, just until the burgers are cooked through and they feel firm when pressed in the centers, about 8 minutes. Top the burgers with the cheese and cover to melt the cheese, about 1 minute.

4. Spread each bun with a generous tablespoon of the chutney mayonnaise. Place the burgers in the buns and serve, with the remaining mayonnaise on the side. Let everyone choose fixings from the lettuce, tomatoes, and onion.

Grilled Cuban Sandwich   Under 30 minutes

Toasted Cuban sandwiches blow boring old ham and cheese out of the water! The classic Cubans are griddled in a sandwich press, but a simple trip to the broiler gives excellent results. In a carefree kitchen, the cook makes extra food for dinner so the leftovers can be used in other meals. This recipe uses leftovers from Caribbean Pork Tenderloin on page 111. Some delicatessens carry roast pork, which can be substituted. But when you want to make more than one sandwich, it is definitely worthwhile to make the tenderloin just for these great sandwiches.

Makes 1 sandwich

1 tablespoon mayonnaise

1 teaspoon spicy brown or Dijon mustard

1 oblong crusty French roll, split (see Note)

2 ounces sliced ham

1½ ounces sliced Swiss cheese

4 thin slices Caribbean Pork Tenderloin (page 111), or use store-bought roast pork

4 dill pickle slices

1. Position a rack 6 inches from the source of heat and preheat the broiler. (Or preheat a toaster oven on Broil.)

2. Mix the mayonnaise and mustard in a small bowl. Spread on one half of the roll. Top with the ham, then the cheese, both cut to fit the roll. Place the pork slices on the other half of the roll. Place on a broiler pan.

3. Broil until the cheese is bubbling, about 3 minutes. Top with the pickles, and close the roll. Cut in half and serve immediately.

Note: The right roll for a Cuban sandwich is crusty but not hard. It should have a soft crumb—the typical sourdough roll is too resilient. In my neighborhood, these are called Portuguese rolls, probably because they are made in Newark, New Jersey, which has a number of Portuguese-American commercial bakeries.

Red Pepper, Prosciutto, and Mozzarella Panini **Under 30 minutes**

A quick trip to the deli for sliced prosciutto (I always have a jar of roasted peppers, some cheese, and some bread in the kitchen), and I'm just minutes away from panini. These pressed toasted sandwiches have always been popular in Italy, and they have recently found their way into American menus. An electric sandwich press is a nice appliance, but not entirely necessary to make a great panino. Preheat the press on medium-low according to the appliance directions, and toast each panino in the press (without the wax paper) until golden brown, about 3 minutes.

Makes 2 sandwiches

4 slices firm white sandwich bread, preferably slightly stale

$^2/_3$ cup shredded mozzarella, provolone, or Italian fontina

2 ounces thinly sliced prosciutto

1 roasted red pepper packed in vinegar, drained, and patted dry

About 8 large basil leaves, optional

2 tablespoons unsalted butter, well-softened

1. Thoroughly heat a large, heavy empty skillet or griddle over medium heat. Cut 2 squares of wax paper slightly larger than a piece of the sliced bread.

2. For each sandwich, top 1 slice of bread with one-fourth of the cheese, then half of the prosciutto and roasted pepper, trimmed to fit the bread. Scatter 4 basil leaves over the red pepper, if using. Sprinkle with another fourth of the cheese. Cover with a second slice of bread. Spread half of the butter in a thin, even layer on the outside of the sandwich and place on a square of wax paper, cut a bit larger than the sandwich.

3. Place 1 sandwich in the skillet (if using a griddle, you should be able to cook both sandwiches at once), wax paper side up, and weight down the sandwich with a flat plate. Cook until the underside is an even golden brown, about 2 minutes. (The idea is to toast the sandwich somewhat slowly, in order to heat the filling and melt the cheese, so lower the heat as needed.) Turn, discarding the wax paper, weight with a plate, and cook until the other side is golden brown, about 2 minutes. Transfer to a cutting board. Repeat with the second sandwich.

4. Cut each sandwich in half on the diagonal, and serve hot.

Hamburgers with Roast Pepper Catsup   Under 30 minutes

For one of my first cookbooks, I created 365 recipes for hamburger and other ground meats. So when I give you advice about hamburgers, it is the voice of experience talking. First, for the juiciest burgers with the most flavor (is there any other way you like them?), use ground round, not sirloin (too dry) or chuck (too fatty). Second, add salt and pepper to the meat before forming the patties so the seasoning can be savored in every bite. As for the roast pepper catsup, you will be surprised at how this simple combination can add a touch of class to the humble burger. This recipe makes enough catsup for the burgers and French fries too—I assume that you will be making Crisp Oven Fries (page 271) or some other potato to go on the side.

Makes 4 servings

One 12-ounce jar roasted red peppers, drained and rinsed, or 2 freshly roasted red peppers (see below)

¾ cup catsup

1⅓ pounds ground round (85 percent lean)

1¼ teaspoons salt

½ teaspoon freshly ground black pepper

4 hamburger buns, split

Mustard, mayonnaise, sliced onion, lettuce leaves, and sliced tomatoes for serving

1. Build a charcoal fire in an outdoor grill and let burn until the coals are covered with white ash. (Or preheat a gas grill on High.)

2. To make the catsup, puree the peppers with the catsup in a blender or food processor. Transfer to a bowl. (You will have about 1 cup.)

3. Working as gently and quickly as possible (overmixing compacts the meat and makes tough burgers), mix the ground round, salt, and pepper. Gently form into four patties about 1 inch thick.

4. Lightly oil the grill. Add the burgers, cover, and cook, turning once, until the outside is browned but the inside is still pink and juicy, 8 to 12 minutes for rare to medium-rare—or longer if desired. If the juices drip onto the coals and cause excessive flare-ups, move the hamburgers to the edges of the grill, away from the coals. (Or, on a gas grill, turn off one burner of the grill, keeping the other one on High, and move the burgers to the cooler area. Cook covered.)

5. Meanwhile, toast the buns on the hot side of the grill until warm and lightly browned. Place the cooked burgers in the buns, and pass the catsup on the side. Let everyone choose fixings from the mustard, mayonnaise, onion, lettuce, and tomatoes.

Roasting Peppers

Every cook knows about the high flavor profile of roasted red peppers. Roasting softens the flesh, condenses the juices, and loosens the bitter skin for easy peeling. (Yellow and orange bell peppers also benefit from roasting, but not green peppers.) Broiling the peppers accomplishes the same thing as roasting or grilling, and it's much quicker and easier.

Cut the pepper as directed on page 14. Position a broiler rack about 6 inches from the source of heat and preheat the broiler. Place the pepper strip, top, and bottom on the rack, skin side up. Broil until the skin is blackened and blistered, 5 minutes or longer, depending on the heat of the broiler. Let cool for a few minutes (I never enclose the peppers in a bag—not only does that slow the cooling, but the collected steam can make the peppers too soft), then peel off the blackened skin. Avoid rinsing the peppers under water, or you will rinse away flavor.

Salmon Burgers Provençale
with Tomato Relish   Under 30 minutes

The fatty flesh of salmon is perfect for grinding and grilling into seafood burgers. The tomato relish adds tang, and arugula provides a peppery note. Use a soft roll, as these burgers are not nearly as firm as ground beef.

Makes 4 sandwiches

Tomato Relish

1 ripe large tomato, seeded and cut into ½-inch dice

1 tablespoon finely chopped shallot

1 tablespoon sherry vinegar or balsamic vinegar

1 tablespoon extra-virgin olive oil

Salt and freshly ground black pepper to taste

Burgers

1½ pounds skinless salmon fillet, cut into 1-inch chunks

2 tablespoons Pesto (page 268), or use store-bought

½ teaspoon salt

¼ teaspoon freshly ground black pepper

2 teaspoons extra-virgin olive oil

4 soft rolls, split

12 large arugula leaves or 4 red-leaf lettuce leaves

1. To make the relish, mix the tomato, shallot, vinegar, and oil in a small bowl. Season with salt and pepper. Set aside while you prepare the salmon.

2. Place the salmon, pesto, salt, and pepper in a food processor and pulse until the salmon is finely chopped. Rinse your hands under cold water, and form the salmon mixture into 4 patties about 4 inches wide.

3. Heat the oil in a large nonstick skillet over medium-high heat. Add the patties and cook until the underside is lightly browned, about 1½ minutes. Turn and cook until the other side is lightly browned, about 1½ minutes for medium-rare salmon burgers; do not overcook.

4. For each sandwich, place a burger on the bottom half of a roll and top with a spoonful of the tomato relish, 3 arugula leaves, and the top of the roll. Serve immediately.

Bistro Skirt Steak Sandwich
on Sourdough Toast **Under 30 minutes**

There is nothing like tearing into a gravy-doused open-faced steak sandwich, and this recipe will have one on your plate in minutes. It features flavors from a French bistro, always one of my favorite places to find inspiration. However, the sauce is best when made with homemade beef stock (use the leftover broth from Viennese Pot Roast on page 108) or high-quality frozen stock, found at many supermarkets—if it is made with canned broth, the sauce will not be nearly as delicious.

Makes 3 or 4 sandwiches

One 1-pound skirt steak, cut into 3 or 4 portions that will fit into the skillet

½ teaspoon salt

¼ teaspoon freshly ground black pepper

1 tablespoon vegetable oil

2 tablespoons unsalted butter

2 tablespoons finely chopped shallots

2 cups beef stock, preferably homemade or thawed high-quality frozen stock

2 tablespoons cognac or other brandy

2 teaspoons cornstarch

2 teaspoons Dijon mustard

1 teaspoon tomato paste

3 or 4 large slices crusty French or Italian bread (one per serving), toasted

1. Season the steak with the salt and pepper. Heat the oil in a large heavy skillet over high heat until very hot. Add the steak. Cook, reducing the heat to medium-high if needed so the steak cooks steadily but doesn't burn, until the underside is well browned, about 5 minutes. Turn and brown the other side, about 5 minutes for medium-rare steak. Transfer the steak to a carving board and let stand while you make the sauce.

2. Let the skillet cool slightly. Then add the butter and shallots and cook over medium heat, stirring often, until the shallots soften, about 2 minutes. Pour the stock and cognac into a small bowl, add the cornstarch, mustard, and tomato paste, and whisk to dissolve the cornstarch. Pour into the skillet and bring to a boil over high heat, scraping up the browned bits in the bottom of the skillet with a wooden spatula. Boil, stirring occasionally, until the sauce reduces and coats the spatula, about 3 minutes. Remove from the heat.

3. Thinly slice the steak *with* the grain (not against the grain), holding the knife at a 45-degree angle to make wider slices. Whisk any of the juices into the gravy.

4. Place a slice of toasted bread on each plate. Top with the sliced meat and the sauce. Serve hot.

Skirt Steak

Skirt steak is a popular cut with French butchers, who call it *bavette*. Most skirt steaks weigh about 1 pound, which allows for three hearty or four modest sandwiches, depending on the diners' appetites. Skirt steak is from the same diaphragm area of beef as flank steak—and has the same reputation for being a chewy, flavorful cut that can be great when prepared correctly—but it should be sliced with the grain, not against it. By doing this, you slice through the tough connective tissue, exposing the juicy, pink interior of the steak.

Beef, Pork, Lamb, and Veal Although Americans are well beyond the "meat and potatoes" mentality, good old red meat is still enormously popular. Beef remains king, but pork, lamb, and veal are showing up more and more on today's dinner tables. ¶ It's all about variety. Mix up your daily fare by type of meat as well as cut and cooking method. Many cooks broil boneless cuts night after night because they're quick to prepare—a sure way to cooking burnout. Stir-fries and sautés are fast, easy, and tasty, and certainly worthwhile, but they cannot compare with the deep, rich flavor of a slowly simmered stew or the satisfying taste of a roast. Make Viennese Pot Roast on a Sunday afternoon, and you'll get a main course, leftovers for sandwiches, and a big pot of homemade beef stock to boot. Or turn your Saturday night Short Ribs Provençale into a pasta sauce for another meal.

Over the years, I have learned to prefer sautéed steaks and chops to broiled. My stove, like so many others, has an inefficient broiler that raises the kitchen temperature to hellish proportions, but doesn't provide enough real heat to brown the food. Sautéing works especially well for meat because it creates pan juices that can be turned into a fast sauce. Pan sauces can be almost infinitely varied by your choice of liquid. Most start out with broth, augmented by wine or a bit of liquor, and are finished off with a swirl of enriching butter. A large heavy skillet is imperative for sautéing success. Of course, along with a good skillet, sautéing also requires a good ventilation system.

So take out the skillet, roasting pan, or braising pot, and get ready to partake in an American tradition, The Red Meat Meal.

The Carefree Cook's Tips for Meat

Always buy the best grade you can afford   The USDA has set standards for beef, pork, lamb, and veal. These standards rate the quality of the meat by age and marbling (the amount of fat in the muscles, which melts and moistens the meat during cooking), among other factors. Higher grades have the best flavor. Beef has seven grades, but only prime, choice, and standard are of any concern to consumers. Restaurants and high-quality butchers snap up prime meat for their discerning clientele; your supermarket probably carries choice beef. If you've ever wondered about how a certain store can consistently sell cheap beef, check out the grade— the market could be selling standard, which may have more waste due to the amount of fat that needs to be trimmed.

Use more economical cuts for variety   Even if I could afford to grill prime-grade steak every night, I'd get tired of it after a while. There's a lot of flavor in some of those less expensive cuts. Sometimes I am in the mood for sautéed lamb loin chops, but most often I actually prefer braised lamb shoulder chops. Some formerly humble cuts are now experiencing newfound popularity, which means that they can demand higher prices. I remember when skirt steak and short ribs were two of the cheapest cuts at the butcher, but they've had a comeback because restaurant chefs rediscovered their flavor. There are many ugly-duckling cuts that are waiting for their time to become glamorous.

Sauté meats in a large heavy skillet A high-quality 12-inch skillet may seem like a lot of pan, but it has vast advantages over smaller, more lightweight models. A large cooking surface gives the amount of meat needed for a typical meal sufficient room for browning. Heavy skillets are typically made from layered metals, and their bulk allows them to absorb and hold heat. This even heating also creates the perfect surface for browning.

The interior surface treatment is up to you. Some cooks like nonstick skillets for their easy cleanup. However, I usually grab my stainless-steel-lined skillet for sautéing meats for the very reason that it makes lots of crusty browned bits in the skillet that can be deglazed and turned into a pan sauce.

What about cast-iron skillets? If you have a well-seasoned one, and take good care of it, it is a wonderful tool. But most cooks don't have the patience to season a cast-iron skillet properly (coat the cleaned pan with vegetable oil and bake at 350°F for an hour, then cool), and someone trying to be helpful eventually ruins the cooked-on slick surface with a good scrubbing of detergent (you should clean the skillet with a generous sprinkle of salt and a wet paper towel—never use soap). A good place to find an already seasoned cast-iron skillet is a garage sale (I bought mine for $5), but factory-preseasoned pans are appearing on the market.

When it comes to doneness, don't be in the dark If meat is underdone, it usually can be cooked a bit longer to the desired doneness. With overdone meat, however, there is no turning back. Take advantage of the many meat thermometers on the market. For more information, see page 136.

Filet Mignon au Poivre
with Bourbon-Shallot Sauce Under 30 minutes

This variation of steak au poivre has an American kick from its bourbon pan sauce. Filet mignon works well because its relatively mild flavor takes well to robust sauces, but feel free to use other boneless cuts, from sirloin to skirt steak. You'll find the four-peppercorn mixture at specialty markets and many supermarkets. If you can't locate it, substitute only 2 teaspoons whole black peppercorns (because the red and green peppercorns aren't as hot as black peppercorns).

Makes 4 servings

1 tablespoon four-peppercorn blend (black, white, red, and green peppercorns)

Four 6-ounce filet mignon steaks

1/2 teaspoon salt, plus more to taste

1 tablespoon vegetable oil

1/2 cup bourbon

4 tablespoons (1/2 stick) chilled, unsalted butter, divided

1/4 cup finely chopped shallots

1 cup beef stock, preferably homemade or thawed high-quality frozen stock

1. Coarsely crush the peppercorns in a mortar and pestle or on a work surface under a heavy skillet. Spread the crushed peppercorns on a plate. Season the steaks with the salt. Sprinkle the peppercorns evenly over both sides of the steaks, pressing them into the meat to adhere.

2. Heat the oil in a 12-inch heavy skillet over medium-high heat, tilting the skillet to slick the bottom with the oil. Add the steaks and cook until the undersides are well browned, about 4 minutes. Turn and brown the other sides for another 4 minutes for medium-rare meat. Transfer to a plate and tent with foil to keep warm.

3. Meanwhile, heat the bourbon in a small saucepan over medium heat until it is warm. Carefully ignite the bourbon with a long match. Let flame for 30 seconds, then, if the flame doesn't burn out on its own, cover the saucepan to extinguish the flame. Set aside.

4. Add 1 tablespoon of the butter and the shallots to the skillet and cook over medium heat, stirring often, until the butter melts and the shallots are softened,

about 2 minutes. Add the stock and bourbon and bring to a boil over high heat, scraping up the browned bits in the skillet with a wooden spatula. Boil until reduced to $1/2$ cup, about 2 minutes. Remove from the heat and whisk in the remaining 3 tablespoons butter, 1 tablespoon at a time. Season carefully with salt—it may need just a pinch, if any at all.

5. Serve each steak on a dinner plate, topped with a spoonful of sauce.

Flank Steak and Arugula
with Warm Balsamic Vinaigrette   Under 30 minutes

The juxtaposition of hot meat and cool salad is very refreshing and I often serve this on warm evenings. Sure, you can grill the meat outside, but cooking on the stove gives you pan juices that are deglazed into the vinaigrette, a simple trick that pulls the whole dish together nicely. While arugula is my first choice to play against the meat, mixed baby greens with a high proportion of radicchio and other bitter greens work well too.

Makes 4 to 6 servings

½ cup plus 2 teaspoons extra-virgin olive oil, divided

1½ pounds flank steak

½ teaspoon salt, divided

½ teaspoon freshly ground black pepper, divided

3 tablespoons balsamic vinegar

12 ounces arugula, tough stems discarded, well washed, and torn into bite-size pieces (about 8 cups)

A large chunk of Parmesan cheese (about 6 ounces—you won't use all of the cheese), for cheese curls

1. Heat 2 teaspoons of the oil in a 12-inch heavy skillet over medium-high heat, tilting the pan to slick the bottom with oil. Season the steak with ¼ teaspoon of the salt and ¼ teaspoon of the pepper. Place in the skillet and cook until the underside is well browned, adjusting the heat as needed to keep the meat from burning, about 6 minutes. Turn and cook until the other side is browned, about 6 minutes for medium-rare steak. Transfer to a carving board. Set the skillet aside.

2. To make the vinaigrette, whisk the vinegar and the remaining ¼ teaspoon salt and ¼ teaspoon pepper in a medium bowl. Gradually whisk in the remaining ½ cup oil. Return the skillet to high heat, pour in the vinaigrette, and scrape up any browned bits in the skillet with a wooden spatula (don't let the vinaigrette reduce). Remove from the heat.

3. Spread the arugula on a large platter. Holding the knife at a 45-degree angle, slice the steak across the grain into thin slices. Spread overlapping slices of the

steak over the arugula. Whisk any meat juices into the vinaigrette, and pour the vinaigrette over the steak and arugula. Using a vegetable peeler, shave a generous amount of curls of Parmesan from the cheese onto the meat and greens. 4. Serve immediately, giving each person a portion of salad topped with steak and cheese curls.

Porterhouse Steak with Vermouth-Glazed Onions

A porterhouse steak makes a dramatic appearance on the table, and it is even more appealing smothered with tender onions. These massive beauties are big enough to serve two steak lovers, but some cooks may be able to get three or even four servings from one large steak. Once considered the private property of steakhouses, porterhouse steaks can now be found at many butchers and supermarkets. Because the steak is so thick, it needs a double-cooking method. Searing on the top of the stove gives the meat a deep brown crust, and baking in the oven completes the cooking. Red vermouth, not a common cooking ingredient (but available at any liquor store), adds just the right sweet note to the onions.

Makes 2 to 4 servings

2 tablespoons unsalted butter

1 pound large onions, cut into ⅛-inch-thick half-moons

½ cup sweet red vermouth

1 tablespoon light or dark brown sugar

¾ teaspoon salt, divided

⅜ teaspoon freshly ground black pepper, divided

One 1¾-pound porterhouse steak, cut about 1¼ inches thick

1. Melt the butter in a medium skillet over medium heat. Add the onions and cook, stirring occasionally, until softened but not tender, about 10 minutes. Stir in the vermouth, brown sugar, ¼ teaspoon of the salt, and ⅛ teaspoon of the pepper and bring to a boil. Reduce the heat to medium-low. Cook, stirring occasionally, until the onions are very tender and the vermouth has reduced to a glaze, about 20 minutes. Transfer the onions to a bowl and set aside.

2. Meanwhile, position a rack in the center of the oven and preheat to 450°F.

3. Heat a 12-inch heavy ovenproof skillet over high heat until very hot. Trim off a piece of the beef fat and, holding it with a pair of tongs, rub the fat onto the bottom of the skillet to create a slick coating. Season the steak with the remaining ½ teaspoon salt and ¼ teaspoon pepper, add to the skillet, and cook until the underside is well browned, about 3 minutes. Turn and brown the other side, about 3 minutes. Discard any rendered fat in the skillet. Transfer the skillet to the oven and roast until an instant-read thermometer inserted in the center

Porterhouse Steak with Vermouth-Glazed Onions; Creamed Spinach (page 274); Crisp Oven Fries (page 271)

of the steak reads 125°F, about 5 minutes. Transfer the steak to a cutting board and let stand for 5 minutes.

4. Meanwhile, pour out the fat in the skillet. Return the skillet to medium heat, add the onions, and cook, stirring up any browned bits in the skillet, until the onions are heated through, about 1 minute. Transfer to a bowl.

5. To carve the steak, cut off the two portions of meat on either side of the bone. Carve each piece crosswise into thin slices. Transfer to plates, making sure each person gets some of the tenderloin, and serve with the onions.

Checking Meat for Doneness

Most cooks hate to cut into a steak to check for doneness, as even the smallest cut will release juices. Unfortunately, when it comes to testing for doneness, there is no substitute for experience. Cooks at a steakhouse work with the same cuts and weights of meat day in and day out, so it doesn't take long for them to learn an average cooking time.

A home cook has two options. The first is the touch test. Meat contains lots of water, and the liquid will evaporate when heat is applied. The longer the steak cooks, the drier and firmer the steak becomes—well-done steak is less moist than rare steak, right? The level of doneness can be established by pressing the cooked steak in the center: if a steak feels relatively soft, it is rare; somewhat firm, medium; firm, well done.

Some meat thermometers can give a reading for steak, but not all. Be sure that the thermometer's sensor (usually indicated by a dimple) is far enough down the stem that it can reach the center of the steak. Those grilling forks with sensors in their prongs actually work quite well because they are designed for thinner cuts like steaks. Some cooks insert the thermometer through the side of the steak to test doneness, but this only works with relatively thick cuts such as filet mignons and porterhouse steaks.

Italian Beef and Vegetable Stir-Fry   Under 30 minutes

When most cooks think of stir-fries, they think of Asian cooking. But the stir-fry technique can, of course, be applied to many ingredients and seasonings. Here I use Mediterranean flavors to make a quick skillet supper. This recipe also works well with thinly sliced pork tenderloin or chicken breast, both of which should be cooked for about 3 minutes in Step 3 to ensure they are thoroughly cooked.

Makes 4 servings

1 pound boneless sirloin steak

2 tablespoons extra-virgin olive oil, divided

1 medium onion, cut into 1/4-inch-thick half-moons

1 medium zucchini, halved lengthwise and cut into
    1/4-inch-thick half-moons

1 garlic clove, minced

1/2 cup drained and chopped sun-dried tomatoes in oil

1/4 cup pitted and coarsely chopped Mediterranean
    black olives

1 teaspoon Italian Herb Seasoning (recipe follows) or
    dried oregano

1/2 teaspoon salt

1/8 teaspoon crushed hot red pepper flakes

1 cup canned low-sodium chicken broth

1 tablespoon tomato paste

1 teaspoon cornstarch

Hot cooked small pasta, such as orzo or ditalini,
    for serving

1. If you have the time, freeze the steak for about 1 hour to firm it and make for easier slicing. Trim off the outside strip of fat from the steak. Holding a large sharp knife at a 45-degree angle, slice the steak across the grain into wide thin slices.

2. Heat 1 tablespoon of the oil in a 12-inch heavy skillet over medium-high heat. Add the onion and zucchini and stir-fry until crisp-tender, about 3 minutes. Add the garlic and cook until it gives off its aroma, about 30 seconds. Stir in the sun-dried tomatoes and olives and stir-fry until heated through, about 1 minute. Transfer the mixture to a plate.

3. Heat the remaining 1 tablespoon oil in the skillet over medium-high heat. Add the steak and season with the herb seasoning, salt, and red pepper flakes. Cook, stirring occasionally, just until it loses its pink color, about 1 1/2 minutes.

(continued)

Return the vegetable mixture to the skillet and stir-fry to mix well, about 1 minute.

4. Whisk the broth, tomato paste, and cornstarch in a small bowl until the cornstarch dissolves. Add to the skillet and stir until the liquid comes to a boil and thickens. Serve immediately, spooned over the pasta.

Seasoning Secret

Italian Herb Seasoning

Take a whiff of this zesty seasoning and you'll immediately think of a restaurant with red-checkered tablecloths and a wonderful Mama cooking in the kitchen. It adds an Italian profile to pasta sauces, meat dishes, grilled chicken and fish, and more (I can't eat delivery pizza without a generous sprinkle of these herbs on top).

Makes about 1/3 cup

2 tablespoons dried basil

2 tablespoons dried oregano

1 tablespoon dried rosemary

1 teaspoon dried thyme

1 teaspoon dried marjoram, optional

Mix all of the ingredients together. Store in an airtight container in a cool, dark place for up to 3 months.

Barbecued Meat Loaves

I am a man of simple tastes . . . sometimes it doesn't take much more than a really good meat loaf recipe to make my day. And everyone should have a good meat loaf recipe in their life. This is how I make meat loaf, with barbecue sauce stepping in for catsup to give a zestier flavor—but choose a red tomato-based sauce, not one that is overly sweet. The only problem with most meat loaves is that they take so long to cook. I solve the problem by making the loaves in individual doughnut shapes— the hole in the center cuts the baking time in half.

Makes 4 servings

½ cup old-fashioned or quick-cooking (not instant) rolled oats

½ cup plus 2 tablespoons store-bought barbecue sauce

1 large egg, beaten

1 small onion, finely chopped

1 garlic clove, crushed through a garlic press

1½ teaspoons salt

½ teaspoon freshly ground black pepper

2 pounds meat loaf mix (equal parts ground beef, pork, and veal)

1. Position a rack in the center of the oven and preheat to 375°F. Line a rimmed baking sheet pan with aluminum foil and lightly oil the foil.

2. Mix the oats, ½ cup of the barbecue sauce, the egg, onion, garlic, salt, and pepper in a large bowl. Add the meat loaf mix and mix with your hands until well combined.

3. Divide the meat mixture into 4 equal portions and place on the baking pan, spacing them a few inches apart. Shape each into a mound about 5 inches wide and 1½ inches thick. Using your finger, create a 1-inch-wide hole in the center of each mound.

4. Bake for 30 minutes. Spread the remaining 2 tablespoons barbecue sauce over the tops of the meat loaves. Continue baking until a meat thermometer inserted in the thickest part of a loaf reads 165°F, about 10 minutes longer. Serve hot.

Roast Beef and Vegetables with Moroccan Spices

For many cooks, the image of beef roasting on a bed of vegetables brings back appetite-inducing memories of Sunday dinners past. This rendition has been intriguingly seasoned with a heady mix of spices. Many cuts of beef are fine candidates for roasting, but for ease of carving and affordability, I usually opt for eye of round. Don't cook this cut past 135°F, or it will toughen.

Makes 6 to 8 servings

1 teaspoon cumin seeds

1 teaspoon coriander seeds

½ teaspoon whole black peppercorns

1¼ teaspoons salt, divided

½ teaspoon ground ginger

⅛ teaspoon ground hot red (cayenne) pepper

One 3-pound beef eye-of-round roast, tied

1 garlic clove, cut into about 12 slivers

4 tablespoons extra-virgin olive oil, divided

2½ pounds baking potatoes, peeled and cut into 1-inch chunks

8 medium carrots, halved lengthwise and cut into 3-inch lengths

¼ teaspoon freshly ground black pepper

2 tablespoons chopped fresh cilantro or parsley

1. Position a rack in the center of the oven and preheat to 350°F. Lightly oil a large roasting pan.

2. In a mortar, or on a work counter using a heavy skillet or saucepan, coarsely crush the cumin, coriander, and peppercorns. Place the crushed spices in a small bowl and stir in ¾ teaspoon of the salt, the ginger, and red pepper.

3. Using the tip of a small knife, make about twelve 1-inch-deep incisions in the beef, and place a garlic sliver in each. Brush 2 teaspoons of the oil over the beef and rub with the spice mixture. In a large bowl, toss the potatoes and carrots with the remaining 2 tablespoons oil and season with the remaining ½ teaspoon salt and the black pepper. Spread in the roasting pan, and place the beef on top.

4. Roast, stirring the vegetables occasionally, until an instant-read thermometer inserted in the center of the beef reads 125°F for medium-rare meat, about 1

hour and 20 minutes. Leaving the vegetables in the pan, transfer the roast to a carving board and let stand for 10 minutes.

5. Meanwhile, increase the oven temperature to 450°F and continue roasting the vegetables until lightly browned, about 10 minutes. Remove from the oven and stir in the cilantro.

6. Remove the string from the roast, carve, and serve hot with the vegetables.

Short Ribs Provençale

A few years ago, the editors of <u>Bon Appétit</u> magazine declared braised short ribs the recipe of the year, and they asked me to create the ultimate version. Combining elements from different short rib dishes I had enjoyed at restaurants, this is the result. I have since received an amazing amount of mail from cooks who have told me that this is the most awesome meat dish they have ever encountered. Hyperbole aside, it has become one of my favorite recipes for entertaining because it can be made well ahead of time and only needs a brief reheating. Leftovers can be easily turned into a terrific pasta sauce. For the best-looking dish, search out the meatiest short ribs, cut between the bones into individual chunks that weigh 12 to 16 ounces each. Buttermilk Mashed Potatoes (page 269) are a must.

Makes 6 servings

2 tablespoons extra-virgin olive oil

6 pounds individual short ribs (not cross-cut flanken)

¾ teaspoon salt, plus more to taste

½ teaspoon freshly ground black pepper, plus more
    to taste

1 large onion, finely chopped

1 medium carrot, finely chopped

1 celery rib, finely chopped

12 garlic cloves, peeled

1 tablespoon Herbes de Provence (page 165), or use
    store-bought

2 tablespoons all-purpose flour

2 cups hearty red wine, such as Zinfandel or Shiraz

1¾ cups beef stock, preferably homemade, or reduced-
    sodium chicken broth

One 14½-ounce can diced tomatoes in juice, drained

1 bay leaf

8 ounces baby-cut carrots

½ cup Mediterranean black olives, such as Niçoise, pitted

3 tablespoons chopped fresh parsley for garnish

1. Position a rack in the center of the oven and preheat to 300°F.

2. Heat the oil in a large (at least 6-quart) Dutch oven or flameproof casserole over medium-high heat. Season the short ribs with the salt and pepper. In batches, without crowding, add the short ribs to the pot and cook, turning occasionally, until browned on all sides, about 8 minutes. Using tongs, transfer the ribs to a platter. (continued)

Shorts Ribs Provençale; Buttermilk Mashed Potatoes (page 269)

3. Pour off all but 2 tablespoons of the fat from the pot. Add the onion, chopped carrot, and celery to the pot and reduce the heat to medium-low. Cover and cook, stirring often, until the vegetables are softened, about 5 minutes. Add the garlic, herbes de Provence, and flour and stir until the garlic gives off its aroma, about 1 minute. Stir in the wine and bring to a boil over high heat, stirring up the browned bits on the bottom of the pan with a wooden spoon. Add the broth, tomatoes, and bay leaf. Return the short ribs, and any juices, to the pot. Add cold water as needed to barely reach the top of the ribs and bring to a boil over high heat.

4. Cover tightly, transfer to the oven, and bake, stirring occasionally to change the position of the ribs, until the meat is falling-off-the-bone tender, about $2\frac{1}{2}$ hours. During last 15 minutes, add the baby carrots.

5. Transfer the short ribs to a deep serving platter and cover with aluminum foil to keep warm. Skim off the fat from the surface of the cooking liquid, and discard the bay leaf. Bring to a boil over high heat and cook until the liquid is reduced to a sauce consistency, about 10 minutes (the exact time depends on the size of the pot). Add the olives and cook to heat them through, about 3 minutes. Season the sauce with salt and pepper.

6. Spoon the sauce with the carrots over the ribs, sprinkle with the parsley, and serve hot.

Short Ribs Pasta Sauce

This hearty sauce is especially excellent with tube-shaped pasta, such as rigatoni or ziti. Pick out and discard most of the baby carrots from the short ribs before measuring, as too many carrots will make an oversweet sauce.

Makes about 4 cups; enough for 1 pound pasta

1 tablespoon extra-virgin olive oil

½ cup chopped onion

3 to 4 cups leftover Short Ribs Provençale—with the
    meat chopped into bite-size pieces, and including
    the vegetables and olives in the sauce

One 28-ounce can crushed tomatoes

½ teaspoon Herbes de Provence (page 165), or use
    store-bought

Heat the oil in a medium saucepan over medium heat. Add the onion and cook, stirring often, until golden, about 5 minutes. Stir in the short ribs, with their vegetables, olives, and sauce, the tomatoes, and herbes de Provence. Bring to a simmer. Reduce the heat to medium-low and simmer until slightly thickened, about 30 minutes.

Viennese Pot Roast with Apple-Horseradish Sauce

Vienna is one of the world's greatest cities, and I visit as often as I can. The signature meat dish of Vienna, Tafelspitz, is nothing more than boiled beef. It is humble, but in the right hands, it is sublime. There are Viennese restaurants that serve nothing but Tafelspitz prepared from various cuts of meat, each one with its own distinctly delicious flavor and texture. I prefer rump roast, which has a deep beefy taste and is easy to carve. One of the secrets of Tafelspitz is a flavorful broth. The really good news here is that you will have leftover broth to use for other recipes. To serve the pot roast in the true Viennese style, offer Creamed Spinach (page 274) and potato pancakes, such as the ones on page 243, on a small plate on the side. The apple-horseradish sauce is a must.

Makes 6 to 8 servings

3 pounds beef soup bones

1 large onion, chopped

2 large celery ribs, cut into 1/2-inch dice

2 medium carrots, cut into 1/2-inch dice

4 garlic cloves, crushed under a knife

2 tablespoons chopped fresh parsley, plus more
   for garnish

1 teaspoon dried thyme

1 bay leaf

One 3 1/2- to 4-pound boneless beef rump roast

1 teaspoon salt, plus more to taste

1/4 teaspoon freshly ground black pepper, plus more
   to taste

Apple-Horseradish Sauce

2 Granny Smith apples, peeled, cored, and cut into
   1-inch chunks

1 teaspoon sugar

2 tablespoons drained prepared horseradish

1. Position the broiler rack 6 inches from the source of heat and preheat the broiler. Spread the beef bones in a broiler pan or shallow metal roasting pan. Broil the bones, turning occasionally, until well browned, about 15 minutes. Transfer the bones to a plate and set aside.

2. Pour 2 tablespoons of the rendered beef fat from the broiler pan into a soup pot and heat over medium heat. Add the onion, celery, carrots, and garlic to the pot. Cook, stirring often, until softened, about 5 minutes.

3. Add the beef bones to the pot. Place the broiler pan over two burners over high heat and heat until the pan is sizzling. Add 2 cups cold water, scraping up the browned bits in the pan with a wooden spatula, and pour the liquid into the pot. Add enough cold water to cover the bones by 1 inch (about $3^1/2$ quarts). Bring to a boil over high heat, skimming off any foam that rises to the surface. Add the parsley, thyme, and bay leaf, partially cover, and reduce the heat to medium-low. Simmer for 2 hours.

4. Season the beef with the salt and pepper and add to the simmering broth. Partially cover and simmer until the meat is tender, about $2^1/2$ hours. (Rump roast has a firm texture, so the best way to test for tenderness is to transfer the roast to a cutting board and carve off a thin slice, cutting across—not with—the grain.)

5. Meanwhile, make the applesauce: bring the apples, sugar, and $^1/4$ cup water to a simmer in a saucepan over medium-low heat. Cover tightly and cook, stirring occasionally, until the apples are tender, about 20 minutes. Transfer to a bowl, add the horseradish, and mash with a fork. Let cool to room temperature.

6. Transfer the meat to a cutting board and cover with aluminum foil to keep warm. Remove the pot from the heat and let stand for 3 minutes. Skim off any fat from the broth. Taste, adding a few grains of salt to your spoon or broth—if you feel the flavor could be stronger, boil over high heat to reduce it slightly, about 10 minutes. Using tongs, remove the bones and the bay leaf. Season the broth with salt and pepper.

7. Carving across the grain, cut the meat into $^1/2$-inch-thick slices and place in soup bowls. Ladle some of the broth and vegetables over each serving and sprinkle with parsley. Serve hot, with the applesauce passed on the side. (The leftover broth, cooled and covered, can be refrigerated for up to three days or frozen for up to three months.)

Beef Brisket with Beer-Smothered Onions

I am crazy about mesquite-smoked brisket, but there are times when cooking brisket outdoors is not feasible. That's when I braise the beef on the stove with lots of onions. Many butchers trim this cut to a fare-thee-well, so look for an untrimmed portion, which will be more flavorful (wholesale shopping clubs are a good source), and remove the excess fat before serving.

Makes 8 to 10 servings

2 tablespoons vegetable oil

One 5- to 6-pound beef brisket (untrimmed)

³/₄ teaspoon salt, plus more to taste

¹/₂ teaspoon freshly ground black pepper, plus more
    to taste

4 large onions, cut into ¹/₄-inch-thick half-moons

4 garlic cloves, minced

One 12-ounce bottle lager beer

¹/₄ cup packed light brown sugar

1 teaspoon dried rosemary

1 teaspoon dried thyme

¹/₄ cup spicy brown mustard

2 tablespoons red wine vinegar

1. Position a rack in the center of the oven and preheat to 300°F.

2. Heat the oil in a Dutch oven over medium-high heat. Add the brisket and brown on both sides, about 10 minutes. Transfer to a plate and season with the salt and pepper.

3. Add the onions and garlic to the pot. Cover and cook, stirring occasionally, until the onions are well softened, about 8 minutes. Stir in the beer, brown sugar, rosemary, and thyme. Bury the beef, with any juices, in the onions.

4. Cover tightly and bake, turning the beef occasionally until the brisket is very tender, about 3 hours. Transfer the beef to a carving board and cover with foil.

5. Let the cooking liquid stand for 5 minutes, then skim off the fat that rises to surface. Bring to a boil over high heat and cook until the liquid has reduced by half, about 5 minutes. Add the mustard and vinegar and cook for 5 minutes to blend the flavors.

6. Slice the brisket across the grain into thin slices and arrange on a deep platter. Season the onions with salt and pepper, then pour over the beef. Serve hot.

Caribbean Pork Tenderloin with Rum-Lime Sauce   **Under 30 minutes**

Pork tenderloin offers lean meat with very little waste. To bring out the flavor, pan-sear it on top of the stove to caramelize the surface, then roast to complete the cooking. If you wish, double the recipe and cook two tenderloins so you are sure to have leftovers for Grilled Cuban Sandwiches (page 80).

Makes 4 servings

One 1-pound pork tenderloin, trimmed

Grated zest of 1 lime

1 teaspoon dried oregano

1/4 teaspoon garlic powder

1/4 teaspoon onion powder

1/4 teaspoon salt, plus more to taste

1/4 teaspoon freshly ground black pepper, plus more to taste

1 tablespoon extra-virgin olive oil

2 tablespoons golden or dark rum

1/2 cup canned reduced-sodium chicken broth

2 tablespoons fresh lime juice

1 tablespoon chilled unsalted butter

1. Position a rack in the center of the oven and preheat to 400°F.

2. To give the tenderloin an even thickness, fold back the thin end and tie with kitchen string or unwaxed dental floss. Mix the lime zest, oregano, garlic and onion powders, salt, and pepper in a shallow dish. Roll the tenderloin in the seasoning mix to coat.

3. Heat the oil in a 12-inch ovenproof skillet over medium-high heat. Add the tenderloin and cook, turning occasionally, until browned on all sides, about 8 minutes. Transfer the pan to the oven and cook until a meat thermometer inserted in the center of the tenderloin registers 145°F, about 12 minutes. Transfer the tenderloin to a plate.

4. Return the skillet to high heat on the stove. Add the rum (it will evaporate almost immediately), then the broth and lime juice and bring to a boil, stirring up the browned bits in the skillet with a wooden spoon. Boil until the liquid is reduced to about 2/3 cup, about 2 minutes. Remove from the heat and stir in the butter until it melts and thickens the sauce. Season with salt and pepper.

5. Holding the knife at a 45-degree angle, cut the tenderloin into 1/2-inch-thick slices. Serve immediately, with a spoonful of the sauce over each serving.

Pork Medallions with Charcuterie Sauce Under 30 minutes

In French cuisine, "à la charcuterie" means chopped cornichons and capers in a pleasantly piquant sauce—probably because the tiny pickles are the classic accompaniment to pâté, one of the masterpieces of the charcutier's art. This quick sauté of thinly sliced pork tenderloin has French style written all over it. Because pork tenderloins usually come in 1-pound portions, I use that amount here. However, for hearty appetites, you may want to double the recipe.

Makes 3 to 4 servings

1 pound boneless pork tenderloin, trimmed

2 tablespoons vegetable oil

1/4 cup all-purpose flour

1/2 teaspoon salt, plus more to taste

1/4 teaspoon freshly ground black pepper, plus more
    to taste

2 tablespoons minced shallots

1 tablespoon unsalted butter

3 tablespoons chopped cornichons (tiny sour pickles) or
    dill pickles

2 tablespoons nonpareil capers, rinsed

1 cup dry white wine, such as Sauvignon Blanc

2 tablespoons white or red wine vinegar

1 tablespoon Dijon mustard

Chopped fresh parsley for garnish

1. Holding the knife at a 45-degree angle, cut the pork tenderloin crosswise into 8 slices about 1/2 inch thick. Gently pound the slices with a meat mallet so they are all about the same size and thickness.

2. Heat the oil in a 12-inch skillet over medium-high heat. Mix the flour, salt, and pepper in a shallow dish. In batches, coat the pork in the flour, shaking off the excess, and add to the skillet. Cook, turning once, until browned on both sides, about 4 minutes. Transfer to a plate.

3. Add the shallots and butter to the skillet and cook over medium heat, stirring often, until the shallots soften, about 2 minutes. Stir in the cornichons and capers. Add the wine and bring to a boil, scraping up the browned bits in the skillet with a wooden spatula. Boil until reduced by half, about 2 minutes.

4. Stir in the vinegar and mustard and reduce the heat to low. Return the pork to the skillet and cook, turning often, until the sauce thickens slightly, about 1 minute. Season with salt and pepper. Serve hot, sprinkled with the parsley.

Oven-Barbecued Pork Chops with Chutney BBQ Sauce

One of the reasons I like cooking with chutney is its range of flavors, from sweet to spicy. It is put to good use to add dimension to a tangy sauce that turns baked pork chops into some pretty good barbecue.

Makes 4 servings

1 tablespoon vegetable oil

Four 10-ounce center-cut pork loin chops, cut

    ¾ inch thick

¼ teaspoon salt

¼ teaspoon freshly ground black pepper

1 tablespoon unsalted butter

1 medium onion, finely chopped

1 garlic clove, minced

½ cup American-style chili sauce or catsup

½ cup mango chutney, such as Major Grey's

1 tablespoon spicy brown or Dijon mustard

1 tablespoon Worcestershire sauce

½ teaspoon liquid smoke seasoning, optional

1. Position a rack in the center of the oven and preheat to 350°F.

2. Heat the oil in a 12-inch ovenproof skillet over medium-high heat. Season the pork chops with the salt and pepper. Add to the skillet and cook until the underside is browned, about 3 minutes. Turn and brown the other side, about 3 minutes. Transfer to a plate.

3. Add the butter to the skillet and melt over medium heat. Add the onion and cook, stirring occasionally, until golden, about 6 minutes. Add the garlic and cook until it gives off its aroma, about 1 minute. Stir in the catsup, chutney, mustard, ⅓ cup water, Worcestershire sauce, and liquid smoke, if using. Bring the sauce to a simmer, scraping up the browned bits in the skillet with a wooden spatula.

4. Return the pork chops to the skillet and baste with the sauce. Cover with a lid or aluminum foil. Transfer to the oven and bake for 25 minutes. Uncover and bake until the chops are glazed and show no sign of pink at the bone when pierced with the tip of a sharp knife. Serve hot.

Pork Chops in Creamy Mushroom Sauce

On my list of favorite comfort foods is my mom's recipe for pork chops simmered in canned cream of mushroom soup. I recently described this dish to a friend, and I was shocked to find out that his mom never made this classic—I thought everyone's mom knew the recipe by heart! Here's an updated, from-scratch version that I love just as much as the original. In fact, the powdered porcini mushrooms, while optional, make it extra special.

Makes 4 servings

Four 10-ounce center-cut pork loin chops, ¾ inch thick

½ teaspoon salt, plus more to taste

¼ teaspoon freshly ground black pepper, plus more to taste

¼ cup all-purpose flour

1 tablespoon vegetable oil

1 tablespoon unsalted butter

1 pound mushrooms, preferably a mix of cremini, button, and stemmed shiitakes, thinly sliced

2 tablespoons chopped shallots

1 tablespoon Porcini Powder (page 179), optional

½ cup dry sherry

1 cup canned low-sodium chicken broth

½ teaspoon dried thyme

½ cup sour cream or plain yogurt

2 teaspoons cornstarch

1. Season the chops with the salt and pepper. Dredge in the flour and shake off the excess.

2. Heat the oil in a 12-inch heavy skillet over medium-high heat. Add the chops and cook, turning once, until browned on both sides, about 4 minutes. Transfer the chops to a plate.

3. Melt the butter in the skillet. Add the mushrooms and cook, stirring often, until they give off their juices and begin to brown, about 6 minutes. Stir in the shallots and cook until they soften, about 2 minutes. Stir in the porcini powder, if using. Add the sherry and bring to a boil. Stir in the broth and thyme. Return the chops to the skillet and reduce the heat to medium-low. Cover tightly and cook until the chops are cooked through, about 25 minutes. Transfer the chops to a platter.

4. Whisk the sour cream and cornstarch together in a small bowl to dissolve the cornstarch. Whisk into the cooking liquid, bring to a simmer, and simmer to slightly thicken the sauce. Season with salt and pepper. Pour the sauce over the chops and serve immediately.

Pork Souvlaki **Under 30 minutes**

While this dish has the classic souvlaki marinade and is grilled on skewers, I don't skewer vegetables with the meat because I find that the vegetables are always overcooked by the time the meat is done. Instead, serve Chopped Greek Salad (page 54) with the pork, along with pita bread. The lemon-onion marinade, which is nothing short of terrific, is great with lamb and swordfish too. The souvlaki can also be cooked on an oiled broiler rack in a preheated broiler. Cook, turning the skewers occasionally, until the pork is cooked through, about 12 minutes.

Makes 4 to 6 servings

2 pounds center-cut boneless pork loin

½ cup chopped onion

⅓ cup fresh lemon juice

¼ cup extra-virgin olive oil

2 garlic cloves, chopped

1 tablespoon dried oregano

½ teaspoon salt

¼ teaspoon freshly ground black pepper

Metal skewers (or wooden skewers that have been
    soaked in water for 30 minutes, then drained)

1. Trim the fat from the pork and cut it into 1½-inch cubes.

2. Puree the onion with the lemon juice, oil, garlic, oregano, salt, and pepper in a food processor or blender. Pour into a zip-tight plastic bag and add the pork cubes. Refrigerate to marinate while you prepare the fire, or for up to 24 hours.

3. Build a charcoal fire in an outdoor grill and let burn until the coals are covered with white ash. (Or preheat a gas grill on High.)

4. Thread the meat onto the skewers, leaving a little space between the cubes. Lightly oil the grill. Grill the skewers, turning occasionally, until the meat is well browned and looks barely pink in the center when prodded with a sharp knife, 10 to 12 minutes.

5. Remove the pork from the skewers and serve hot.

Pork Souvlaki; Chopped Greek Salad
with Feta and Olives (page 54)

Pork Souvlaki Sandwich

Here's how to turn leftover pork souvlaki into a great sandwich. Or, instead of the cucumber, tomato, and onion, use leftover chopped salad.

Makes 1 sandwich

4 to 6 cubes Pork Souvlaki, reheated in a microwave or at room temperature

1 pita bread, one edge trimmed off, opened into a pocket, and toasted

$1/3$ cup thinly sliced cucumber

$1/2$ ripe tomato, seeded and cubed

A few thin slices of onion

3 tablespoons plain yogurt

$1/4$ teaspoon ground cumin

1 small garlic clove, crushed through a press

Stuff the pork cubes into the pita, and fill the sandwich with the cucumber, tomato, and onion. Combine the yogurt, cumin, and garlic and spoon inside the sandwich.

Tuscan Roasted Spareribs

Certain dishes fill the kitchen with incredibly appetizing aromas that make the diners half-crazed with anticipation—and then these dishes live up to their promise. These effortless spareribs are such a recipe. I am a huge fan of barbecued ribs, but I have never served these without someone at the table saying that they like these oven-roasted ribs just as much as grilled ribs, if not better. That is quite a recommendation! You will need a very large roasting pan, about 18 by 14 inches, to hold both racks of ribs. If you don't have one, bake the ribs on two rimmed baking sheets, on two oven racks. To make the sauce, deglaze one baking sheet with all of the wine, then use the resulting liquid to deglaze the second sheet. Serve the ribs with soft polenta and sautéed green beans.

Makes 4 servings

3 garlic cloves

1 teaspoon salt, divided

1½ teaspoons dried basil

1½ teaspoons dried oregano

1½ teaspoons dried rosemary

1½ teaspoons dried sage

¾ teaspoon freshly ground black pepper

2 tablespoons extra-virgin olive oil

5½ pounds spareribs

¾ cup dry white wine

1. Position a rack in the center of the oven and preheat to 350°F.

2. On a cutting board, crush the garlic under the side of a knife, then coarsely chop. Sprinkle with ½ teaspoon of the salt, and continue chopping and smearing the garlic on the board until it forms a paste. Scrape into a small bowl. Add the basil, oregano, rosemary, sage, pepper, and the remaining ½ teaspoon salt. Stir in the oil to make a paste.

3. Rub the herb paste all over the spareribs. Place the ribs in a very large roasting pan, about 18 x 14 inches. The ribs can overlap slightly. Roast, basting occasionally with the juices in the pan, for 1 hour. Turn the ribs and continue baking and basting until they are browned and tender, about 1 more hour. Transfer to a cutting board and let stand while you make the sauce.

(continued)

4. Tilt the roasting pan and spoon off the fat, leaving the dark juices in the pan. Place on two burners over high heat and heat until the pan is sizzling. Add the wine and use a flat wooden spatula or spoon to scrape up the browned bits in the pan. Cook until the wine is slightly reduced, about 2 minutes. Pour the sauce into a small bowl.

5. Cut the ribs between the bones and place on a serving platter. Serve immediately, topping each serving with a spoonful of the sauce.

Pan Juices

Never, ever throw out the juices left in the bottom of a roasting pan or skillet. These browned bits are a treasure trove of flavor and should be used, not washed down the drain! Most recipes call for deglazing the pan to collect the juices, a technique that is akin to rinsing out the pan with a flavorful liquid.

Heat the pan on top of the stove, over two burners if necessary, being sure that the pan is sizzling hot before adding the liquid, which is often wine. When the wine hits the pan, the heat makes a blast of steam that forces out the raw alcohol taste to make a more mellow sauce. Even if the liquid isn't alcoholic, the high heat will make the sauce come to a boil quickly. Scrape up the flavor-packed browned bits on the bottom of the pan—a flat wooden spatula does the best job, but a wooden spoon works if care is taken to reach all over the pan. Boil the liquid until it reaches a slightly thickened consistency. To make any pan sauce richer and a bit thicker, remove the pan from the stove and whisk in a tablespoon or two (or three) of chilled unsalted butter, a tablespoon at a time.

Tuscan Roasted Spareribs;

Herbed Polenta with Corn (page 265);

Braised Escarole (page 262)

Smoked Pork Chops
with Honey-Mustard Glaze **Under 30 minutes**

Smoked pork chops deliver the flavor of ham without requiring you to cook a whole leg. They can be found in most supermarkets, but a local European butcher (I get mine from a Polish shop) will doubtless carry a superior product. Be sure to get chops on the bone.

Makes 4 servings

Four 3/4-inch-thick smoked pork chops on the bone (about 2 1/4 pounds)

3 tablespoons whole-grain mustard, such as moutarde de Meaux

1 1/2 tablespoons honey

1 small garlic clove, crushed through a press

1. Position an oiled broiler rack 6 inches from the source of heat and preheat the broiler.

2. Place the chops on the rack and broil until the tops are lightly browned, about 4 minutes. Turn and cook to lightly brown the other side, about 4 minutes.

3. Stir the mustard, honey, and garlic together in a small bowl. Spread over the tops of the chops and cook until the glaze is bubbling, about 1 minute. Serve hot.

Tandoori-Style Boneless Leg of Lamb Under 30 minutes

Boneless leg of lamb takes beautifully to the grill or broiler. It is often marinated, but I don't always have the time for a long soak. This Indian yogurt-and-spice coating is so thick and flavorful that a marinating period is totally optional. Remember that marinades do not really tenderize meat, so, for the tenderest eating, be sure to cut the lamb across the grain into fairly thin slices. Serve with basmati rice and Tomato and Cucumber Salad (page 67).

Makes 4 to 6 servings

1 small onion, coarsely chopped

2 tablespoons fresh lemon juice

1 tablespoon shredded fresh ginger (use the large holes on a box grater)

2 garlic cloves, crushed through a press

½ cup plain low-fat yogurt

1½ teaspoons Madras-style curry powder

½ teaspoon salt

⅛ teaspoon ground hot red (cayenne) pepper

One 2⅓-pound boneless leg of lamb, trimmed of excess fat, butterflied and opened out

1. Position a lightly oiled broiler rack 6 inches from the source of heat and pre-heat the broiler.

2. Process the onion with the lemon juice, ginger, and garlic in a food processor until finely minced. Transfer to a large bowl and stir in the yogurt, curry, salt, and red pepper. (Do not be tempted to mix the yogurt and seasonings in the food processor—the yogurt will thin too much.) Add the lamb and turn to coat with the marinade. (The lamb can be marinated, covered tightly with plastic wrap and refrigerated, for up to 8 hours.)

3. Place the lamb on the rack and broil for 6 minutes. Turn and broil until an instant-read thermometer inserted in the thickest part of the lamb reads 125°F for medium-rare lamb, about 6 minutes more. Transfer to a carving board and let stand for 5 minutes.

4. Cut the lamb across the grain into thin slices and serve hot.

Roman Lamb Sauté
with White Wine and Herbs   Under 30 minutes

You can hardly go to a trattoria in Rome without seeing <u>abbacchio alla cacciatore</u> (hunter-style spring lamb) on the menu. Fragrant with herbs and garlic, with a piquancy provided by vinegar, this will become a favorite.

Makes 4 servings

2 tablespoons extra-virgin olive oil, divided, plus more as needed

2¾ pounds boneless leg of lamb, trimmed of fat and sinew and cut into 1½-inch cubes (2 pounds trimmed weight)

2 garlic cloves, thinly sliced

1 teaspoon anchovy paste

1 tablespoon finely chopped fresh rosemary or 1½ teaspoons crumbled dried rosemary

1 teaspoon finely chopped fresh sage or ½ teaspoon dried sage

¼ teaspoon crushed hot red pepper flakes

2 teaspoons all-purpose flour

½ cup dry white wine

¼ cup white or red wine vinegar

Salt to taste

Fresh rosemary or sage sprigs for garnish, optional

1. Heat 1 tablespoon of the oil in a 12-inch skillet over high heat. In batches, without crowding, adding more oil as needed, cook the lamb, turning occasionally, until browned on all sides, about 3 minutes. Transfer to a plate.

2. Add the remaining 1 tablespoon oil to the pan and heat. Add the garlic and anchovy paste and cook, stirring often, until the garlic softens, about 1 minute. Return the lamb, with its juices, to the pan and stir in the rosemary, sage, and red pepper flakes. Cook until the lamb juices are reduced to a glaze, about 1 minute. Sprinkle with the flour and mix well.

3. Add the wine and vinegar and bring to a boil, scraping up the browned bits in the bottom of the skillet. Reduce the heat to medium and simmer until the sauce thickens slightly and loses any flour taste, about 3 minutes. Season with salt.

4. Serve hot, garnished with the herb sprigs, if using.

Lamb Sauté with Tomatoes and Feta   Under 30 minutes

When you have a longing for the fresh, clean flavors of Greek cuisine, make this fast sauté of lamb chunks in a mint-flecked tomato sauce. The salty feta cheese brings it all together. For a sharper flavor, substitute fresh or dried oregano for the mint. Serve with Orzo with Parmesan and Peas (page 264).

Makes 4 servings

2 tablespoons extra-virgin olive oil, divided, plus more as needed

2¾ pounds boneless leg of lamb, trimmed of fat and sinew and cut into 1½-inch cubes (2 pounds trimmed weight)

½ teaspoon salt, plus more to taste

¼ teaspoon freshly ground black pepper, plus more to taste

⅔ cup finely chopped red onion

1 garlic clove, minced

One 28-ounce can diced tomatoes in juice, drained

⅓ cup pitted and coarsely chopped Kalamata olives

2 tablespoons chopped fresh mint, plus more for garnish, or 2 teaspoons dried mint

⅓ cup crumbled feta cheese

1. Heat 1 tablespoon of the oil in a 12-inch skillet over high heat. Season the lamb with the salt and pepper. In batches, without crowding, adding more oil as needed, cook the lamb, turning occasionally, until browned on all sides, about 3 minutes. Transfer to a plate.

2. Heat the remaining 1 tablespoon oil in the skillet, then reduce the heat to medium. Add the onion and cook, stirring often, until softened, about 3 minutes. Add the garlic and cook until it gives off its aroma, about 1 minute. Add the tomatoes and cook until they give off their juices, about 3 minutes. Stir in the olives and mint.

3. Return the lamb, and any juices, to the skillet and cover tightly. Cook until the lamb is medium-rare when pierced with the tip of a knife, about 5 minutes.

4. Remove from the heat and sprinkle with the feta. Serve immediately, garnishing each serving with a sprinkle of fresh mint.

Veal Chops with Sweet Peppers and Paprika

Shoulder chops are an economical way to enjoy veal. The large bone-in chops should be cut crosswise in half to make two smaller servings. This is how I learned to make veal chops when I was in Budapest working on a cookbook on the desserts of Austro-Hungarian cafés. (Yes, many cafés serve more than sweets.) For a true Magyar meal, serve the chops with buttered noodles tossed with poppy seeds.

Makes 4 servings

2 tablespoons vegetable oil, divided

Two 1-pound shoulder veal chops, cut into 4 chops

$1/2$ teaspoon salt, plus more to taste

$1/4$ teaspoon freshly ground black pepper, plus more to taste

1 large onion, cut into $1/4$-inch-thick half-moons

1 large red bell pepper, cored, seeds and ribs removed, and cut into $1/2$-inch-wide strips

1 large green bell pepper, cored, seeds and ribs removed, and cut into $1/2$-inch-wide strips

2 garlic cloves, minced

1 tablespoon sweet paprika, preferably Hungarian or Spanish

1 cup canned reduce-sodium chicken broth

1 tablespoon tomato paste

1 tablespoon cornstarch

1. Heat 1 tablespoon of the oil in a 12-inch skillet over medium-high heat. Season the veal chops with the salt and pepper. In two batches, without crowding, adding more oil if needed, add the chops to the skillet and cook until the undersides are browned, about 3 minutes. Turn and brown the other sides, about 3 minutes. Transfer to a plate.

2. Heat the remaining 1 tablespoon oil in the skillet over medium heat. Add the onion and red and green peppers and cook, stirring often, until they soften, about 6 minutes. Add the garlic and stir until it gives off its aroma, about 30 seconds. Stir in the paprika. Stir the broth and tomato paste together to dissolve the paste, then stir into the skillet, scraping up the browned bits in the pan with a wooden spatula.

3. Return the veal chops to the skillet and bring the cooking liquid to a boil. Cover tightly, reduce the heat to medium-low, and simmer until the chops are very tender, about 45 minutes. Transfer the veal to a deep platter.

4. Sprinkle the cornstarch into 2 tablespoons cold water and stir to dissolve. Pour into the skillet and whisk until the sauce thickens. Pour over the veal and serve hot.

Sour Cream Variation

Whisk the cornstarch into $1/2$ cup sour cream instead of the water. The cornstarch will stabilize the sour cream so it won't curdle when heated. Add to the skillet in Step 4 and whisk until the liquid comes to a boil and thickens.

Lamb Chops with Spiced Apricots and Garbanzos

Shoulder lamb chops are reasonably priced and loaded with flavor, but they do need a tenderizing simmer. The intriguingly spiced sauce is great for spooning over couscous or rice. Do place the apricots on top of the lamb chops to soften them—if added to the cooking liquid, they will absorb it and reduce the amount of sauce.

Makes 4 servings

4 shoulder lamb chops, cut about ½ inch thick

½ teaspoon salt, or more to taste

¼ teaspoon freshly ground black pepper, or more to taste

2 tablespoons extra-virgin olive oil, divided

1 medium onion, chopped

½ teaspoon ground cumin

½ teaspoon dried oregano

½ teaspoon ground ginger

½ teaspoon ground cinnamon

1 cup dry white wine, such as Sauvignon Blanc

1 packed cup (7 ounces) dried apricots, soaked in water to cover for 10 minutes and drained

One 15- to 19-ounce can garbanzo beans (chickpeas), drained and rinsed

Chopped fresh cilantro for garnish, optional

1. Season the lamb chops with the salt and pepper. Heat 1 tablespoon of the oil in a 12-inch skillet over high heat. Add the lamb and cook, turning once, until browned on both sides, about 5 minutes. Transfer to a plate.

2. Add the remaining 1 tablespoon of oil to the skillet and heat. Add the onion and reduce the heat to medium. Cook, stirring often, until the onion is golden, about 5 minutes. Add the cumin, oregano, ginger, and cinnamon and stir until fragrant, about 30 seconds. Pour in the wine and bring to a boil over high heat, scraping up the browned bits in the skillet with a wooden spatula.

3. Return the lamb to the skillet. Scatter the apricots and garbanzo beans over the lamb chops, being sure the apricots do not fall into the cooking liquid. Cover tightly, reduce the heat to medium-low, and simmer until the lamb chops are tender, about 30 minutes.

4. Transfer the lamb chops to a deep platter. Season the sauce with additional salt and pepper if needed. Pour over the chops, sprinkle with the cilantro, if using, and serve immediately.

Veal Scaloppine with Apples and Cider–Balsamic Vinegar Sauce   Under 30 minutes

The most difficult part about cooking veal scaloppine is finding the right butcher for cutting the meat. Most butchers understand that it must be cut from the round, but not enough know that it must be cut across the grain. If cut incorrectly, the meat will curl and toughen during cooking. That being said, this dish comes together quickly.

Makes 4 servings

8 slices veal scaloppine (about 1 pound), cut from the round

1/3 cup all-purpose flour

1/2 teaspoon salt, plus more to taste

1/4 teaspoon freshly ground black pepper, plus more to taste

2 tablespoons vegetable oil, or as needed

2 tablespoons unsalted butter, divided (1 tablespoon chilled)

2 Granny Smith apples, peeled, cored, and cut into 1/4-inch-thick slices

2 tablespoons finely chopped shallots

1/2 teaspoon finely chopped fresh thyme or 1/4 teaspoon dried thyme

3/4 cup apple cider

2 tablespoons balsamic vinegar

Fresh thyme sprigs for garnish, optional

1. Pound the veal with a meat mallet to a little less than 1/4 inch thick. Mix the flour, salt, and pepper in a small shallow dish. Coat the veal in the flour, shaking off the excess.

2. Heat the oil in a 12-inch skillet over medium-high heat. In batches, without crowding, adding more oil to the skillet as needed, cook the veal, turning once, until browned on both sides, about 2 minutes. Transfer the veal to a platter and tent with aluminum foil to keep warm.

3. Add 1 tablespoon butter (not the chilled butter) to the skillet and melt over medium heat. Add the apples and cook, stirring occasionally, until they begin to brown, about 2 minutes. Stir in the shallots and thyme and cook, stirring occasionally, until the shallots soften, about 1 minute. Add the cider and balsamic vinegar and bring to a boil over high heat, scraping up the browned bits in the bottom of the skillet with a wooden spatula. Return the veal to the skillet and

turn to coat with the sauce. Reduce the heat to low and simmer for 1 minute to lightly thicken the sauce. Remove from the heat.

4. Using a slotted spoon, transfer the veal and apples to the platter. Add the 1 tablespoon chilled butter to the sauce and stir until it melts. Season the sauce with salt and pepper. Pour the sauce over the veal, garnish with the thyme sprigs, if using, and serve immediately.

Poultry Chicken, turkey, and duck are indeed our fine-feathered friends. Chicken, in particular, has a chameleonlike quality that allows it to work well with an enormous variety of seasonings, flavors, and cooking techniques. Grilled chicken simply tastes different from braised chicken. Turkey was once the king of the holiday table, but, thanks to the availability of separate parts, it has broken out to become a choice for everyday cooking as well. Duck has also benefited from new marketing that makes it more accessible for quick preparation, and now you can sauté duck breasts rather than roasting a whole bird.

It was difficult to choose my favorite poultry recipes, so I offer representative recipes for different parts. For example, you could probably roast a whole chicken a hundred different ways, but the Roast Chicken with Olivada is a standout, and it has a simple pesto variation too. Cut-up chicken, chicken wings, breasts, and thighs are all here, braised, grilled, roasted, sautéed, or fried.

For turkey and duck, I've concentrated on the most popular supermarket cuts. Duck Breasts with Warm Pineapple-Cherry Chutney is probably the most restaurant-y recipe in the book, but one that can be easily made at home without tears.

The Carefree Cook's Tips for Poultry

Use common sense when handling poultry All poultry, meat, seafood, and even produce has a certain amount of bacteria, and of course you must avoid the harmful kind. However, some people practically put on Haz-Mat uniforms when handling poultry. Just use a little common sense, and all will be well.

Take the poultry out of its wrapper over the sink to let any juices drain away. Rinse under a gentle stream of cold water—a strong stream could splash raw poultry juices all over. Pat the poultry dry with paper towels, as a dry exterior encourages browning. Before handling other ingredients, wash your hands, cutting board, and any utensils that have come in contact with the raw poultry with soap and hot water. That's it.

Don't overcook the bird! Overcooked poultry is tough and dry. The trick is to stop cooking when the poultry has reached its optimum point for juiciness and flavor. For roast chicken and turkey breast, a meat thermometer does the best job. For dark meat, such as thighs, transfer a piece to a white plate and make a small cut down to the bone—the juices should be clear with no sign of pink. To check the doneness of a sautéed or grilled chicken breast, press it in the center, which should feel firm and spring back.

Roast Chicken with Olivada

There are many ways to enliven classic roast chicken, but this method, with a rub of olivada under the skin, is one of my favorites. You won't be able to loosen the skin around the wings, so don't even try. As the roasted bird is carved, some of the olive spread will find its way onto the cutting board, and you can dip the wings in these juices to pick up the olive flavor. Roast a large bird so you have leftovers for sandwiches and more.

Makes 6 servings

One 6½-pound roasting chicken, rinsed and patted dry

½ cup Olivada (recipe follows)

1 tablespoon extra-virgin olive oil

⅓ cup dry white wine

1. Position a rack in the center of the oven and preheat to 425°F.

2. Starting at the tail area, slip your hand under the chicken skin (cut any membrane between the skin and flesh with a small knife if necessary) and loosen the skin all over the chicken, ignoring the wings and drumstick ends. Using your fingers, spread the olivada under the chicken skin as evenly as possible, then massage the chicken skin to better distribute the olivada. Rub the chicken with the oil. Fold the wings under the chicken and tie the drumsticks together. Place on an oiled rack in a roasting pan.

3. Roast, basting occasionally with the pan juices, until an instant-read thermometer inserted in thickest part of the thigh reads 170°F, about 1 hour and 20 minutes. Tip the juices from the cavity into the pan, transfer the chicken to a carving board, and let stand while you make the sauce.

4. Pour the pan juices into a gravy strainer or a large glass measure and let stand for 5 minutes; set the roasting pan aside. Pour or skim off and discard the clear yellow fat that rises to the surface of the juices. Add the wine and enough water to the juices to make 1⅓ cups liquid. Place the roasting pan over two burners on high heat. Add the wine mixture and bring to a boil, scraping up the browned bits in the pan with a wooden spatula. Boil until reduced to ½ cup, about 5 minutes. Pour into a sauceboat. (continued)

5. Carve the chicken, removing the wings last. To give the wings more olive flavor, roll in the olivada and juices on the carving board. Transfer the chicken to a platter and pour the juices over the top. Serve the chicken, with the sauce on the side.

Roast Pesto Chicken
Substitute $1/3$ cup Pesto (page 268) for the olivada.

Instant-Read Thermometers

With a reliable meat thermometer, there's no need to guess when your roasts are done. An instant-read thermometer gives fast results and should be in every cook's kitchen. Unlike the old-fashioned glass thermometer, it should not be left in meat or poultry during roasting, because its face is made from plastic, not glass. The probe-type thermometer with a digital readout is a recent improvement, as is the remote model that beeps when the chicken is done, and you can hear it even if you are in the garage. Suit your fancy.

Seasoning Secret

Olivada

A spoonful of olivada, an Italian olive paste, can give a Mediterranean accent to many dishes. Specialty markets carry many different variations on the olive paste theme—some are made with green olives, some with black, and some are spicier than others. I like to make my own olivada so I can personalize it. It only takes a few minutes to prepare, especially when you use pitted Kalamata olives, and it keeps for quite a while in the refrigerator.

Makes about 1 cup

1½ cups pitted and coarsely chopped Mediterranean black olives

1 tablespoon finely chopped fresh rosemary or 1½ teaspoons dried rosemary

1 garlic clove, crushed through a press

½ teaspoon crushed hot red pepper flakes

¼ cup extra-virgin olive oil

Pulse the olives, rosemary, garlic, and red pepper flakes in a food processor fitted with the metal blade. With the machine running, add the oil, and process until the mixture has the consistency of a paste. Transfer to a small covered container. (The olivada will keep, refrigerated, for up to 3 weeks.)

Chicken Jambalaya

When I was working on a cookbook for the Delta Queen Steamboat Company, I spent a good amount of time in the New Orleans region learning the specialties of Cajun and Creole cuisine. While it is true that jambalaya can be an ornate affair studded with seafood, most of the home cooks I met considered it just the thing to serve up to a hungry family. I forget who taught me how to make jambalaya by stirring cooked rice into the spicy tomato sauce (as opposed to cooking the raw rice in the sauce itself, which never works well), but I will always be thankful. If you have about 3 1/2 cups leftover cooked rice on hand, skip the first step.

Makes 6 servings

1¼ cups long-grain rice

¾ teaspoon salt, plus more to taste

1 tablespoon vegetable oil

One 4-pound chicken, cut into 2 breasts, 2 drumsticks, 2 thighs, and 2 wings

4 ounces spicy sausage, such as andouille or kielbasa, cut into ½-inch dice

1 small onion, chopped

2 scallions, white and green parts, chopped

2 medium celery ribs, cut into ½-inch dice

½ green bell pepper, cored, seeds and ribs removed and cut into ½-inch dice

2 garlic cloves, minced

1 tablespoon Cajun Seasoning (page 36), or use store-bought salt-free Cajun/Creole seasoning

One 28-ounce can crushed tomatoes in puree

Freshly ground black pepper to taste

1. Combine the rice, 2½ cups water, and the salt in a medium saucepan. Bring to a boil over high heat. Cover tightly, reduce the heat to medium-low, and cook until the rice is tender, about 17 minutes. Remove from the heat and set aside.

2. Meanwhile, heat the oil in a large Dutch oven over medium-high heat. In batches, add the chicken, skin side down, and cook, turning once, until browned, about 5 minutes. Using a slotted spoon, transfer to a platter, leaving the fat in the pot.

3. Add the sausage to the pot and cook, stirring occasionally, until lightly browned, about 3 minutes. Add the onion, scallions, celery, green pepper, and garlic, reduce the heat to medium, cover, and cook, stirring occasionally, until

the onion softens, about 5 minutes. Uncover, add the Cajun seasoning, and stir until fragrant, about 30 seconds. Stir in the crushed tomatoes, and scrape up the browned bits in the bottom of the pan with a wooden spatula. Return the chicken to the saucepan and bring the sauce to a simmer. Reduce the heat to medium-low and simmer, uncovered, until chicken shows no sign of pink when pierced at the bone, about 35 minutes.

4. Stir in the rice and cook, stirring often, until it absorbs some of the sauce, about 2 minutes. Season with salt and pepper. Serve hot.

Italian Lemon-Garlic Chicken

Lemon chicken seems to be a staple of the Italian-American kitchen, and there are innumerable versions. Some are made in a skillet, a few are roasted. Because my standards for lemon chicken include crisp poultry skin and a brown, tangy sauce, I combine the methods for optimum results. When I have fresh rosemary handy, I like to make the Rosemary Lemon Chicken variation.

Makes 4 servings

3 large lemons

1 tablespoon extra-virgin olive oil

One 4-pound chicken, cut into 2 breasts, 2 drumsticks, 2 thighs, and 2 wings

1/2 teaspoon salt, plus more to taste

1/4 teaspoon freshly ground black pepper, plus more to taste

1/2 cup canned reduced-sodium chicken broth

1 teaspoon cornstarch

1 garlic clove, minced

Chopped fresh parsley for garnish

1. Position a rack in the top third of the oven and preheat to 400°F.

2. Slice 1 lemon into 1/4-inch-thick rounds. Grate the zest from 1 lemon. Squeeze the juice from both whole lemons; you should have 1/4 to 1/3 cup.

3. Heat the oil in a large ovenproof skillet over medium-high heat. Season the chicken with the salt and pepper. In batches, add the chicken to the pan, skin side down, and cook until the skin is well browned, about 4 minutes. Turn and brown the other side, about 2 minutes. Transfer the browned chicken to a platter.

4. Pour off all but 2 tablespoons of the fat from the pan. Return the chicken to the pan, skin side up, and top with the lemon slices. Roast in the oven, basting occasionally with the pan juices, until an instant-read thermometer inserted in the thickest part of a breast reads 170°F, about 35 minutes. Transfer the chicken, with the lemon slices, to a deep serving platter. Set the skillet aside.

5. Mix the lemon juice and chicken broth in a small bowl. Sprinkle the cornstarch over the liquid and stir to dissolve. Place the skillet over medium heat, add the garlic, and cook, stirring often, until the garlic is softened, about 1 minute. Add the lemon mixture and lemon zest. Bring to a boil, whisking to

Italian Lemon-Garlic Chicken;

Smashed Potatoes with Pesto (page 267)

scrape up the browned bits in the pan—the sauce will thicken lightly when it comes to a boil. Season the sauce with salt and pepper.

6. Pour the sauce over the chicken, sprinkle with the parsley, and serve immediately.

Rosemary Lemon Chicken

Add 1 tablespoon chopped fresh rosemary or 1½ teaspoons dried rosemary to the pan just after the garlic has softened.

Fried Chicken Breasts
with Blue Cheese Sauce Under 30 minutes

Here's a quick version of fried chicken for when a craving for golden crunchy breasts strikes (which is more often than I care to admit). And because the ubiquitous Buffalo chicken wings have proven the successful match of fried chicken and blue cheese dressing, why not make the meal a full-scale indulgence?

Makes 4 servings

Blue Cheese Sauce

1/2 cup mayonnaise

1/3 cup crumbled blue cheese, such as Danish Blue

1/4 teaspoon celery seeds

1 garlic clove, crushed through a press

Freshly ground black pepper to taste

Chicken Breasts

Four 7-ounce boneless, skinless chicken breasts

1 cup buttermilk

1 tablespoon hot red pepper sauce

1 cup all-purpose flour

1 teaspoon salt

Vegetable oil for frying

1. To make the sauce, mix the mayonnaise, blue cheese, celery seeds, and garlic in a small bowl. Season with pepper. Set aside at room temperature while you make the chicken.

2. Using a meat mallet, pound the chicken breasts to flatten slightly. Mix the buttermilk and red pepper sauce in a shallow dish. Mix the flour and salt in another shallow dish. Dip each chicken breast in the buttermilk to coat, then dip in the flour, shaking off the excess flour. Transfer to a wax paper–lined baking sheet. Let stand while you heat the oil (a few minutes' wait helps to set the crust).

3. Pour enough oil into a heavy 12-inch skillet to come 1/2 inch up the sides. Heat over high heat until the oil is very hot but not smoking (it will have a slight shimmer on the surface). Add the chicken breasts and adjust the heat so the oil bubbles steadily around the edges of the breasts. Cook until the underside is golden brown, about 5 minutes. Turn the chicken and cook until the other side is golden, about 5 minutes. Transfer to paper towels to drain briefly.

4. Serve hot, with the sauce served alongside.

Grilled Five-Spice Chicken

With just a few ingredients, this Vietnamese-inspired marinated chicken has become one of my favorites. Served with jasmine rice and the Tomato and Cucumber Salad on page 67, it is one of my most-requested meals. I've marinated and grilled quite a few chickens in my time, and I've also seen too many cooks overmarinate their birds, making for grilled poultry with a tough, cottony texture. A reaction between the acids in the marinade and the meat's proteins causes this phenomenon. But with a bold marinade (and most are), you don't really get additional flavor with a long soak, as the marinade won't reach any deeper than an eighth-inch or so. Because grilling adds a smoky note, I prefer this chicken cooked outdoors, but it can certainly be broiled in the oven.

Makes 4 servings

¼ cup Japanese soy sauce

¼ cup fresh lime juice

¼ cup shredded fresh ginger (use the large holes on a
   box grater)

1 tablespoon light brown sugar

1 tablespoon dark Asian sesame oil

2 teaspoons Five-Spice Powder (recipe follows), or use
   store-bought

4 garlic cloves, minced

One 4-pound chicken, cut into quarters

Lime wedges for serving

1. Combine the soy sauce, lime juice, ginger, brown sugar, oil, five-spice powder, and garlic in a large zip-tight plastic bag. Seal the bag and shake to dissolve the sugar. Add the chicken, seal the bag, and refrigerate to marinate for at least 30 minutes, or up to 8 hours.

2. Build a charcoal fire in an outdoor grill and let burn until the coals are covered with white ash; leave the coals heaped in the center of the grill. (Or preheat a gas grill on High, then turn one burner off.)

3. Lightly oil the grill grate. Remove the chicken from the marinade; reserve the marinade. Place the chicken on the cooler areas on the perimeter of the grill, around, not over, the coals. (On a gas grill, arrange the chicken over the turned-

Grilled Five-Spice Chicken;

Tomato and Cucumber Salad with

Sherry-Ginger Vinaigrette (page 67)

off burner.) Cover the grill. Grill, turning the chicken once or twice and basting when you do so with the marinade, until the chicken shows no sign of pink when pierced at the bone, about 45 minutes. Do not baste the chicken during the last 10 minutes of grilling. Serve hot, with the lime wedges.

Five-Spice Powder

A staple of Chinese cooking, this wonderfully aromatic blend is said to represent the five elements of fire, water, earth, metal, and wood. It is readily available in plastic bags at Asian markets, where it's much less pricey than in the spice rack of the supermarket. However, unless you are a dedicated fan of Chinese cooking, you may not be able to use up the entire bag before it starts to lose its flavor. So if you have the ingredients on hand, it's a good idea to grind your own blend in a coffee grinder. Try it in your next apple pie—unconventional but delicious.

Makes about 4 teaspoons

2 star anise, broken into points

1 teaspoon Sichuan peppercorns

$\frac{1}{2}$ teaspoon fennel seeds

1 teaspoon ground cinnamon

$\frac{1}{4}$ teaspoon ground cloves

In a coffee grinder, finely grind the star anise, peppercorns, and fennel. Add the cinnamon and cloves and pulse to blend. Store in an airtight container in a dark place for up to 3 months.

Spice Grinders

Serious cooks have a coffee grinder that is used only for grinding spices. If you don't want to take the plunge, you can use your everyday grinder. It must be the type that uses a blade, not a burr, for grinding. To remove unwanted flavors before and after grinding spices (you probably don't want five-spice-flavored coffee, or coffee-flavored five-spice powder), grind about $\frac{1}{4}$ cup raw rice or granulated sugar to a powder—it will pick up the residual flavors.

Cajun Oven-Fried Chicken

Could I serve this every night for dinner and get away with it? Probably. Even if you have to mail-order the panko, you'll be glad you have this dish in your repertoire. As a change of pace, substitute curry powder for the Cajun seasoning. I rarely use aerosol nonstick cooking oil spray anymore, as the oil isn't the best quality. Instead, look for oil spray dispensers, available at kitchenware stores, which can be filled with whatever oil you prefer.

Makes 4 servings

Vegetable oil in a sprayer or nonstick cooking spray

One 4-pound chicken, cut into 2 breasts, 2 drumsticks, 2 thighs, and 2 wings

½ cup buttermilk

1 tablespoon Cajun Seasoning (page 36), or use store-bought

½ teaspoon salt (omit if using salted store-bought seasoning)

1½ cups panko (Japanese bread crumbs)

1. Preheat the oven to 400°F. Spray a baking sheet with cooking spray.

2. Pull off and discard the skin from the breasts, drumsticks, and thighs. Don't bother to remove the skin from the wings—the wings won't be as crispy as the rest of the chicken, but they will still be delicious.

3. In a medium bowl, mix the buttermilk, Cajun seasoning, and salt. Spread the panko in a shallow dish. One piece at a time, dip the chicken in the buttermilk, shake off the excess so there is only a thin layer clinging to the chicken, and roll in the panko to coat. Arrange on the baking sheet. Spray the chicken lightly with oil.

4. Bake for 20 minutes. Turn and spray the chicken lightly with oil. Bake until the coating is golden brown and the chicken shows no sign of pink when cut in the thickest part, 25 to 30 minutes.

Note: If you don't have buttermilk, substitute ⅓ cup plain low-fat yogurt whisked with 3 tablespoons milk.

Panko

Panko are crisp, flaky bread crumbs. A Japanese product, they make an especially crunchy coating for food, and they can be substituted for regular bread crumbs in just about any recipe. Panko can be found at Asian markets and some supermarkets.

Grilled Chicken Breasts
with Orange Jerk Marinade Under 30 minutes

Jerk is Jamaica's grandest contribution to world cooking. Its ingredients reflect the jumble of cultures that came to the Caribbean to work in the sugar industry: soy sauce and allspice from Asia, scallions and thyme from France, and the indigenous chiles. Scotch bonnet chiles, tiny little firebombs that look like colorful tam-o'-shanters, have a unique flavor that combines incendiary heat with an underlying vegetal note. They are popping up in supermarkets, so use them if you can, but any other available hot chile is acceptable, if not authentic. Unless you are a chile head who loves the hottest food imaginable, it is inadvisable to use an entire Scotch bonnet chile in a single dish, so I suggest using a measured amount and adding more only after tasting. Any leftover chiles can be easily turned into a fine hot sauce—simply mix the coarsely chopped chiles with dry sherry (about 1 chile per 1/4 cup sherry) in a small jar, and let stand at room temperature for a few days before using. Refrigerated, the hot sauce will keep indefinitely.

Makes 4 servings

3 garlic cloves, peeled

4 scallions, white and green parts, coarsely chopped

1 teaspoon seeded, minced Scotch bonnet chile, or
   1 jalapeño, seeded and minced

Grated zest of 1 large orange

1/4 cup fresh orange juice (1 large orange)

2 tablespoons cider vinegar

1 tablespoon Japanese soy sauce

1 teaspoon dried thyme

1/2 teaspoon ground allspice

Four 6- to 7-ounce boneless, skinless chicken breasts

1. To make the marinade, with the machine running drop the garlic through the feed tube of a food processor to chop it. Add the scallions, chile, orange zest and juice, vinegar, soy sauce, thyme, and allspice and puree. Transfer to a glass or stainless-steel bowl, add the chicken; turn the chicken to coat. Cook immediately, or cover and refrigerate for up to 8 hours.

2. Position an oiled broiling rack 6 inches from the source of heat and preheat the broiler.

3. Place the chicken on the rack and broil for 5 minutes. Turn and broil until the chicken springs back when pressed in the center, about 5 more minutes. Serve immediately.

Chicken Thighs Osso Buco—Style

Osso buco, the Italian dish of veal shanks, is traditionally served with a sprinkle of gremolata, a mix of parsley, lemon zest, and garlic. Chicken thighs can be prepared in the same delicious manner. Saffron Rice (page 276) is the perfect side dish, along with a steamed green vegetable, such as green beans.

Makes 4 servings

1 tablespoon extra-virgin olive oil

8 chicken thighs

½ teaspoon salt

¼ teaspoon freshly ground black pepper

1 medium onion, chopped

1 medium carrot, cut into ½-inch dice

1 large celery rib, cut into ½-inch dice

2 garlic cloves, minced

¾ cup dry white wine

One 28-ounce can diced tomatoes in juice

1 teaspoon dried rosemary

1 teaspoon dried basil

3 tablespoons chopped fresh parsley

Grated zest of 1 lemon

1 garlic clove, minced

1. Heat the oil in a large saucepan over medium-high heat. Season the chicken with the salt and pepper. In batches, without crowding, add to the pan skin side down and cook until the skin is browned, about 3 minutes. Turn the chicken and brown the other side, about 3 minutes. Transfer to a platter.

2. Pour off all but 1 tablespoon of the fat in the pan. Add the onion, carrot, celery, and garlic, cover, and cook, stirring occasionally, until the vegetables soften, about 5 minutes. Add the wine, scraping up the browned bits with a wooden spatula. Stir in the tomatoes, with their juice, the rosemary, and basil.

3. Return the chicken to the pan, nestling the pieces in the sauce, and bring to a boil. Cover and reduce the heat to medium-low. Simmer until the chicken shows no sign of pink when pierced at the bone with the tip of a sharp knife, about 40 minutes. During the last 5 minutes, uncover the pan to help reduce the juices.

4. Just before serving, make the gremolata by mixing the parsley, zest, and garlic. Serve the chicken with the sauce, sprinkling each serving with gremolata.

**Chicken Thighs Osso Buco–Style;
Saffron Rice (page 276—variation on
Perfect Rice recipe)**

Farmhouse Turkey Breast with Root Vegetables

Turkey is much too delicious to be served only on Thanksgiving. When I'm in the mood for an old-fashioned turkey supper without the long list of side dishes that tyrannically go with the bird, I make this home-style main course. Turkey breast halves are easy to find in most supermarkets, but when whole ones are available, ask the butcher to saw one in half down the breastbone and roast both halves (don't increase the amount of vegetables). You'll be glad you did when you have the bonus of a second roasted breast for sandwiches and casseroles.

Makes 6 to 8 servings

5 medium red-skinned potatoes, cut into 1-inch chunks

3 medium carrots, cut on a diagonal into 1-inch lengths

3 medium parsnips, cut on a diagonal into 1-inch lengths

1 medium turnip, cut into 1½-inch lengths

12 large garlic cloves, unpeeled

2 tablespoons extra-virgin olive oil

2 teaspoons Herbes de Provence (page 165), or use store-bought, divided

1½ teaspoons salt, divided, plus more to taste

½ teaspoon freshly ground black pepper, divided, plus more to taste

4 tablespoons (½ stick) unsalted butter, divided

One 2¾-pound turkey breast half (with skin and bones)

2 tablespoons all-purpose flour

1½ cups canned reduced-sodium chicken broth

1. Position a rack in the center of the oven and preheat to 350°F. Lightly oil a large roasting pan.

2. Mix the potatoes, carrots, parsnips, turnip, garlic, oil, 1 teaspoon of the herbes de Provence, 1 teaspoon of the salt, and ¼ teaspoon of the pepper in the roasting pan.

3. Soften 2 tablespoons of the butter (use a microwave, if you wish). Spread it over the top of the turkey breast and sprinkle with the remaining 1 teaspoon herbes de Provence. Season the turkey with the remaining ½ teaspoon salt and ¼ teaspoon pepper, and place on top of the vegetables.

4. Roast, stirring the vegetables occasionally, until an instant-read thermometer

inserted in the thickest part of the turkey reads 170°F, about 1 1/2 hours. Transfer the turkey to a carving board and cover loosely with foil to keep warm.

5. Increase the oven temperature to 450°F. Continue roasting the vegetables until they are lightly browned, about 10 minutes. Transfer the vegetables to a serving dish and cover with foil to keep warm.

6. Place the roasting pan over two burners over medium heat. Add the remaining 2 tablespoons butter and let it melt. Whisk in the flour, to make a roux. Reduce the heat to medium-low and let the roux bubble without browning for 1 minute. Whisk in the broth and bring to a boil over high heat. Reduce the heat to medium-low and simmer until no raw flour taste remains, about 5 minutes. Season the gravy with salt and pepper.

7. Carve the turkey and serve hot with the vegetables and gravy.

Turkey Breast Cutlets with Roasted Peppers and Mozzarella   Under 30 minutes

Turkey breast cutlets have lots of flavor and are a welcome change from chicken breasts. Like chicken breasts, they are very versatile and lend themselves to a variety of seasonings. Here, they go Italian, with roasted red pepper and mozzarella cheese. I love this recipe because I usually have all of the ingredients but the turkey on hand, so it means just a short trip to the market for dinner's groceries. A word of caution: turkey cutlets are very lean and must be cooked over medium heat, as they will toughen if the flame is too high. Try with the Israeli Couscous with Vegetables on page 259.

Makes 4 servings

Four ½-inch-thick turkey breast cutlets (about 1¼ pounds)

½ teaspoon salt

¼ teaspoon freshly ground black pepper

1 tablespoon extra-virgin olive oil

2 teaspoons chopped fresh sage or 1 teaspoon crumbled dried sage

1 large vinegar-packed roasted red bell pepper (see page 46), cut into 2-inch-wide strips and trimmed to fit the cutlets

2 ounces thinly sliced mozzarella cheese, cut into 2-inch wide strips and trimmed to fit the cutlets

¼ cup dry Marsala wine

¼ cup canned reduced-sodium chicken broth

1 tablespoon chilled unsalted butter

1. Season the turkey with the salt and pepper. Heat the oil in a large nonstick skillet over medium heat. Add the turkey and cook until the underside is browned, about 3 minutes. Turn and cook to brown the other side, about 3 minutes.

2. Sprinkle the turkey with the sage. Top with the pepper strips, then the cheese. Add the Marsala and broth and bring to a simmer. Cover and cook until the cheese melts, about 1 minute. Using a slotted spoon, transfer the turkey to plates.

3. Increase the heat to high and boil the wine mixture until it reduces to ¼ cup, about 2 minutes. Remove from the heat and whisk in the butter. Pour the sauce over the cutlets and serve.

Duck Breasts with Warm Pineapple-Cherry Chutney Under 30 minutes

I had always considered duck breasts to be restaurant fare until I learned how to make them from Alfred Portale when we worked together on his Gotham Bar and Grill Cookbook. I will always be grateful for learning his method for cooking the breasts to yield crisp skin and rare meat. It's difficult to find a quicker, more sophisticated main course, and it is my secret weapon for special dinner parties, or even a fast weeknight supper when a celebration is in order. For side dishes, serve basmati or jasmine rice and a simple stir-fried Asian vegetable, such as bok choy.

Makes 4 servings

Pineapple-Cherry Chutney

½ ripe pineapple, peeled, cored, and cut into ½-inch
  cubes (about 2 cups)

⅓ cup dried cherries

2 tablespoons sugar

2 tablespoons cider vinegar

1 tablespoon shredded fresh ginger (use the large holes
  on a box grater)

1 tablespoon minced shallot

1 teaspoon seeded, minced red serrano chile or jalapeño

2 tablespoons chopped fresh cilantro, plus a few sprigs
  for garnish

Duck Breasts

Two 14-ounce boneless duck breasts (magrets)

¾ teaspoon Five-Spice Powder (page 147), or use store-
  bought

½ teaspoon salt

⅛ teaspoon freshly ground black pepper

1. Position a rack in the center of the oven and preheat to 450°F.

2. To make the chutney, in a medium nonreactive saucepan, combine all the ingredients except the cilantro and bring to a boil over medium heat. Cover and cook, stirring often, until the juices are syrupy, about 10 minutes. Set aside.

3. Score the duck breast skin in a crisscross pattern, with a small sharp knife, taking care not to cut through the skin to the flesh. Season the breasts with the five-spice powder, salt, and pepper. Place the breasts skin down in a large nonstick ovenproof skillet. Place the skillet over medium heat and cook until the

skin is a rich golden brown, about 12 minutes. Pour off the fat in the skillet. Turn and cook until the meaty sides are browned, about 3 minutes.

4. Transfer the pan to the oven and bake until an instant-read thermometer inserted in the thickest part of the breasts reads 125°F, about 5 minutes. Transfer the duck breasts to a carving board.

5. Pour off any remaining fat in the pan. Add the chutney to the skillet and cook over medium heat for 1 minute, scraping up the browned bits in the pan. Stir in the cilantro. Remove from the heat.

6. Carve each duck breast on the diagonal into $1/4$-inch-thick slices. Slide a large knife under half of the slices from one breast, transfer to a plate, and fan out the slices on the plate. Repeat with the remaining sliced breasts. Garnish with cilantro sprigs, and serve with the chutney.

Magrets

Upscale markets now carry boneless Moulard duck breasts (often called magrets) as a matter of course. One half-breast weighs in at about a hefty 14 ounces, so you can serve half a breast per person. If your market carries only the smaller White Pekin (Long Island) duck breasts, serve one breast per serving, and allow a bit less cooking time.

Crispy Chicken Wings with Chutney Dip

The seasoning combination of cinnamon, garlic salt, and pepper is as irresistible as it is unlikely. The original recipe comes from my dear friend, cooking teacher Arlene Ward—the chutney dip is my embellishment. Because most chicken drummettes are frozen and give off excessive juice, it is best to take a couple of minutes to cut up fresh wings. If you are using drummettes and they aren't browning well, increase the oven temperature to 425°F.

Makes 4 servings

4 pounds chicken wings

1 teaspoon garlic salt

1 teaspoon ground cinnamon

½ teaspoon freshly ground black pepper

One 9-ounce jar mango chutney, such as Major Grey's

¼ cup balsamic vinegar

2 tablespoons light brown sugar

1. Position a rack in the center of the oven and preheat to 400°F.

2. Using a heavy cleaver or large knife, cut the wings between the joints to make three pieces. Discard the wing tips, or save for another use (such as chicken stock). Transfer the wings to a large bowl. In a small bowl, mix the garlic salt, cinnamon, and pepper. Season the chicken with the spice mixture, tossing well to coat.

3. Spread the wings in a large roasting pan. (Do not crowd the wings or they will steam, not brown as they should.) Bake, stirring the wings occasionally, until crisp and browned, about 1 hour. Using a slotted spoon, transfer the wings to a platter.

4. Pour out and discard the fat from the roasting pan. Place the pan over two burners on medium-high heat until the pan is sizzling. Add ½ cup water, the chutney, vinegar, and brown sugar and bring to a boil, scraping up the browned bits in the pan with a wooden spatula. Boil until slightly thickened, about 1 minute. Pour the dip into a small bowl. (For a smoother sauce, puree in a blender.)

5. Serve the wings hot, with the dip.

Fish and Shellfish For a great meal in a hurry, seafood (a broad category encompassing fish, shellfish, and crustaceans) can be the answer. Because of the delicate texture of these "fruits of the sea," every effort should be made to avoid overcooking them, and most seafood recipes can be prepared in a very short time. Check out the Halibut with Herbed Oil—a very special dish that any Italian trattoria would be proud to serve, it can be on your plate in less than 15 minutes. For a simple but classy main course for company, depend on Porcini-Crusted Sea Bass on Spinach and Cremini to make a favorable impression.

In these recipes, I use readily available fish fillets, steaks, and shellfish. While cooking whole fish or lobster may seem like a simple chore to chefs, most home cooks consider it a daunting task that requires special equipment. In my days as a caterer, I routinely simmered a whole salmon in a coffinlike poacher. However, for home meals, baking salmon fillets, as in the recipe for Oven-Poached Salmon Fillets with Watercress Mayonnaise, accomplishes the same effect with a fraction of the effort. Chilled, these fillets can be served as a cold entrée, and the leftovers used to make deliciously moist salmon patties, such as the Asian Salmon Cakes.

Poached, baked, sautéed, even roasted... seafood is endlessly versatile and ready to become meals in minutes.

The Carefree Cook's Tips for Fish and Shellfish

Buy your fish from a top-notch purveyor   Most cooks buy seafood from a supermarket, but the quality of the product varies greatly from store to store. A good fish department has a wide selection of fresh fish, and it does not automatically wrap everything in plastic. Search out the best independent fish store in your neighborhood. Such fishmongers often supply local restaurants as well as home cooks, and chefs are notoriously picky about ingredients—especially something as perishable as fish.

With seafood, the nose knows   The best way to check a fish for freshness is the sniff test, as your nose will immediately reject over-the-hill specimens. Fresh fish have a faint aroma of the sea with no hint of ammonia. To be able to apply the test, it is preferable to buy fish that has not been prewrapped in plastic. At supermarkets with a seafood display case, the clerk should allow you to smell (if not touch) the fish before weighing and wrapping it.

Soak shellfish in salted water before cooking   Clams and mussels can be gritty and the sand can ruin a wonderful sauce. See "Cleaning Shellfish" on page 183 for details on how to prepare your shellfish before cooking.

Use large nonstick skillets for sautéing fish fillets   Seafood is naturally low-fat, and many cooks prefer nonstick skillets so they can use the minimum amount of oil needed for sautéing. A large (12-inch) heavy-bottomed nonstick skillet gives you plenty of room to manipulate the delicate fillets, and I rarely use anything else. To ensure break-free turning, use a slotted offset spatula, which is thin and angled to slip easily under the fish. With a large nonstick skillet and an offset spatula, you will be able to flip the fish over without flipping out.

Be creative—substitute fish varieties   Fish are often categorized by shape, round (salmon, sea bass, and the like) or flat (flounder, sole, and halibut are good examples). Nonetheless, it is also useful to consider the relative fat content of the fish, which is an indication of its flavor and texture. This way of thought also allows you to substitute one fish for another. The three categories are lean (sole, flounder, halibut, cod, snapper, tilapia, orange roughy, catfish, sea bass), moderate (striped bass, swordfish, mahi-mahi, trout), and oily (bluefish, salmon, mackerel, tuna). Of course, you should consider the other ingredients in the recipe, but in general, feel free to mix and match different varieties of fish to accommodate what you find in the market.

Cod Fillets in Bouillabaisse Sauce

Simone Beck is one of my favorite cookbook writers. She was the coauthor of Mastering the Art of French Cooking *with Julia Child and Louisette Bertholle, and her solo books are also exceptional. This easy twist on the classic bouillabaisse is based on one of her recipes. It is especially useful for dinner parties, because the sauce can be prepared a couple of hours ahead—and the house will be filled with a mouth-watering saffron aroma to welcome your guests. On the Côte d'Azur, potatoes are almost always served with bouillabaisse, so add a couple of small, boiled red-skinned potatoes to each bowl, if you wish.*

Makes 4 servings

2 tablespoons extra-virgin olive oil

1 large onion, cut into ¼-inch-thick half-moons

½ medium fennel bulb, cored and cut into ½-inch dice
   (about 1½ cups)

2 garlic cloves, minced

½ cup dry white wine or dry vermouth

One 28-ounce can diced tomatoes in juice

½ cup bottled clam juice or canned reduced-sodium
   chicken broth

1½ teaspoons Herbes de Provence (recipe follows), or
   use store-bought

½ teaspoon crumbled saffron threads

¼ teaspoon crushed hot red pepper flakes

Four 7-ounce skinless cod fillets

¼ teaspoon salt, plus more to taste

¼ teaspoon freshly ground black pepper

1. Heat the oil in a 12-inch skillet over medium heat. Add the onion and fennel, cover and cook, stirring occasionally, until the onion is tender, about 6 minutes. Add the garlic and cook, uncovered, until it gives off its aroma, about 1 minute. Add the wine and cook until it reduces by half, about 1 minute. Stir in the tomatoes, with their juices, the clam juice, herbes de Provence, saffron, and red pepper flakes. Bring to a simmer. Reduce the heat to medium-low, partially cover, and simmer until the sauce is slightly reduced, about 30 minutes.

2. Season the fillets with the salt and pepper. Place in the sauce, cover, and cook until the fish looks opaque when pierced in the thickest part with the tip of a sharp knife, about 10 minutes.

3. Transfer each fillet to a soup bowl with a slotted spatula. Season the sauce with salt. Spoon the bouillabaisse sauce around the fillets and serve immediately.

Seasoning Secret

Herbes de Provence

This wonderfully fragrant blend of herbs enhances many of the most delicious dishes of Provençal cuisine. Rather than buy it at the market, make it from the herbs in your kitchen cabinet. Even without the savory, fennel, and lavender, which are not commonly found in American spice racks, you will have an excellent blend.

Makes about 1/4 cup

1 tablespoon dried basil

1 tablespoon dried oregano

1 tablespoon dried rosemary

1 tablespoon dried thyme

1 teaspoon dried savory

$1/2$ teaspoon fennel seeds, coarsely crushed in a mortar or under a heavy saucepan

$1/2$ teaspoon dried lavender

Mix all of the ingredients together. Store in an airtight container in a cool, dark place for up to 3 months.

Catfish en Papillote
with Cilantro Tomato Sauce   Under 30 minutes

A dish cooked <u>en papillote</u> has a lot going for it, as the flavors mingle as in no other cooking technique. The traditional method calls for wrapping the food in paper, but it is much easier to work with aluminum foil. The firm texture and mild flavor of farmed catfish has made new friends for this fish, and it takes well to this treatment. It is difficult to test a packet for doneness, as you want your guests to open their individual servings at the table so they can savor the wonderful aromas, so be sure your oven is thoroughly preheated to the correct temperature. Serve with French Rice (page 276).

Makes 4 servings

Four 6-ounce catfish fillets

¼ teaspoon salt, plus more to taste

⅛ teaspoon freshly ground black pepper, plus more
   to taste

5 tablespoons unsalted butter, divided

2 tablespoons chopped shallots

1½ tablespoons shredded fresh ginger (use the large
   holes on a box grater)

2 garlic cloves, minced

One 28-ounce can diced tomatoes in juice, drained

2 tablespoons chopped fresh cilantro

1. Position a rack in the center of the oven and preheat to 375°F.

2. Season the fillets with the salt and pepper. Melt 1 tablespoon of the butter in a medium skillet over medium heat. Add the shallots, ginger, and garlic and cook until the shallots soften, about 2 minutes. Add the tomatoes and cook until heated through, about 3 minutes. Season with salt and pepper.

3. Tear off four 14-inch-long sheets of aluminum foil. Fold each sheet of foil in half, then open it out. For each serving, place one-quarter of the sauce on the bottom half of one sheet of foil. Top with a fillet, 1 tablespoon butter, and a sprinkle of cilantro. Fold the foil over, and crimp the three open sides to seal. Place the four packets on a large baking sheet.

4. Bake for 15 minutes. If you must test for doneness, carefully open one packet

(watch out for steam) and flake the thickest part of the fish with the tip of a knife—it should look opaque.

5. Transfer each packet to a plate and serve, allowing each guest to cut open his or her own serving with a sharp knife. The fish and sauce can be eaten directly out of the foil, or slide out of the foil onto the plate.

Flounder in Parmesan Herb Crust

This savory topping adds a flavorful dimension to ubiquitous flounder fillets. Think of it when looking for a way to zip up tilapia, orange roughy, or any other thin fish fillets. The trick is folding the fillets to make them thicker, a technique that keeps them from overcooking.

Makes 4 servings

Four 6-ounce flounder fillets

½ cup fresh bread crumbs (made from crusty French or Italian bread in a blender or food processor)

2 tablespoons freshly grated Parmesan cheese

1 tablespoon chopped fresh parsley

½ teaspoon Herbes de Provence (page 165), or use store-bought

1 garlic clove, finely chopped

Pinch of freshly ground black pepper

1 tablespoon extra-virgin olive oil, divided

1. Position a rack in the top third of the oven and preheat to 400°F. Lightly oil a 9 x 13-inch baking dish.

2. Arrange the fillets in the baking dish, folding the thin ends of each fillet under to meet in the center, to make triple-thick "packets."

3. Mix the bread crumbs, Parmesan, parsley, herbes de Provence, garlic, and pepper in a small bowl. Stir in 2 teaspoons of the oil to moisten the crumbs. Spread evenly on the tops of the fillets. Drizzle the crumbs with the remaining 1 teaspoon oil.

4. Bake until the topping is golden brown and the fish looks opaque when flaked in the center with the tip of a sharp knife, about 15 minutes. Serve hot.

Parmesan Cheese

I have often considered specifying freshly grated Parmigiano-Reggiano in my recipes that call for Parmesan cheese. There are a lot of Parmesan cheeses out there, but there is only one real McCoy. When I ask for Parmesan cheese, I am talking about the one from Parma, Italy, not Wisconsin or Argentina. (We won't even go into the grated stuff that comes in cans.) It has the nuttiest flavor and smoothest melting texture, and I insist on it in my kitchen. Buy Parmigiano in wedges and grate it yourself. Grana padano or Romano cheeses are sometimes suggested as budget-minded substitutes, but the former is not nearly as lush and the latter has a sharpness that is not as adaptable as true Parmesan.

Halibut with Herbed Oil Under 30 minutes

The mild flavor of halibut really gets a lift from this bright green, fragrant olive oil. Herbed oils can be found on gourmet market shelves, but I prefer to make a small fresh batch whenever I need it. While a slab of cooked halibut steak looks uninspiring, it is very easy to cut the clunky steak into more delicate fillets that are easier to sauté. Serve one fillet per person for average appetites, or allow one and a half fillets each for hungrier people.

Makes 4 to 6 servings

Herbed Oil

¼ cup plus 2 tablespoons extra-virgin olive oil

1 tablespoon finely chopped fresh basil

1 tablespoon finely chopped fresh chives

1 tablespoon finely chopped fresh parsley

1 tablespoon fresh lemon juice

Salt to taste

Pinch of crushed hot red pepper flakes

Halibut

Three 12-ounce halibut steaks, cut about ¾ inch thick

¼ teaspoon salt

⅛ teaspoon freshly ground black pepper

1 to 2 tablespoons extra-virgin olive oil

1. To make the oil, stir the oil, herbs, and lemon juice in a small bowl until combined. Season with the salt and red pepper flakes. Set aside.

2. Using a sharp knife, cut off the halibut skin. Cut off the two lobes of meat from the center bone in each steak to make 6 boneless fillets in all. Season with the salt and pepper.

3. Heat 1 tablespoon of oil in a 12-inch nonstick skillet over medium-high heat (if using a skillet with a regular surface, use 2 tablespoons oil). Add the halibut and cook until golden brown on the underside, about 3 minutes. Turn and cook until the other side is browned and the fish is barely opaque when flaked in the center with the tip of a sharp knife, about 2 minutes.

4. Transfer the fillets to dinner plates. Spoon the herbed oil over and around each fillet. Serve hot.

Sesame Seed—Crusted Tuna with Ponzu Dip Under 30 minutes

Coating fish steaks with crunchy seeds is a way to impart an instant burst of flavor. Sesame is an excellent complement to the rich taste of tuna, and for contrasting color, I always mix in a tablespoon of another darker spice such as black sesame or cumin seeds. If you can find them at an Indian market, try black onion seeds (also called nigella), which are not related to the onion but share its flavor—these seeds are also great as a topping for rolls and other savory baked goods. Ponzu, a Japanese dipping sauce, is authentically made with some very esoteric ingredients (kombu seaweed, sour orange juice, dried fish flakes, and the like). I think you'll find my easy version just as tasty. This colorful recipe is for lovers of rare tuna.

Makes 4 servings

¼ cup fresh lime juice

¼ cup Japanese soy sauce

1 tablespoon shredded fresh ginger (use the large holes
    on a box grater)

1 teaspoon light brown sugar

⅓ cup white sesame seeds

2 teaspoons black sesame seeds, cumin seeds, or black
    onion seeds

Four 6-ounce tuna steaks, cut ¾ inch thick

1. To make the dip, mix the lime juice, soy sauce, 2 tablespoons water, the ginger, and brown sugar in a small bowl, stirring to dissolve the sugar. Pour into four small bowls or ramekins and let stand while you prepare the tuna.

2. Mix the white sesame and black sesame seeds and spread in a pie plate. Coat both sides of each tuna steak in the seeds, pressing to help the seeds adhere.

3. Heat an empty 12-inch nonstick skillet over medium-high heat until the pan is very hot. Add the tuna steaks and cook until the seeds on the underside are lightly toasted, about 1½ minutes. If the seeds start to pop, partially cover the skillet. Turn the tuna and cook until the seeds on the other side are toasted, about 1½ minutes.

4. Serve immediately, with the ponzu for dipping the tuna.

Sesame Seed–Crusted Tuna with
Ponzu Dip; Chinese Cabbage and
Sesame Slaw (page 49)

Salmon Fillets with Hoisin Glaze Under 30 minutes

This has become my preferred way to cook salmon, as the sweet-saltiness of the hoisin sauce balances the buttery salmon flesh. Ginger juice (available bottled at specialty markets, but very easy to extract by hand) gives the glaze a nice kick. Grill a double batch of fillets so you'll have leftovers to make Asian Salmon Cakes with Ginger Tartar Sauce (page 175). Serve jasmine rice and sautéed snow peas as side dishes.

Makes 4 servings

1/4 cup hoisin sauce

2 tablespoons dry sherry

1 scallion, chopped, white and green parts kept separate

1/2 garlic clove, crushed through a press

2 tablespoons shredded fresh ginger (use the large holes in a box grater)

Four 6-ounce salmon fillets, with skin

1. Position an oiled broiler rack 6 inches from the source of heat and preheat the broiler.

2. In a small bowl, mix the hoisin sauce, sherry, the white part of the scallion, and the garlic. Working over the bowl, squeeze the ginger hard in your hand to extract the juice, and stir it in. Set the glaze aside.

3. Arrange the fillets, skin side down, on the broiler rack and broil for 3 minutes. Slather with the glaze and continue broiling until the glaze is bubbling, about 2 minutes for medium-rare salmon. Using a spatula, transfer the salmon to dinner plates (the skin may remain stuck to the broiler rack). Sprinkle the fillets with the chopped scallion greens. Serve immediately.

Hoisin Sauce

Sweet and salty, thick, dark red hoisin sauce is a versatile Chinese condiment with a base of fermented soybeans. Many Asian cooks use it as the start of a barbecue sauce, and it is a must for mu shu pork and Mandarin pancakes. Although it is also available in cans, buy it in jars to store in the refrigerator, where it will keep almost indefinitely.

Asian Salmon Cakes
with Ginger Tartar Sauce   Under 30 minutes

OK, I admit that when I was a kid, I loved fish sticks. As a grownup, when I have a craving for a crunchy fish dish, I make these salmon cakes with their crisp coating and moist interior. The ginger tartar sauce may sound like gilding the lily, but it really adds to the dish—and besides, it uses some of the same ingredients as the cakes, so it is easy to whip up. For the cakes, use leftovers from Salmon Fillets with Hoisin Glaze (page 174) or Oven-Poached Salmon with Watercress Mayonnaise (page 177), or poach salmon from scratch. Serve with Chinese Cabbage and Sesame Slaw (page 49).

Makes 4 servings

Ginger Tartar Sauce

$1/3$ cup mayonnaise

1 scallion, white and green parts, minced

1 tablespoon shredded fresh ginger (use the large holes on a box grater)

1 teaspoon hot Chinese or Dijon mustard

Salmon Cakes

2 scallions, white and green parts, minced

2 tablespoons shredded fresh ginger (use the large holes on a box grater)

1 cup panko (Japanese bread crumbs; see page 146)

$1/4$ cup mayonnaise

1 tablespoon hoisin sauce (omit if using leftover Grilled Salmon with Hoisin Glaze)

1 tablespoon Japanese soy sauce

1 tablespoon hot Chinese or Dijon mustard

1 large egg, beaten

$1/2$ teaspoon salt

$1/4$ teaspoon freshly ground black pepper

$1 1/2$ pounds salmon fillets, cooked, skinned, and flaked (about $3 1/2$ cups; see Note)

$1/3$ cup vegetable oil

Lime wedges for serving

1. To make the tartar sauce, mix the mayonnaise, scallion, ginger, and mustard in a small bowl. Let stand at room temperature while you make the cakes.

2. Line a baking sheet with wax paper. Mix the scallions, ginger, $1/3$ cup of the panko, the mayonnaise, hoisin sauce, soy sauce, mustard, egg, salt, and pepper in a bowl. Add the salmon and mix. Let stand for 5 minutes, then shape into four 4-inch-wide patties and place on the baking sheet.

(continued)

3. Place the remaining panko in a shallow dish. Coat the patties in the panko and return to the baking sheet.

4. Heat the oil in a 12-inch nonstick skillet over medium heat until very hot. Add the patties and cook until the undersides are golden, about 3 minutes. Turn and cook until the other sides are golden, about 3 minutes. Using a slotted spoon, transfer to paper towels to drain briefly.

5. Serve the cakes immediately, with the tartar sauce and lime wedges.

Note: To poach salmon fillets, place them in a skillet and add just enough lightly salted cold water to cover. Bring to a boil over high heat. Cover tightly and reduce the heat to medium-low. Simmer until the salmon is opaque with a hint of rosy color in the center when flaked with the tip of a knife, about 8 minutes. Remove from the skillet with a slotted spatula. Depending on your time frame, the salmon can be used immediately or allowed to cool.

Oven-Poached Salmon with Watercress Mayonnaise

Poaching fish in an herbed liquid adds both flavor and moisture. Salmon is one of the best fish for this technique, as it holds its shape so well. After serving poached salmon at countless weddings as a caterer, I can testify that cooking the fillets in the oven is the easiest and most reliable way.

Makes 6 servings

1 shallot, thinly sliced

4 sprigs parsley, with stems

1 sprig fresh thyme, leaves stripped from the stem, or 1/8 teaspoon dried thyme

1/3 cup dry white wine

Four 8- to 10-ounce salmon steaks, cut about 3/4 inch thick

1/4 teaspoon salt

1/8 teaspoon freshly ground black pepper

1/2 cup packed watercress leaves

1/3 cup mayonnaise

1 tablespoon whole-grain Dijon mustard

2 teaspoons fresh lemon juice

1. Position a rack in the center of the oven and preheat to 350°F. Lightly oil a 9 x 13-inch glass or ceramic baking dish. (The wine could react with a metal pan and give the fish a metallic flavor.)

2. Scatter the shallot, parsley, and thyme over the bottom of the baking dish. Pour in the wine and 1/3 cup water. Place the salmon on top. Season with the salt and pepper. Cover tightly with aluminum foil.

3. Bake until the salmon is barely opaque with a rosy center when prodded with the tip of a knife, about 25 minutes. Uncover and let cool in the dish, then cover tightly with plastic wrap and refrigerate until chilled (the cooking juices will jell), at least 4 hours, or overnight.

4. To make the mayonnaise sauce, pulse the watercress in a food processor to finely chop. Add the mayonnaise, mustard, and lemon juice and process to combine. Transfer to a small serving bowl, cover, and refrigerate. (The sauce can be prepared up to 1 day ahead.)

5. Using a slotted spatula, transfer the salmon steaks to a platter. Serve chilled, with the sauce passed on the side.

Porcini-Crusted Bass on Spinach and Cremini Mushrooms Under 30 minutes

Porcini mushroom powder is a terrific ingredient with many uses. Here it coats striped bass fillets, which have a meaty flavor that can stand up to the earthy porcini. The cooking procedure is a little unusual, so I'll give you an outline: The fish are briefly sautéed and removed from the skillet. A bed of spinach and mushrooms is prepared in the same skillet, and then the fish are returned to finish cooking. Voilà.

Makes 4 servings

Four 5- to 6-ounce sea bass fillets, skinned

1/4 teaspoon salt, plus more to taste

1/8 teaspoon freshly ground black pepper, plus more to taste

1 tablespoon Porcini Powder (recipe follows), or use store-bought

1 to 2 tablespoons vegetable oil

1 tablespoon unsalted butter

8 ounces cremini mushrooms (also called baby portobellos), sliced

2 tablespoons chopped shallots

1 garlic clove, minced

1 1/4 pounds flat-leaf spinach, stems removed if necessary, or use baby spinach

1. Season the fillets on the rounded side with the salt and pepper, then sprinkle with a generous coating of the porcini powder.

2. Heat 1 tablespoon oil in a 12-inch nonstick skillet over medium-high heat (if using a skillet that is not nonstick, use 2 tablespoons oil). Add the fillets, skinned sides down, and cook until seared, about 1 minute. Turn and sear the other side, about 1 minute. Transfer the fillets to a plate.

3. Melt the butter in the skillet over medium heat. Add the mushrooms and cook until they give off their juices, about 5 minutes. Add the shallots and garlic and cook until the shallots soften, about 2 minutes. Add 1/3 cup water to the skillet. A handful at a time, coarsely tearing the leaves as you go, add the spinach, letting each batch wilt before adding another. Season with salt and pepper to taste.

4. Return the fillets to the skillet, cover, and cook until a fillet looks opaque when pierced in the thickest part with the tip of a sharp knife, about 3 minutes.

5. Using a slotted spoon, transfer the spinach and mushrooms to dinner plates, and top with the fillets. Serve immediately.

Seasoning Secret

Porcini Powder

One of my favorite cooking secrets is porcini powder, another ingredient that can be found at some specialty stores but is so easy to make in your own kitchen. A dusting of this powder on fish or meats adds a sensational flavor that will have your guests guessing the source. Stir a tablespoon or two into pasta sauces, soups, and stews to add a taste of the Italian countryside.

Makes about ¹/₄ cup

1 cup loosely packed dried porcini mushrooms (about 1¹/₂ ounces)

Using a pastry brush, brush away any grit from each mushroom slice. Place the mushrooms in an electric spice grinder (see Note) or blender. Process the mushrooms until finely ground to a powder. Transfer to a small covered jar and store in a cool, dark place for up to 6 months.

Note: Reserve an electric coffee grinder with a rotary blade (not a burr-operated grinder) to grind spices. If your coffee grinder must do double duty for coffee and spices, grind about ¹/₄ cup raw rice or granulated sugar between uses—unwanted flavors will transfer to the ground rice.

Scallops with Grape Tomatoes and Mint Under 30 minutes

Plump sea scallops need a slightly acidic accent to balance their sweetness, and tomatoes are the perfect foil. The best fish markets sell "dry" scallops (these are almost always large sea scallops and not the smaller sea scallops) that have not been treated with moisture-causing preservatives. "Day boat" or "diver" scallops are equally fine, for they are collected close to shore and never subjected to preservatives. Serve Orzo with Parmesan and Peas (page 264) with these delectable morsels.

Makes 4 servings

3 tablespoons extra-virgin olive oil, divided

1 pound "dry" sea scallops, patted dry with paper towels

2 tablespoons minced shallots

1 pint grape tomatoes, cut lengthwise in half, or use
   2 cups diced (1-inch cubes) ripe plum tomatoes

1 tablespoon finely chopped fresh mint, plus small sprigs
   for garnish

¼ cup dry vermouth or dry white wine

Salt and freshly ground black pepper to taste

Hot cooked rice for serving

1. Heat 2 tablespoons of the oil in a 12-inch nonstick skillet over high heat until very hot. Add the scallops and cook, turning once, until opaque when pierced in the center with the tip of a sharp knife, about 5 minutes. (If you have scallops of varying sizes, remove the smaller scallops as they are cooked.) Transfer to a platter.

2. Add the remaining 1 tablespoon oil to the skillet and reduce the heat to medium. Add the shallots and cook, stirring often, until softened, about 1 minute. Add the tomatoes and mint and cook, stirring occasionally, until heated through, about 3 minutes. Add the vermouth and cook until the juices are thickened, about 1 minute. Return the scallops to the skillet and stir a few times to combine. Season with salt and pepper.

3. Spoon over the hot rice, garnish with mint sprigs, and serve immediately.

Lager-Steamed Mussels
with Mustard Dipping Sauce Under 30 minutes

If you've ever been to Belgium, then you know that mussels (and beer, for that matter) can be found on just about every menu. I think I like mussels cooked in beer even better than the well-known white wine version. Be sure to use a lager, as other beers may be too bitter. A Flemish cook would serve these with French fries. For an easier option, make the Crisp Oven Fries on page 271, and be sure to dip them in the mustard sauce too—also a Belgian tradition.

Makes 4 servings

1 cup mayonnaise

2 tablespoons Dijon mustard

2 garlic cloves, crushed through a press

2 tablespoons unsalted butter

2 large leeks, white and pale green parts only, well rinsed and cut into ¼-inch dice (1 cup)

2 medium celery ribs, cut into ¼-inch dice

1 medium carrot, cut into ¼-inch dice

2 garlic cloves, minced

One 12-ounce bottle lager beer

4 pounds mussels, preferably cultivated mussels, well scrubbed and debearded if necessary

Salt and freshly ground black pepper to taste

1. To make the sauce, mix the mayonnaise, mustard, and garlic in a bowl. Divide among four small bowls or ramekins. Set aside.

2. Melt the butter in a large soup kettle over medium heat. Add the leeks, celery, carrot, and garlic, cover, and cook, stirring occasionally, until the vegetables are tender, about 8 minutes. Add the beer and ½ cup water. Bring to a boil over high heat.

3. Add the mussels and cover tightly. Cook, stirring the mussels occasionally with a long spoon, until they open, 5 to 7 minutes.

4. Using tongs or a long spoon, transfer equal portions of the mussels to four deep bowls, discarding any unopened mussels. Taste the cooking liquid and season with salt and pepper as necessary. Ladle the cooking liquid over the mussels. Serve immediately, with the bowls of mustard sauce for dipping. (Don't forget a large bowl on the table to collect the empty shells.)

Cleaning Shellfish

I always soak mussels (cultivated mussels need no soaking) or clams to help them expel any sand. Fill a large bowl with cold water and add enough salt so it tastes distinctly salty (about 1 tablespoon salt for every quart of water); the shellfish could die if soaked in plain water. Stir in about $1/4$ cup cornmeal. Add the scrubbed shellfish and refrigerate for at least 30 minutes, or up to 2 hours. The shellfish will eat the cornmeal and any grit will pass through their systems. Drain the shellfish and rinse before cooking.

Mussels

It used to be that the only mussels one could buy were blue mussels (even though they are mainly black with a blue sheen). Harvested from the sea, often encrusted with barnacles, and sporting a tough "beard" (the cord used by the mussel to attach itself to rocks, pilings, and the like) that had to be pulled from each mollusk, they required a bit of work from the cook before finding their way into a pot. Now many markets carry smaller cultivated mussels with smooth, shiny shells. Their thin beards have usually been trimmed during harvesting. Large, plump New Zealand mussels, with green shells and flesh that is white (male) or orange (female) when cooked, are also popping up in stores. These varieties are interchangeable.

As with clams, avoid broken or gaping shells (or at least shells that don't close after being tapped with another mussel shell). If a blue mussel feels especially heavy, it may be full of mud and should be discarded. A particularly light mussel of any variety means the shell is empty for one reason or another, and it should also be tossed out. If you have the time, soak the mussels as directed above.

Roasted Clams with Peppers and Spicy Sausage **Under 30 minutes**

Until I tasted them roasted, I invariably steamed clams with wine. I am now a convert to the roasted version. As the juices spill out of the clams, they concentrate in the heat of the oven, creating an especially flavorful sauce that cries out for plenty of crusty bread for dipping. Be sure to use a large roasting pan so the shellfish have plenty of room. I use a 14 by 18-inch roasting pan, but an oval turkey roaster also works well.

Makes 4 servings

48 littleneck or cherrystone clams (about 4$\frac{1}{2}$ pounds),
   well scrubbed (see Note)

$\frac{1}{4}$ cup cornmeal

4 ounces chorizo or other hard, smoked spicy sausage,
   cut into $\frac{1}{2}$-inch dice

$\frac{1}{4}$ cup extra-virgin olive oil

1 large onion, chopped

1 large red bell pepper, cored, seeded, and cut into
   $\frac{1}{2}$-inch dice

2 garlic cloves, thinly sliced

1 cup dry white wine, such as Sauvignon Blanc, or dry
   vermouth

Salt and freshly ground black pepper to taste

1 tablespoon chopped fresh thyme, preferably lemon
   thyme

1. Place the clams in a large bowl and add enough salted cold water to cover. Stir in the cornmeal. Let stand while the oven is preheating. (Or, if you have the time, refrigerate the clams for up to 2 hours.)

2. Position a rack in the center of the oven and preheat to 500°F.

3. Cook the chorizo in the oil in a large roasting pan on top of the stove over medium-high heat, stirring occasionally, until the chorizo begins to brown, about 3 minutes. Add the onion, red pepper, and garlic. Cook, stirring often, until the vegetables soften, about 5 minutes. Drain the clams and rinse well under cold water. Add to the roasting pan, pour in the wine, and bring to a boil over high heat.

4. Transfer the pan to the oven and roast, stirring the clams occasionally, until

all of the clams open, about 15 minutes. Taste the cooking liquid. If it is too salty (the saltiness will vary with the clams), add a little hot water to dilute it slightly. Season with salt and pepper, if needed.

5. Spoon the clams and broth into large bowls, sprinkle with the thyme, and serve immediately.

Note: If the exteriors of the clams are well scrubbed, most of their grit will be removed. The soaking in Step 1 is for insurance.

Clams

When discussing the common Atlantic hard-shell clam, the clam's specific name indicates its variety but not its size. Littleneck clams are smallest and cherrystones are considered moderately sized. Manila or mahogany clams, which hail from the warmer waters of the Pacific, are smaller than littlenecks. Any of these will be delicious for Roasted Clams (above). Or you can try vongole, a small clam popular with Italian cooks. Large hard-shell chowder clams or quahogs, soft-shell or steamer clams, or the enormous geoducks are not good choices for this recipe.

Do not buy any clams that are broken or aren't tightly closed. However, if an open clam shuts when rapped, it's fine. See page 183 for instructions on cleaning clams.

Sweet-and-Sour Shrimp with Pineapple Under 30 minutes

Whenever I make this for dinner, the reaction is "Why can't we get Chinese food this good from the delivery place?" It has all of the flavors of classic sweet-and-sour but is lighter and fresher. To save time, buy peeled pineapple and shelled, deveined shrimp, both of which are becoming more available at supermarkets.

Makes 4 servings

1 tablespoon cornstarch

1/4 cup canned reduced-sodium chicken broth

1/4 cup Japanese soy sauce

1/4 cup rice vinegar

3 tablespoons dry sherry

1 1/2 tablespoons sugar

1/2 teaspoon crushed hot red pepper flakes

2 tablespoons vegetable oil, divided

1 pound large (21 to 25 count) shrimp, shelled and deveined (see Note)

1 medium red bell pepper, cored, seeds and ribs removed, and cut into 1-inch squares

3 scallions, white and green parts, cut into 2-inch lengths

1/2 ripe pineapple, peeled, cored, and cut into 1-inch cubes (about 2 cups)

3 garlic cloves, minced

Hot cooked rice for serving

1. To make the sauce base, sprinkle the cornstarch over 1/3 cup water in a small bowl and whisk to dissolve the cornstarch. Add the broth, soy sauce, vinegar, sherry, sugar, and red pepper flakes and mix well. Set aside.

2. Heat a 12-inch nonstick skillet over high heat. Add 1 tablespoon of the oil and swirl the skillet to slick the bottom with oil. Add the shrimp and stir-fry just until the shrimp turn opaque, about 2 minutes. Using a slotted spoon, transfer to a plate.

3. Add the remaining 1 tablespoon oil to the skillet and heat over medium-high heat. Add the red pepper and stir until it begins to soften, about 1 minute. Add the scallions and stir until they begin to wilt, about 1 minute. Add the pineapple and cook, stirring occasionally, until heated through, about 2 minutes. Stir in the shrimp and garlic and stir-fry until the garlic gives off its aroma, about 1 minute. Pour in the sauce base and bring to a boil to thicken the sauce, stirring occasionally.

4. Serve hot, spooned over the rice. (continued)

Note: There is no USDA standard for shrimp sizes. One store's large can be another's extra large. The best way to establish size is the number of shrimp per pound. For example, 21 to 25 shrimp to the pound (often indicated by "21–25 count" on the label), can be considered large, and an acceptable size for almost all cooking needs.

Pineapple

There is only one word for a ripe and juicy pineapple: luscious. It all starts with choosing the right pineapple. The newer varieties, often with the word "gold" in their brand names and from Central America, can be relied on for especially sweet flavor. A ripe pineapple will "give" slightly when squeezed, but perhaps the best test is your nose—it should have a rich, sugary scent.

While many supermarkets now sell pared and cored pineapple, that is a convenience that not all of us enjoy. To pare a pineapple, cut off the top crown, then cut a thin slice off the bottom. Stand the pineapple on the work surface. Using a heavy chef's knife or a strong serrated knife, cut down the side from top to bottom where the flesh meets the thick skin. Repeat all around the pineapple. To remove the eyes, you can simply dig them out with the tip of the knife. However, if you look closely, notice that the eyes actually run in rows that spiral around the fruit. Holding the knife at an angle, you can cut out a few at a time, working around the pineapple until all the eyes have been removed. When you're finished, the pineapple will sport a jaunty spiral pattern cut into its sides.

To core the pineapple, cut it lengthwise into quarters. Working with one pineapple quarter at a time, stand it on end, and slice off the tough core that runs along the pointed edge.

Shrimp in Green Tomatillo Sauce Under 30 minutes

Tomatillos, which have nothing to do with tomatoes (they are actually related to gooseberries, as evidenced by their papery husks), are the basis of spicy green Mexican salsa. Formerly available only at Latino markets, they are stocked by many supermarkets as well. At a farmers' market in California, one of my favorite stands sells shrimp and tomatillo tamales. Tamales are wonderful, but very time-consuming to make by hand. I spoon the pink shrimp in their pretty pale green sauce over Herbed Polenta with Corn (page 265) to mimic the Southwestern flavor of the tamales without the fuss.

Makes 6 servings

1 pound tomatillos, husked

1 small onion, coarsely chopped

2 tablespoons chopped fresh cilantro, plus a few sprigs
    for garnish

1 tablespoon seeded, minced jalapeño, or more to taste

1 garlic clove, crushed

2 tablespoons extra-virgin olive oil, divided

1½ pounds large (21 to 25 count) shrimp, peeled and
    deveined

¼ teaspoon salt

Hot soft polenta for serving

1. Bring a medium pot of lightly salted water to a boil over high heat. Add the tomatillos and cook until they are barely tender and olive green (for tomatillos of varying sizes, remove the smaller ones with a slotted spoon as they become tender), about 5 minutes. Do not overcook, or the tomatillos will burst. Using a slotted spoon, transfer the tomatillos to a food processor or blender. Add the onion, cilantro, jalapeño, and garlic, and puree.

2. Heat 1 tablespoon of the oil in large nonstick skillet over medium heat. Season the shrimp with the salt. In batches, without crowding, cook the shrimp, turning once, until they turn just opaque, about 2 minutes. Transfer to a plate.

3. Heat the remaining 1 tablespoon oil in the same pan. Add the tomatillo sauce and bring to a boil. Reduce the heat to medium-low and cook, stirring often, until lightly thickened, about 5 minutes. Stir in the shrimp and simmer just to heat through, about 1 minute.

4. Spoon over the polenta, garnish with the cilantro sprigs, and serve hot.

Shrimp, Chorizo, and Peas in Saffron Sauce Under 30 minutes

When I want the flavors of paella in a hurry, I make this quck sauté and serve it over rice. Saffron is an expensive but worthwhile addition to your spice cabinet, as its unique flavor adds distinction to many Mediterranean-inspired recipes. (The tiny brick-red threads are actually the stigmas of a crocus, and the painstaking hand-harvesting contributes to the high cost.) While rice is the most obvious bed for the luscious shrimp and its sauce, consider orzo or couscous as alternatives. Overcooked shrimp will ruin the dish, so during their first trip to the skillet, take care to just sear them, as they will cook through when they are added to the sauce.

Makes 4 to 6 servings

½ teaspoon saffron threads

½ cup dry white wine, such as Sauvignon Blanc or
    Pinot Grigio

2 tablespoons extra-virgin olive oil, divided

1½ pounds large (21 to 25 count) shrimp, peeled and
    deveined

3 ounces smoked chorizo, or other hard spicy sausage,
    cut into thin slices

1 medium onion, chopped

1 medium red bell pepper, seeded and cut into
    ½-inch dice

1 garlic clove, minced

½ teaspoon dried oregano

2 teaspoons cornstarch

1½ cups canned reduced-sodium chicken broth

1 cup thawed frozen peas

Salt to taste

Crushed hot red pepper to taste

Perfect Rice (page 276), for serving

1. Heat a small skillet over medium heat. Add the saffron and cook, stirring often, just until the threads are very aromatic and lightly toasted, about 1 minute. (This step intensifies the saffron flavor, but can be omitted.) Transfer a small bowl, add the wine, and set aside to steep while cooking the remaining ingredients.

2. Heat 1 tablespoon of the oil in a 12-inch nonstick skillet over medium-high heat. Add the shrimp and cook, stirring occasionally, just until the exteriors turn opaque, 2 to 3 minutes. Do not overcook the shrimp—they should be rare and translucent on the inside. Transfer the shrimp to a plate.

3. Heat the remaining oil in the skillet over medium heat. Add the chorizo and cook, stirring occasionally, until the sausage is lightly browned, about 2 minutes. Add the onion, red pepper, and garlic. Cook, stirring occasionally, until the vegetables are tender, about 5 minutes. Stir in the oregano.

4. Sprinkle the cornstarch over the broth and whisk to dissolve. Add the wine-saffron mixture, then the broth to the skillet and stir well. Add the shrimp and peas and bring the liquid to a boil. Cook until the shrimp are cooked through and the sauce is lightly thickened, about 1 minute. Season with salt and crushed red pepper.

5. Serve hot, spooned over the rice.

Shrimp

Few members of the seafood family are as versatile as shrimp—a friend of mine refers to them as "chicken breast of the sea." Almost all shrimp in America has been frozen, even if the market sells it thawed. Knowing that virtually all shrimp has been frozen once already, don't refreeze thawed shrimp.

Many supermarkets sell frozen shrimp, which is a great item to store in the home freezer, ready to thaw for impromptu meals (shrimp thaw quickly at room temperature, but if you're in a hurry, rinse them under cold, not warm or hot, running water to speed the process).

Buy shell-on shrimp for the best flavor, and to have the shells to cook in chicken broth or claim juice to make a quick seafood broth. Easy-peel shrimp, whose shells have already been split to make for easy removal, are a good option. Unless you are in a big hurry, avoid peeled shrimp, because some flavor has been lost during processing.

Shrimp is sorted according to size, but there is no common standard. For example, one fish store's large shrimp will be another market's medium or extra-large. If you see the label that says "21–26" count," that means that there are twenty-one to twenty-six shrimp to a pound, which is a good, meaty size (they can go up to about sixty shrimp per pound, which are too small for anything except soup). Shrimp in the 21 to 31 count range are best for most dishes, as they won't overcook as quickly as their smaller counterparts.

Pasta and Grains Here's a common scenario in my kitchen: I stumble in after a busy day, and it hits me: there isn't a thing to eat for dinner! But the initial shock is almost immediately replaced by a wave of relief, because I am never without a box of pasta in the cupboard and frozen pasta sauce in the freezer. Never. ¶ Some weekends I spend a part of one afternoon simmering up a big pot of tomato sauce specifically for packing into

1-quart freezer containers. The entire house is filled with the aroma of mingling toma-toes, onions, garlic, and herbs, which invites frequent tasting—I am often surprised that there is any sauce left in the pot from all the tasting that has gone on. I have quite a dif-ficult time deciding between the easy classic meat sauce on page 200, the pork meat-balls and sauce on page 202, Bolognese Sauce (page 218), and Turkey Sausage Ragù (page 216). Even when I am cooking one of these sauces for a single meal, I always make a double batch and reserve half for a future dinner—or share it with my neighbors who, lured by the wafting scent of pasta sauce, have found their way to my door. As with soup, you may spend a little time chopping up the ingredients for pasta sauce, but considering the amount of food you get in return, it is time well spent.

The pleasures of long-simmered pasta sauce are well known, but just as often, I make a quick sauce that can be cooked up in the time it takes the water to come to a boil. And on the occasions when a comforting dish is the order of the day, baked pasta fills the bill like no other meal.

The Carefree Cook's Tips for Pasta and Grains

When boiling pasta, don't skimp on the water Pasta loves to swim, so allow plenty of water for cooking: at least 4 quarts of water for a pound of pasta. You don't have to measure the water precisely, though—estimate according to the size of the pot: for example, fill a 5-quart pot four-fifths full. Cover the pot while the water heats to speed up the boiling.

Don't forget the salt Pasta does not contain salt, so the cooking water must be salted for proper seasoning. How much salt is enough? Well, I never measure, but if I had to, I would specify about 2 teaspoons of regular table salt for 4 quarts of water.

Don't rinse or oil cooked pasta After the pasta is cooked al dente, drain in a large colander. (Before you drain the pasta, check to see if your recipe uses some of the cooking water to dilute a thick sauce.) Unless the pasta is for lasagna or salad, don't rinse it, as this removes starches that help the sauce cling. And never oil pasta, or the sauce will slide off into a puddle at the bottom of the bowl.

Toss the pasta in the cooking pot to retain heat   Return the drained pasta to its cooking pot, add the sauce, and mix well. The retained heat from the pot will keep everything nice and warm. The serving bowl should be warm too—I put the bowl under the colander in the sink. When the pasta is drained, the hot water goes into the bowl, and heats it up while the pasta is sauced. Pour out the water, give the bowl a quick wipe dry with a towel, and add the pasta.

Use the right rice for risotto   Rice is categorized by the length of the grain: short, medium, or long. The shorter the grain, the more starch the rice contains. For this reason, medium-grain rice, an Italian specialty, is the rice for risotto, as its starch is released into the cooking liquid to make a creamy-textured sauce. (When I learned to make risotto in Italy, my friends there warned me that adding cream to risotto is cheating, and that cheese and butter are the only acceptable dairy embellishments. Modern chefs have changed this, but I still hesitate before adding cream to my risotto recipes.) You cannot make risotto with American long-grain rice, and although some producers are now growing domestic Arborio, I still prefer the Italian variety.

American cooks automatically think of Arborio as the only rice for risotto. As Arborio is the easiest Italian rice variety to grow and harvest, it is the one most frequently exported, but there are three other excellent varieties that you might come across at a specialty market or Italian delicatessen, and they are worth trying. Carnaroli and Vialone Nano have tied for my first choice for risotto, as they share a firm texture and copious starch to make an especially creamy sauce. Baldo is another Italian medium-grain rice that has its fans, but I save it for Italian rice desserts. The truth is, you can make great risotto with any of these four Italian beauties.

Farfalle with Arugula, Sausage, and Garlic Under 30 minutes

Arugula can be spicy in a salad (the older large leaves are the most peppery), but its heat is reduced by cooking. Like other greens, it wilts dramatically, so make this rustic but sophisticated dish when the summer crop of arugula is plentiful and reasonably priced. This pasta is moistened with olive oil, not tomato sauce, and the better the oil, the more delicious the final dish. Resist the temptation to use more sausage, as this small amount allows the arugula to shine through.

Makes 4 to 6 servings

1 pound arugula

1/4 cup plus 1 tablespoon extra-virgin olive oil, preferably estate-quality, divided

1 medium onion, chopped

2 garlic cloves, chopped

4 ounces sweet Italian pork or turkey sausage, casings removed

1/4 teaspoon crushed hot red pepper flakes

1 pound farfalle (bow-tie pasta)

1/2 cup (2 ounces) freshly grated Parmesan cheese, plus more for serving

Salt to taste

1. Remove and discard the tough stems from the arugula. Wash the arugula well in a sink or large bowl of cold water. Lift the arugula from the water and shake off the excess water, but do not spin-dry.

2. Heat 1 tablespoon of the oil in a large skillet over medium heat. Add the onion and cook until it softens, about 3 minutes. Add the garlic and stir until it gives off its aroma, about 1 minute. Add the sausage and red pepper flakes and cook, breaking up the meat into small pieces with the side of a spoon, until the meat loses its pink color, about 4 minutes. In four or five additions, add the arugula, stirring until each batch wilts before adding another. Cover, reduce the heat to medium-low, and simmer until the arugula is tender, about 5 minutes.

3. Meanwhile, bring a large pot of lightly salted water to a boil over high heat. Add the pasta and cook until barely tender, about 9 minutes.

4. Scoop out about $1/2$ cup of the cooking water, then drain the pasta, and return it to the pot. Add the arugula-sausage mixture and the remaining $1/4$ cup olive oil and mix well. Add the Parmesan and toss again, adding enough of the reserved pasta water to moisten the pasta. Season with salt.

5. Serve hot, with additional cheese passed on the side.

Fettuccine with Asparagus and Ricotta   Under 30 minutes

This creamy pasta dish is perfect for a quick spring supper. If at all possible, use fresh ricotta, which can be found at cheese shops and Italian delicatessens—but don't skip over this recipe if only the supermarket variety is available. Please be sure the ricotta is at room temperature, as chilled ricotta would cool the pasta too much—simply place the ricotta in a bowl on the stove as you prepare the rest of the ingredients, and it will warm up nicely. And as egg fettuccine (which is richer than plain semolina pasta and better for this dish) usually comes in 12-ounce packages, the recipe reflects these proportions.

Makes 4 to 6 servings

1 pound asparagus

12 ounces dried egg fettuccine

1 cup ricotta cheese, preferably fresh ricotta, at room
   temperature

½ cup (2 ounces) freshly grated Parmesan cheese, plus
   more for serving

3 tablespoons unsalted butter, at room temperature

2 tablespoons finely chopped fresh chives and/or
   tarragon (preferably a combination)

Salt and freshly ground black pepper to taste

1. Bring a large pot of lightly salted water to a boil over high heat.

2. Snap off and discard the woody stems from the asparagus. Cut off the spears about 1 inch below the tips; reserve the tips. Cut the bottoms of the asparagus stalks into 1-inch lengths. Add the asparagus stalks (not the tips) to the boiling water and cook for 1½ minutes. Add the tips and cook until the asparagus is barely tender, about 3 minutes more. Using a large skimmer or a wire sieve, remove the asparagus from the water and transfer to a bowl. (Resist the temptation to rinse the asparagus under cold water—you want it to stay warm.)

3. Add the fettuccine to the boiling water and cook until it is barely tender. During the last minute of cooking, add the asparagus to the water to reheat it. Scoop out and reserve about ½ cup of the cooking water, then drain the fettuccine and asparagus and return them to the pot.

4. Add the ricotta, Parmesan, butter, and chives to the pot and mix, adding enough of the reserved cooking water to make a creamy sauce. Season generously with salt and pepper.

5. Serve hot in individual bowls, with additional Parmesan cheese passed on the side.

Wide Noodles with Meat Sauce and Basil Ricotta

When you have a longing for the flavors of lasagne but don't have the time to bother with the layering and baking, toss together this easy version. You should be able to find mafalde (also known as tripoline) at an Italian grocery. These look like long narrow lasagna noodles with one edge of curly waves—but any wide noodle will do.

Makes 4 to 6 servings

One 15-ounce container ricotta cheese

1/3 cup chopped fresh basil, plus additional for serving

1/2 teaspoon salt

1 tablespoon extra-virgin olive oil

1 medium onion, chopped

2 garlic cloves, minced

1 pound ground round (85 percent lean)

1/2 cup hearty red wine, such as Shiraz or Zinfandel

One 28-ounce can crushed tomatoes in puree

One 14 1/2-ounce can diced tomatoes in juice

2 teaspoons dried oregano

1 pound mafalde, fettuccine, or pappardelle

Freshly grated Parmesan cheese for serving

1. Mix the ricotta, basil, and salt in a medium bowl. Let stand at room temperature while you prepare the pasta, so the ricotta loses its chill.

2. Heat the oil in a large skillet over medium heat. Add the onion and cook, stirring occasionally, until softened, about 3 minutes. Add the garlic and cook until it gives off its aroma, about 1 minute. Add the ground round, increase the heat to medium-high, and cook, breaking up the meat with a spoon, until it loses its pink color, about 5 minutes. Add the wine and bring to a boil. Stir in the crushed tomatoes, diced tomatoes, with their juices, and oregano. Bring to a boil, then reduce the heat to medium-low. Simmer, uncovered, stirring often, until the sauce thickens, about 25 minutes.

3. Meanwhile, bring a large pot of lightly salted water to a boil over high heat. Add the pasta and cook until barely tender, about 9 minutes. Drain well, and return the pasta to the pot.

4. Add the sauce to the pasta and mix well. Serve immediately in individual bowls, topping each serving with a large spoonful of the basil ricotta and a sprinkle of chopped basil. Pass the Parmesan cheese on the side.

Spaghetti with Pork Meatballs

Not your grandmother's meatballs, unless Nonna came from Sicily. Pine nuts and currants add interest to these meatballs, which are made with ground pork instead of the familiar beef, the latter being a rare commodity in southern Italy. A quick trip to the broiler browns the outside of the meatballs—much easier than sautéing. Don't let the length of the ingredients list deter you—many of the same ingredients are used in the sauce and the meatballs.

Makes 4 to 6 servings

Tomato Sauce

2 tablespoons extra-virgin olive oil

1 large onion, chopped

2 garlic cloves, minced

One 28-ounce can crushed tomatoes in puree

One 14½-ounce can diced tomatoes in juice

1 tablespoon Italian Herb Seasoning (page 100), or use
    store-bought

⅛ teaspoon crushed hot red pepper flakes

Meatballs

1 tablespoon extra-virgin olive oil

1 small onion, finely chopped

1 garlic clove, minced

⅓ cup dried bread crumbs

1 large egg, beaten

1½ teaspoons Italian Herb Seasoning (page 100), or use
    store-bought

3 tablespoons pine nuts, toasted

3 tablespoons dried currants

1½ teaspoons salt

½ teaspoon crushed hot red pepper flakes

1½ pounds ground pork

1 pound spaghetti

Freshly grated Parmesan cheese for serving

1. To make the sauce, heat the oil in a large saucepan over medium heat. Add the onion and cook, stirring occasionally, until golden, about 5 minutes. Add the garlic and cook, stirring, until aromatic, about 1 minute. Stir in the crushed tomatoes, the diced tomatoes, with their juice, the herb seasoning, and red pepper flakes. Bring to a boil. Reduce the heat to low and simmer, uncovered, stirring often, until the sauce reduces by about one-quarter, about 30 minutes.

2. Meanwhile, to make the meatballs, position an oiled broiler rack about 6 inches from the source of heat and preheat the broiler.

3. Heat the oil in a small skillet over medium heat. Add the onion and cook, stirring often, until tender, about 5 minutes. Stir in the garlic and cook until it gives off its aroma, about 1 minute. Transfer to a large bowl. Add the bread crumbs, egg, herb seasoning, pine nuts, currants, salt, and red pepper flakes and mix. Add the pork and mix well with your hands. Rinse your hands in cold water, and shape the meat into 18 meatballs.

4. Arrange the meatballs on the broiler rack and broil, turning occasionally, until browned, about 8 minutes. After the sauce has cooked for 20 minutes, transfer the meatballs to the sauce and simmer until the meatballs are cooked through, about 20 minutes.

5. Meanwhile, bring a large pot of lightly salted water to a boil over high heat. Add the pasta and cook, stirring often, until barely tender, about 9 minutes. Drain well and return to the pot.

6. Transfer the meatballs and about 1 cup of the sauce to a serving bowl or platter. Toss the remaining sauce with the pasta. Serve immediately, topping each serving with meatballs, and pass the Parmesan cheese on the side.

Pine Nuts

Small and pale beige, with a sweet flavor, pine nuts are a favorite ingredient in Mediterranean cooking, and they are most easily found at Italian grocers. However, the pine nuts we buy are not necessarily Italian. The typical Italian pine nut is bullet shaped, with a mild flavor, and expensive—though less costly when purchased in bulk. Cheaper pine nuts are most likely the triangular Chinese variety, which some cooks feel have a strong taste that isn't compatible with Mediterranean food. In either case, oily pine nuts can turn rancid easily, so store them in an airtight container in the refrigerator or freezer.

Baked Macaroni with Four Cheeses

I used to make my macaroni and cheese with only Cheddar, and maybe some Velveeta, if no one was looking. Then, on the personal advice from that great cook and singer Patti LaBelle, I started adding more cheeses to the recipe. Now I use a quartet of sharp Cheddar, nutty Gruyère, and tangy blue cheese with a Parmesan crust. If you have onion-soup bowls or individual casseroles, this is fun to bake in single portions.

Makes 4 to 6 servings

1 pound elbow macaroni

5 tablespoons unsalted butter, divided

¼ cup all-purpose flour

3 cups milk, heated until hot in the microwave or in a
   saucepan

1¼ cups (5 ounces) shredded extra-sharp Cheddar
   cheese

1¼ cups (5 ounces) shredded Gruyère or Swiss cheese

⅓ cup (about 1½ ounces) crumbled Danish blue or
   Roquefort cheese

2 teaspoons Dijon mustard

Salt to taste

Hot red pepper sauce to taste

½ cup (2 ounces) freshly grated Parmesan cheese

2 tablespoons dried bread crumbs

1. Position a rack in the center of the oven and preheat to 350°F. Lightly butter a deep 2-quart baking dish.

2. Bring a pot of lightly salted water to a boil over high heat. Stir in the macaroni and cook until almost but not quite done, about 8 minutes. Drain well.

3. Add 4 tablespoons (½ stick) of the butter to the pasta pot and melt over medium heat. Whisk in the flour and reduce the heat to low. Let the roux bubble without browning for 2 minutes. Whisk in the hot milk. Stir in the Cheddar, Gruyère, blue cheese, and mustard. Return the macaroni to the pot and mix well. Season with salt and hot pepper sauce. Transfer to the baking dish.

4. Mix the Parmesan and bread crumbs and sprinkle over the macaroni. Dot with the remaining 1 tablespoon butter. Bake until the macaroni is bubbling throughout, about 25 minutes. Let stand for 5 minutes, then serve hot.

Penne with Cauliflower and Sage Under 30 minutes

If a definition of eternity is a ham and two people (thank you Irma S. Rombauer and Marion R. Becker for those words of wisdom), a whole head of cauliflower isn't far behind. Cauliflower isn't a common pasta sauce ingredient, but once you taste this dish, you'll wonder why it isn't.

Makes 4 to 6 servings

4 ounces sliced (1/8-inch-thick) pancetta or bacon, cut into small dice

2 tablespoons extra-virgin olive oil

One 2-pound cauliflower, cut into florets about 1 inch wide

2 garlic cloves, minced

One 14 1/2-ounce can chopped tomatoes in juice

2 tablespoons chopped fresh sage, plus more for garnish

Salt to taste

Crushed hot red pepper flakes to taste

1 pound penne or other tubular pasta

Freshly grated Parmesan cheese for serving

1. Bring a large pot of lightly salted water to a boil over high heat.

2. Combine the pancetta and oil in a 12-inch heavy skillet and cook over medium-high heat, stirring occasionally, until the pancetta is crisp and brown, about 5 minutes. Using a slotted spoon, transfer the pancetta to paper towels to drain.

3. Add the cauliflower to the fat in the skillet. Cook uncovered, turning occasionally, until the cauliflower is lightly browned, about 4 minutes. Add the garlic and stir until it releases its fragrance, about 1 minute. Stir in the tomatoes, with their juice, the pancetta, sage, and the salt and red pepper flakes. Bring the sauce to a simmer. Reduce the heat to low, cover, and simmer until the cauliflower is quite tender, about 15 minutes.

4. Meanwhile, cook the penne in the boiling water until al dente. Drain and return the pasta to the hot pot.

5. Add the sauce to the pasta and mix well, allowing the cauliflower to break up. Serve immediately, topping each serving with a sprinkle of sage, and pass the Parmesan on the side.

Cappellini with Olivada and Caper Sauce Under 30 minutes

Cappellini, the very thin "angel hair" pasta, requires a light-bodied sauce that doesn't weigh down the tiny ribbons, but that doesn't mean the sauce can't be boldly flavored. Here's a tomato sauce that gets plenty of oomph from olive paste, capers, and red pepper flakes. Olivada's saltiness precludes the use of Parmesan, but you can add a sprinkle of cheese as a garnish, if you wish.

Makes 4 to 6 servings

1 tablespoon extra-virgin olive oil

1 garlic clove, minced

One 28-ounce can crushed tomatoes

1/4 teaspoon crushed hot red pepper flakes

About 1/2 cup Olivada (page 137), or use store-bought olive paste

2 tablespoons nonpareil capers, rinsed

1 pound cappellini

1. Bring a large pot of lightly salted water to a boil over high heat.

2. Meanwhile, heat the oil and garlic in a large saucepan over medium heat until the garlic softens, about 2 minutes. Stir in the tomatoes and red pepper flakes and bring to a simmer. Cook, uncovered, until slightly thickened, about 5 minutes. Stir in 1/4 cup of the olivada and the capers and return to a simmer. Remove from the heat and keep warm.

3. Add the pasta to the boiling water and cook just until tender, about 2 minutes. Drain the pasta well, and return to the pot.

4. Add the sauce to the pasta and mix well. Serve immediately in bowls, each garnished with an additional tablespoon or so of olivada.

Fettuccine with Shrimp and Creamy Lemon Sauce

My friend Pat Rowan came back from a trip to Italy raving about a pasta dish with an unusual lemon sauce. Here's what I came up with so she could enjoy it at home too. Rosemary, not a common herb with shrimp, cuts through the richness of the sauce and works beautifully here. Because of the high cream content, you may want to serve it the Italian way, in small portions as an appetizer. However, it is so delicious that I usually serve it as a main course, calories be damned.

Makes 4 to 6 servings

2 tablespoons unsalted butter, divided

1 pound large (21 to 25 count) shrimp, peeled and
   deveined

⅓ cup chopped shallots

Grated zest of 1 large lemon

3 tablespoons fresh lemon juice

2 cups heavy cream

¾ cup canned reduced-sodium chicken broth

4 teaspoons finely chopped fresh rosemary, plus small
   sprigs for garnish

Salt and freshly ground black pepper to taste

1 pound fettuccine

1. Melt 1 tablespoon of the butter in a large skillet over medium-high heat. Add the shrimp and cook, stirring occasionally, just until they turn opaque, about 2 minutes. Do not overcook the shrimp, as they will be subjected to more heat later. Transfer the shrimp to a plate.

2. Add the remaining 1 tablespoon butter to the skillet and melt it. Add the shallots and cook, stirring often, until softened. Add the lemon zest and juice—the juice will immediately evaporate into a glaze. Stir in the heavy cream, chicken broth, and chopped rosemary, bring to a boil, and cook until the sauce has reduced to about 1¾ cups, 5 to 7 minutes. During the last minute, return the shrimp to the skillet. Season the sauce with salt and pepper.

3. Meanwhile, bring a large pot of lightly salted water to a boil over high heat. Add the fettuccine and cook just until tender, about 9 minutes. Drain well. Return the fettuccine to the pot.

4. Add the sauce to the pasta and mix well. Serve hot in individual bowls, garnished with the rosemary sprigs.

Spaghetti with Spicy Tomato and Pancetta Sauce

One of the benefits of having pancetta in the freezer is being able to make this pasta sauce without a trip to the local Italian delicatessen. Most of the pancetta is simmered in the peppery sauce, and the remainder is used as a garnish to add crunch and up-front flavor.

Makes 4 to 6 servings

2 tablespoons extra-virgin olive oil

6 ounces sliced (1/8-inch-thick) pancetta or bacon, coarsely chopped (3/4 cup)

1 medium onion, chopped

3 garlic cloves, minced

1/2 teaspoon crushed hot red pepper flakes

2 teaspoons crumbled dried rosemary

2 teaspoons dried oregano

One 28-ounce can tomatoes in juice, coarsely chopped, with their juices

1 pound spaghetti

Freshly grated Parmesan cheese for serving

1. Combine the oil and pancetta in a large saucepan and cook over medium-high heat, stirring occasionally, until the pancetta is browned, about 5 minutes. Using a slotted spoon, transfer the pancetta to paper towels, leaving the fat in the pan.

2. Add the onion to the saucepan and cook over medium heat, stirring often, until translucent, about 5 minutes. Stir in the garlic and red pepper flakes and cook until the garlic gives off its aroma, about 1 minute. Stir in the rosemary and oregano, then the tomatoes, with their juices, and about two-thirds of the cooked pancetta. Bring to a simmer. Reduce the heat to medium-low and cook, uncovered, until the sauce is slightly thickened, about 20 minutes.

3. Meanwhile, bring a large pot of lightly salted water to a boil over high heat. Add the pasta and cook until barely tender, about 9 minutes. Drain well and return the pasta to the pot.

4. Stir the sauce into the pasta. Transfer to a warmed serving dish and sprinkle with the remaining pancetta. Serve hot, with a bowl of Parmesan passed on the side.

Spaghetti with Slow-Roasted Tomatoes

I prefer this roasted tomato sauce to the simmered variety, but I admit it can only be made during the summer tomato season. The low oven temperature concentrates the tomato juices and brings out the flavor of the tomatoes in a way that is superior to cooking on the stove. If you have a bumper crop of tomatoes, slow-roast a big batch, use some for the pasta, and preserve the rest in the refrigerator. Layer the roasted tomatoes in a small covered container, cover with olive oil, and refrigerate; they will keep for a week or so. Remove the tomatoes from the oil and use as a garnish or salad ingredient, or in any recipe that calls for drained canned tomatoes.

Makes 4 to 6 servings

¼ cup extra-virgin olive oil, divided, plus more for serving

3 pounds ripe plum tomatoes

½ teaspoon salt, plus more to taste

¼ teaspoon freshly ground black pepper, plus more to taste

6 large garlic cloves, unpeeled

½ cup packed fresh basil leaves

1 pound spaghetti

Freshly grated Parmesan cheese for serving

1. Position a rack in the center of the oven and preheat to 300°F. Line a large baking sheet with aluminum foil and oil well with 1 tablespoon of the oil.

2. Cut the tomatoes lengthwise in half. Using your finger, poke the seeds out of the tomatoes—don't worry if you don't remove every last seed. Turn the tomatoes cut side up on the baking sheet and season with the salt and pepper. Turn the tomatoes cut sides down and brush with 2 tablespoons of the oil. Bake for 1½ hours.

3. Toss the garlic with the remaining 1 tablespoon oil in a small bowl. Drizzle the garlic and oil over the tomatoes. Bake until the tomatoes and garlic are very tender, about 1 hour longer. If the garlic cloves are soft before the tomatoes are done, remove them.

4. Place the tomatoes in a food processor. Squeeze the softened garlic flesh from the skins onto the tomatoes and add the basil. Pour ¼ cup boiling water onto the baking sheet and use a rubber spatula to scrape up as much of the

caramelized tomato juice as possible. Add the juices to the food processor. Pulse until the tomatoes are pureed. Season with salt and pepper.

5. Meanwhile, bring a large pot of lightly salted water to a boil over high heat. Add the spaghetti and cook until barely tender, about 8 minutes. Drain and return to the pot. Add the sauce and mix well.

6. Serve the pasta hot in individual bowls, with a bowl of Parmesan and extra olive oil passed on the side.

Bucatini Carbonara with Peas   Under 30 minutes

Possibly named for the coal miners who often sustained themselves with this delicious meal of pasta, pork (Italians use guanicale, a cured pork not available here), and eggs, pasta alla carbonara is a very special treat. Over the years, I've perfected my recipe with a splash of cream (without it, the egg sauce can be a bit dry), the addition of peas, and Parmesan cheese instead of sharp, salty Romano. Note that this recipe uses raw eggs, which will cook when they come into contact with the hot pasta. To be sure that they reach the proper temperature to kill any dangerous bacteria, I warm them first in hot water.

Makes 4 to 6 servings

1 pound bucatini, perciatelli, or spaghetti

3 large eggs

5 ounces sliced ($\frac{1}{4}$-inch-thick) pancetta, cut into $\frac{1}{4}$-inch-wide slivers

1 garlic clove, finely chopped

$\frac{1}{3}$ cup heavy cream

$\frac{1}{4}$ teaspoon crushed hot red pepper flakes

$\frac{1}{2}$ cup (2 ounces) freshly grated Parmesan cheese, plus more for serving

$1\frac{1}{2}$ cups thawed frozen peas

Salt and freshly ground black pepper to taste

1. Bring a large pot of lightly salted water to a boil over high heat. Add the pasta and cook until barely tender, about 9 minutes.

2. Meanwhile, cover the eggs with hot tap water in a small bowl. Let stand for about 5 minutes to warm the eggs.

3. Place the pancetta in a medium skillet and cook over medium heat, stirring occasionally, until crisp and browned, about 5 minutes. Using a slotted spoon, transfer the pancetta to paper towels to drain, leaving the fat in the skillet.

4. Add the garlic to the fat and cook, stirring often, just until it gives off its aroma, about 1 minute. Add the cream and red pepper flakes and bring to a boil over high heat, scraping up any browned bits in the skillet with a wooden spatula. Remove from the heat. (continued)

5. Drain the pasta and return it to the cooking pot. Crack the warm eggs into a large bowl and beat them. Gradually beat in hot cream mixture, then the Parmesan cheese. Add to the pasta and toss well. Add the peas and cooked pancetta and toss again. Season with salt and pepper.

6. Serve hot, with Parmesan cheese passed on the side.

Spaghetti with Cool Tomato Sauce, Green Olives, and Goat Cheese

This light tomato pasta sauce is almost, but not quite, uncooked. The pastas with raw tomato sauces I've had in the past have been a little underpowered, but I solved the problems with a few tweaks. First, salting the tomatoes releases excess watery juices from the tomato flesh, intensifying their flavor. And the briefest cooking of the pasta and sauce together allows the ingredients to blend. When the weather is really hot, serve the pasta at room temperature.

Makes 4 to 6 servings

3 pounds large ripe tomatoes, cored, seeded, and cut into 1-inch cubes

$1/2$ teaspoon salt, plus more to taste

1 pound spaghetti

$1/4$ cup extra-virgin olive oil, plus more for serving

2 garlic cloves, crushed through a press

$1/2$ cup pitted and coarsely chopped Mediterranean green olives

$1/2$ cup coarsely chopped fresh basil

$1/4$ teaspoon crushed hot red pepper flakes

$3^1/2$ ounces goat cheese, crumbled

1. A few hours before serving, toss the tomatoes and $1/2$ teaspoon salt together in a large colander over a large bowl. Let stand to drain off excess juices, at least 2 and up to 4 hours.

2. Strain the collected tomato juice through a wire sieve over a bowl to remove the seeds; set aside.

3. Bring a large pot of lightly salted water to a boil over high heat. Add the spaghetti and cook, stirring often, until just tender, about 9 minutes. Drain well.

4. Combine oil and garlic in the pasta pot and cook over medium heat until the garlic gives off its fragrance, about 2 minutes. Add the tomatoes, olives, basil, and red pepper flakes and cook, until the tomatoes soften, about 2 minutes. Add the spaghetti and enough of the strained tomato juice to moisten the dish, and cook until piping hot, about 1 minute. Season with salt.

5. Transfer to individual bowls, and top each serving with goat cheese. Serve immediately.

Ziti with Turkey Sausage Ragù

This has become our house pasta sauce, and I make it in double or triple batches to freeze. Turkey sausage has all the flavor of pork sausage with reduced fat and calories, so this is a rare instance where substituting a more healthful ingredient doesn't affect the flavor of the dish.

Makes 4 to 6 servings

1 ounce (1 loosely packed cup) dried porcini mushrooms

1 tablespoon extra-virgin olive oil

1 pound sweet or hot turkey sausage, casings removed

10 ounces cremini mushrooms (also called baby portobellos), quartered

1 medium onion, chopped

1 medium carrot, cut into ½-inch dice

1 medium celery rib, cut into ½-inch dice

2 garlic cloves, minced

1 cup hearty red wine, such as Zinfandel or Shiraz

One 28-ounce can crushed tomatoes in puree

1½ teaspoons dried basil

1½ teaspoons dried oregano

¼ teaspoon crushed hot red pepper flakes (optional if using hot sausage)

1 pound ziti or other tubular pasta, such as rigatoni or mostaccioli

Freshly grated Parmesan cheese for serving

1. In a small bowl, soak the porcini in 1 cup boiling water until soft, 20 to 30 minutes. Lift the porcini out of the water and coarsely chop. Strain the liquid through a moistened paper towel–lined wire sieve into a bowl, and reserve.

2. In a large saucepan, heat the oil over medium-high heat. Add the sausage and cook, breaking up the sausage with a wooden spoon, until it loses its raw look, about 5 minutes. Add the cremini mushrooms, onion, carrot, celery, and garlic. Cover and cook, stirring occasionally, until the vegetables soften, about 10 minutes. Add the wine and bring to a boil. Stir in the crushed tomatoes, chopped porcini, reserved mushroom liquid, basil, oregano, and red pepper flakes, if using, and bring to a boil. Reduce the heat to low and simmer, uncovered, stirring occasionally, until thickened, about 45 minutes.

3. Meanwhile, bring a large pot of lightly salted water to a boil over high heat. Add the ziti and cook until barely tender, about 9 minutes. Drain well, and return the ziti to the pot.

4. Add the sauce to the pasta and mix well. Serve hot, passing the cheese on the side.

Porcini Mushrooms

Porcini are prized for their deep, earthy flavor. While some high-level supermarkets carry fresh porcini ("little pigs," in Italian, as the fresh ones are so plump) during their brief season in the autumn, most porcini are sliced and dried. Dried porcini need to be rehydrated before serving. Buy them in bulk at specialty markets or Italian grocers, as when they are stored in a cool, dry place, they will keep for months.

Some cooks soak the mushrooms in a small bowl of hot water for 20 minutes or so, then strain the soaking liquid to remove any grit and use the liquid in the recipe as a mushroom-flavored broth, as it were. If the dish is going to cook for 20 minutes or longer anyway, I often add the dried mushrooms (first rinsed quickly under cold water to clean away what little dirt there may be) directly to the pot. Porcini powder (page 179) is an even easier way to get that complex woodland flavor into your food.

Layered Polenta with Bolognese Sauce

With precooked polenta on hand, you can have a warm and comforting casserole on the table with very little effort. Simply make a saucepan of your favorite pasta sauce (for example, this meaty, creamy Bolognese), layer the sliced polenta with shredded mozzarella, and bake. For a satisfying vegetarian dish, substitute one pound of sliced mushrooms for the ground meat.

Makes 4 to 6 servings

2 tablespoons unsalted butter

1 medium onion, chopped

1 medium carrot, cut into ¼-inch dice

1 medium celery, cut into ¼-inch dice

1½ pounds ground meat loaf mix (equal parts beef, pork, and veal) or ground veal

½ teaspoon salt

¼ teaspoon freshly ground black pepper

½ cup dry white wine, such as Pinot Grigio

One 28-ounce can crushed tomatoes

1 teaspoon dried basil

⅓ cup heavy cream

One 1½-pound tube precooked polenta, cut into 20 rounds about ½ inch thick

1 cup (4 ounces) shredded mozzarella cheese

1. To make the sauce, melt the butter in a large saucepan over medium-high heat. Add the onion, carrot, and celery and cook, stirring often, until the onion is tender, about 7 minutes. Add the meat loaf mix, salt, and pepper and cook, breaking up the meat with the side of a spoon, until the meat loses its pink color, about 10 minutes.

2. Add the wine and cook until it has almost completely evaporated, about 5 minutes. Stir in the tomatoes and basil and bring to a boil. Reduce the heat to medium-low and simmer, uncovered, until slightly thickened, about 30 minutes. Stir in the heavy cream. Remove from the heat.

3. Meanwhile, position a rack in the center of the oven and preheat to 350°F. Lightly oil an 8 x 11½-inch baking dish.

4. Arrange half of the polenta rounds in the baking dish. Spread with 2 cups of the sauce. Top with the remaining polenta rounds and sauce. Sprinkle with the mozzarella.

5. Bake until the sauce is bubbling and the cheese is melted, about 25 minutes. Let stand for 5 minutes, then serve hot.

The New Polenta

Traditional polenta recipes advise the cook to stir the polenta constantly for 45 minutes or so, until it is perfectly soft. While I support the "slow food movement," I can't often find the time to cook polenta the old-fashioned way. Happily, two polenta products are available that provide polenta without elbow grease.

Instant polenta, which comes in boxes, is parcooked, then dehydrated. It reconstitutes quickly in boiling water or broth to make soft polenta perfect for serving with stews or roasts. If allowed to cool and firm, it can be cut up and baked and fried, but there is an easier way.

Precooked polenta is completely cooked, shaped into a tube, and packaged aseptically so it can be shelved at the market without refrigeration. This is the polenta to use for sautéing and baking when you're in a hurry. Some Italian delicatessens carry unseasoned precooked polenta, but more often it comes flavored with basil, sun-dried tomatoes, or garlic. Usually these seasonings are compatible with the sauce and don't pose a problem.

Viennese Noodles with Ham and Sour Cream

Vienna has a reputation for setting a delicious, if sinfully rich table, and the city's version of macaroni and cheese lives up to that reputation. Called <u>Schinkenfleckerl</u>, pork with noodles, it is the kind of recipe that would make an American personal trainer break out in a cold sweat. I say, make this wonderfully creamy dish tonight and go to the gym tomorrow.

Makes 6 servings

2 tablespoons unsalted butter, 1 tablespoon at room temperature, 1 tablespoon diced and chilled

12 ounces egg noodles

One 15-ounce container sour cream

1½ cups (6 ounces) shredded Gruyère or Swiss cheese

3 large eggs, beaten, at room temperature

¾ teaspoon salt

¼ teaspoon freshly ground black pepper

8 ounces smoked ham, cut into ½-inch dice

1. Position a rack in the center of the oven and preheat to 375°F. Generously butter a 9 x 13-inch baking dish with the 1 tablespoon room-temperature butter.

2. Bring a large pot of lightly salted water to a boil over high heat. Add the noodles and cook until tender, about 9 minutes. Drain well, and return the noodles to the pot.

3. Add the sour cream, cheese, eggs, salt, and pepper to the noodles and mix well. Stir in the ham. Spread evenly in the prepared dish and dot with the 1 tablespoon chilled butter.

4. Bake until the noodles feel set when pressed in the center and the tips are lightly browned, about 30 minutes. Let stand for 5 minutes.

5. Cut the noodles into squares to serve.

Italian "Fried Rice" with Shrimp, Pancetta, and Basil Under 30 minutes

On a recent evening, it seemed as though there was nothing in the house for dinner. But I had leftover cooked rice in the refrigerator, and my usual supply of shrimp, pancetta, lima beans, and peas in the freezer. I decided to apply the Asian method of "frying" rice to the ingredients on hand. It was a very successful experiment, and has since warranted many repeat performances. Note that the cooked rice for fried rice must be chilled, or the ingredients will stick together into a lumpy mass.

Makes 4 servings

2 ounces sliced (¼-inch-thick) pancetta, cut into ½-inch dice (½ cup)

2 tablespoons extra-virgin olive oil, divided

12 ounces large (21 to 25 count) shrimp, peeled and deveined

1 medium onion, finely chopped

2 garlic cloves, minced

3½ cups cooked rice, chilled

2 cups thawed frozen peas and/or lima beans (preferably a combination)

½ cup dry white wine

½ cup canned reduced-sodium chicken broth

½ cup (2 ounces) freshly grated Parmesan cheese, plus more for serving

2 tablespoons chopped fresh basil

Salt and freshly ground black pepper to taste

1. Combine the pancetta and 1 tablespoon of the oil in a 12-inch skillet and cook over medium heat until the pancetta is browned, about 5 minutes. Using a slotted spoon, transfer the pancetta to paper towels, leaving the fat in the skillet.

2. Increase the heat to medium-high and add the shrimp to the skillet. Cook, stirring occasionally, just until the shrimp turn opaque, about 2 minutes. Transfer to a plate.

3. Add the remaining 1 tablespoon oil to the skillet and heat. Add the onion and cook, stirring often, until translucent, about 3 minutes. Stir in the garlic and cook until it softens, about 30 seconds. Add the rice and peas. Cook, stirring often to break up the clumps of rice, until the rice is heated through, about 3 minutes.

(continued)

Add the wine, then the broth, stirring up any browned bits in the bottom of the pan with a wooden spatula. Add the shrimp and pancetta and stir until piping hot, about 1 minute.

4. Remove from the heat and stir in the Parmesan and basil. Season with salt and pepper. Serve hot, with additional Parmesan passed on the side.

Shrimp and Baby Spinach Risotto

Casual but elegant, this is a risotto that could double as a first course at a dinner party, but I serve it most often as an entrée. To get additional seafood flavor into the risotto, the shrimp are cooked in the broth, an easy trick that works perfectly. Many cooks believe that Italian seafood dishes never include cheese, but that is only so in the southern part of the country, where cows, milk, and cheese are in short supply (in fact, many pasta dishes from that area use toasted bread crumbs as a topping). If you have a knee-jerk aversion to combining seafood with cheese, just leave out the Parmesan, but I think it's delicious.

Makes 4 to 6 servings

6 cups canned reduced-sodium chicken broth

1 pound large (21 to 25 count) shrimp, peeled and deveined

2 tablespoons unsalted butter

2 tablespoons extra-virgin olive oil

1 medium onion, chopped

2 garlic cloves, minced

1½ cups (11 ounces) rice for risotto, such as Arborio,

Carnaroli, or Vialone Nano

¾ cup dry white wine, such as Pinot Grigio

6 ounces baby spinach

1 large ripe tomato, seeded and cut into ½-inch dice

½ cup (2 ounces) freshly grated Parmesan cheese, plus more for serving

2 tablespoons chopped fresh basil

Salt and freshly ground black pepper to taste

1. Bring the broth to a boil in a medium saucepan over high heat. Add the shrimp and cook just until they turn pink and opaque, about 2 minutes. Using a slotted spoon, transfer the shrimp to a bowl, and cover with foil to keep warm. Reduce the heat to low and keep the broth hot.

2. Heat the butter and oil in a large heavy-bottomed saucepan over medium heat. Add the onion and cook, stirring often, until golden, about 5 minutes. Add the garlic and cook until it gives off its aroma, about 1 minute. Add the rice and cook, stirring often, until it turns from translucent to chalky white (do not brown), about 2 minutes. Add the wine and cook until almost evaporated, about 2 minutes.

3. Stir about 1 cup of the hot broth into the rice. Cook, stirring almost con-

stantly, until the rice absorbs almost all of the broth, about 3 minutes. Stir in another cup of broth, and stir until it is almost absorbed. Repeat, keeping the risotto at a steady simmer and adding more broth as it is absorbed, until you have used all of the broth and the rice is barely tender, about 20 minutes total. If you run out of broth and the rice isn't tender, use hot water. During the last 3 minutes of cooking, in batches, stir in the spinach, until it is wilted.

4. Remove the risotto from the heat and stir in the shrimp, tomato, cheese, and basil. Season with salt and pepper. Spoon into individual bowls and serve hot, with additional Parmesan passed on the side.

Tips for Risotto

Yes, risotto must be stirred almost constantly for about 20 minutes, but that shouldn't stop you from including it in your repertoire of carefree recipes. When I make it, I invite friends or family into the kitchen so we can chat while I'm stirring away. And note that I say to stir "almost" constantly. With a heavy-bottomed pot to discourage scorching, you can walk away from the pot for a minute or two without disaster.

Once you are familiar with the risotto routine, you can vary the dish according to what you have on hand. As with pasta, I usually base my risotto on what is in the refrigerator, without shopping for specific ingredients. I've made a great risotto with leftover chicken and some frozen peas and lima beans. And I've stretched a previous night's meal of sausage and green cabbage into a fine risotto. And while the best risotto is made from homemade stock, canned chicken broth is an acceptable substitute for weeknight meals.

While risotto is usually considered a meal that must be eaten immediately after preparation, it can be made ahead. (Why do you think risotto is such a popular restaurant dish? It is not because each portion must be prepared to order!) Cook the risotto in the broth until it is almost, but not quite done, about 5 minutes less than required. If you bite into a grain of rice, it will have a visible white core. Line a large baking sheet with parchment paper, and spread out the parcooked risotto on the parchment. As soon as it cools, tightly cover the risotto on the sheet with plastic wrap, and refrigerate for up to 4 hours. When ready to serve, bring about 1 cup chicken broth to a boil in the pot over medium heat. Add the risotto and stir, adding more hot broth as needed, until the risotto is hot and barely tender, 3 to 5 minutes.

Radicchio and Sausage Risotto

Here, radicchio's mildly bitter flavor is nicely tempered by sweet sausage and creamy rice to create a memorable risotto. Cooking the maroon radicchio will tint the risotto a dull brown, but a topping of fresh leaves brightens up the color and provides a textural contrast as well.

Makes 4 to 6 servings

2 medium heads (1 pound) radicchio

3 cups canned reduced-sodium chicken broth

2 tablespoons extra-virgin olive oil, divided

1 pound sweet Italian pork or turkey sausage, casings removed

1 medium onion, chopped

2 garlic cloves, minced

1½ cups (11 ounces) rice for risotto, such as Arborio, Carnaroli, or Vialone Nano

1 cup dry white wine

½ cup (2 ounces) freshly shredded Parmesan cheese

Salt and freshly ground black pepper to taste

1. Core the radicchio and cut crosswise into ⅛-inch shreds. You should have about 6 cups loosely packed radicchio; reserve about 1½ cups to use as a garnish.

2. Bring the broth and 3 cups of water to a boil in a medium saucepan over high heat. Turn the heat to very low to keep the broth hot.

3. Heat 1 tablespoon of the oil in a large heavy-bottomed saucepan over medium heat. Add the sausage and cook, breaking up the sausage with the side of a spoon into small pieces, until it loses its pink color, about 5 minutes. Add the onion and garlic and cook, stirring occasionally, until the onion softens, about 3 minutes. Using a slotted spoon, transfer the sausage mixture to a plate.

4. Add the remaining 1 tablespoon oil to the saucepan and heat. Add the rice and cook, stirring often, until it turns from translucent to opaque (do not brown), about 2 minutes. Return the sausage mixture to the pan. Add the wine and cook until almost evaporated, about 2 minutes.

5. Stir about 1 cup of the hot broth mixture into the rice. Cook, stirring almost constantly, until the rice absorbs almost all of the broth, about 3 minutes. Stir in another cup of broth, and stir until it is almost absorbed. Repeat, keeping the

risotto at a steady simmer and adding more broth as it is absorbed, until you have used all of the broth and the rice is barely tender, about 20 minutes total. If you run out of broth and the rice isn't tender, use hot water. During the last 5 minutes of cooking, in batches, stir in the radicchio until all but the reserved 1 1/2 cups has been added and wilted.

6. Remove the risotto from the heat and stir in the cheese. Season with salt and pepper. Spoon the risotto into individual bowls, and top each serving with a mound of the reserved radicchio.

Vegetarian Main Courses For years, most American cooks considered vegetables only as auxiliary ingredients—they were good enough for side dishes and salads, but they were rarely the stars of the show. ¶ Well, all that's changed, and some of my most requested main courses are now vegetable-based —and we are a household of confirmed carnivores. There are many good reasons for the rise of vegetables as a major component in daily cooking. ¶ First, there's the health factor. Vegetables are good for us, supplying vitamins and fiber to our daily diets. However, people aren't going to eat vegetables if they aren't tasty. Too many of us remember vegetables as uninspired, generally abused side dishes. With the newfound popularity of rustic cuisines, which often use vegetables more than meat as a main ingredient, those days are happily over.

These vegetable main courses are favorites from my kitchen, and reflect my personal tastes. The vegetarian cooking of the Far East and India is renowned for its complexity and variety, but I don't usually have the required spices at hand, so I don't cook those dishes often. And because I haven't found a canned brand that I like, I never use vegetable stock. I much prefer to let the vegetables in the recipe provide the flavor, and simply use water (sometimes with a bit of miso, the Japanese soybean paste, for added flavor) to supply liquid. Of course, if you have homemade vegetable stock on hand, it can be substituted for water in a recipe for a more complex flavor. To add protein to a vegetarian dish, I use cheese or dairy products. True vegetarians often combine grains and beans to create the necessary amino acids for good nutrition, but that's not a worry for those of us who cook vegetarian meals only occasionally.

Forget equating a vegetarian meal with a bowl of greens—these are recipes for every taste. Even the hungriest meat eater will tear into a bowl of Vegetable Chili with Corn and Pink Beans or a wedge of Zucchini Pie with Polenta Crust. Santa Fe Corn Pudding with Year-Round Salsa is a delicate dish suitable for supper or brunch, as are the Potato-Carrot Pancakes and Potato and Rosemary Fritatta. You'll find other meatless main courses in the Pasta and Grains chapter.

The Carefree Cook's Tips for Vegetarian Main Courses

Discover rustic cooking The rediscovery of Old World cooking (whether from Europe, Asia, or elsewhere) was a big reason for the emergence of vegetarian cooking. A few years ago, for example, only cooks of Italian heritage were familiar with polenta, one of the humblest of Italian foods, but now it's a staple in many kitchens.

Shop at your local farmers' market If you have a local farmers' market that you have been meaning to visit, make the effort and drop by—I guarantee that it will become a habit. Most of my vegetarian main course recipes were developed after an especially enthusiastic shopping spree at a farmers' market made me think up ways to cook the bounty heaped on the counter. The big-city cousin to the farmers' market is the upscale natural foods supermarket, and these are popping up all over the map like so many cornstalks in a field. They may not have the same charm as the old-fashioned market, but they provide high-quality produce that was unavailable at any price just a few years ago.

Let the season dictate your menu Today there are few vegetables or fruits that aren't available all year round, but just because they look beautiful doesn't mean they taste good. Produce will always be best when purchased from local farmers (whenever possible) within its traditional season. Spring asparagus from a nearby farmstand or farmers' market is the gold standard; asparagus flown in by jet from thousands of miles away in November will most likely disappoint even the most unsophisticated palate.

Vegetable Chili with Corn and Pink Beans

A big bowl of vegetable chili is a beautiful thing, especially on a chilly (no pun intended) night. But chili can also be the topping for a crunchy tostada, or be tucked into warm tortillas for burritos. My friend Steven Evasew shared his trick for preparing the vegetables in a food processor, a technique that gives them texture that simulates ground-meat chili. Ordinarily I never chop vegetables in the processor, in part because it tends to release too many juices. However, for this chili, where the juices are beneficial, I make an exception. Use any beans you prefer, but I like the neutral flavor and color of pink beans. Some cooks swear by black beans in their chili, but they turn the bright and vibrant stew a dark and murky color.

Makes 6 to 8 servings

2 garlic cloves, minced

1 jalapeño, seeded and finely chopped

1 large onion, coarsely chopped

2 medium zucchini, coarsely chopped

2 medium celery ribs with leaves, coarsely chopped

1 large red bell pepper, cored, seeds and ribs removed, coarsely chopped

1 medium carrot, coarsely chopped

2 tablespoons extra-virgin olive oil

1 tablespoon pure ground ancho chiles or use regular chili powder

1 teaspoon dried oregano

1 teaspoon ground cumin

One 28-ounce can tomatoes in juice, chopped, juices reserved

1½ cups fresh or thawed frozen corn kernels

One 15- to 19-ounce can pink beans, drained and rinsed

¼ cup chopped fresh cilantro, plus more for garnish

Salt and freshly ground black pepper to taste

Sour cream and shredded Cheddar cheese for serving

1. Fit a food processor with the metal chopping blade. With the machine running, drop the garlic and jalapeño through the feed tube to finely chop. In two or three batches, add the onion, zucchini, celery, red pepper, and carrot and pulse until finely chopped into approximate 1/4-inch dice.

2. Heat the oil in a large saucepan over medium heat. Add the chopped vegetables, cover, and cook, stirring occasionally, until the vegetables give off their juices, about 10 minutes.

(continued)

**Vegetable Chili with Corn
and Pink Beans; Easy Yogurt
Corn Bread (page 283)**

3. Add the ground chiles, oregano, and cumin and stir until they give off their aroma, about 30 seconds. Stir in the tomatoes, with their juices, and bring to a boil over medium-high heat. Cover again, reduce the heat to medium-low, and simmer until the vegetables are tender, about 20 minutes.

4. Stir in the corn, beans, and cilantro and cook, uncovered, until heated through, about 5 minutes. Season with salt and pepper.

5. Serve hot, with bowls of sour cream, cheese, and chopped cilantro passed on the side for toppings.

Ground Chiles

There is chili powder, and there are powdered chiles, also known as pure ground chiles. The difference is more than semantics. Every supermarket carries chili powder, which is a blend of spices destined to season a pot of Texas chili. While it has a base of powdered hot or mild chiles, it can also include cumin, oregano, garlic or onion powder, and the like. Pure ground chiles are unadulterated chiles ground into a powder, so you get a truer flavor. You'll find them at upscale supermarkets and gourmet shops with Mexican or Southwestern items. Some of the most popular are ancho (somewhat mild with a sweet note), chipotle (smoked and dried jalapeños), and habanero (famously incendiary). If you can't find pure ground chiles, simply use chili powder.

Santa Fe Corn Pudding with Year-Round Salsa

These individual custards make single servings of a deliciously creamy corn pudding enlivened with Southwestern flavors. Serve it for a comforting supper or keep it in mind when you want a special brunch main course.

Makes 4 servings

1 tablespoon unsalted butter, plus more for the custard cups

3 tablespoons dried bread crumbs

1 small onion, chopped

1/2 cup chopped red bell pepper

1 teaspoon seeded and minced jalapeño

1 garlic clove, minced

2 cups fresh or thawed frozen corn kernels, divided

2 large eggs

1 large egg yolk

3/4 teaspoon salt

1/4 teaspoon freshly ground black pepper

1 cup milk

1/2 cup (2 ounces) shredded extra-sharp Cheddar cheese

Year-Round Salsa (recipe follows)

1. Position a rack in the center of the oven and preheat to 325°F. Lightly butter the inside of four 10-ounce custard cups. Coat the insides of the cups with the bread crumbs, tapping out the excess crumbs.

2. Melt 1 tablespoon butter in a medium skillet over medium heat. Add the onion, red pepper, jalapeño, and garlic. Cook, stirring occasionally, until the onion is tender, about 4 minutes. Remove from the heat and let cool slightly.

3. Combine 1 cup of the corn, the eggs, yolk, salt, and pepper in a food processor and process until the corn is pureed. With the machine running, add the milk. Transfer to a medium bowl. Stir in the cheese, vegetables, and the remaining 1 cup corn. Ladle the mixture into the custard cups.

4. Place the cups on a baking sheet. Bake until the tops are puffed and lightly browned and the custards feel set when pressed in the centers, about 45 minutes. Let stand for 5 minutes, then run a knife around the inside of each cup. Protecting your hands with a kitchen towel, invert each custard onto a dinner plate. Serve hot, with the salsa passed on the side.

Year-Round Salsa

The season for fresh ripe tomatoes, unfortunately, isn't very long, but my desire for a zesty salsa lasts all year. Recently I've taken to using canned diced tomatoes, an excellent product, to make a great homemade version that will remind you of your favorite gourmet shop salsa. The flavor and heat level can be varied by the choice and amount of pure ground chiles. Ancho is my favorite, with its warm heat and sweet notes. Watch out for hotter chiles, as you'll need to reduce the amount. For a hot and smoky chipotle salsa, use only 1/2 teaspoon ground chiles. And only 1/8 teaspoon ground habanero chiles will provide enough heat to set a batch of salsa on (figurative) fire.

Makes about 1 1/2 cups

1 tablespoon olive oil

1/2 cup chopped onion

1 teaspoon seeded and minced jalapeño

1 garlic clove, chopped

1 teaspoon pure ground chiles, such as ancho, optional (see page 234)

One 14 1/2-ounce can diced tomatoes in juice

2 tablespoons chopped fresh cilantro

1. Heat the oil in a medium skillet over medium heat. Add the onion, jalapeño, and garlic. Cook, stirring often, until the onion is translucent, about 5 minutes. Stir in the ground chiles, if using.

2. Add the tomatoes, with their juices, and bring to a boil. Cook, stirring often, until the juices thicken to the desired consistency, about 3 minutes for a juicy salsa and 5 minutes for a thick-and-chunky version. Remove from the heat and stir in the cilantro. Transfer to a bowl and let cool completely. (The salsa can be made ahead and refrigerated, covered, for up to 5 days.)

Eggplant Parmesan Gratin

Anyone who has gone through the tedium of frying sliced eggplant for eggplant Parmesan knows that it is a kitchen chore in need of a fresh approach. My version of the dish, made with broiled eggplant, is quicker and the final result is much lighter. There are just a few simple steps, but do allow time to salt the eggplant to draw off the bitter juices before broiling it.

Makes 6 to 8 servings

2 medium eggplants (about 1¼ pounds each), trimmed and cut into ½-inch-thick rounds

2 teaspoons salt

2 tablespoons extra-virgin olive oil, plus more for brushing the eggplant

1 medium onion, chopped

2 garlic cloves, minced

2 teaspoons dried oregano

⅛ teaspoon crushed hot red pepper flakes

One 28-ounce can crushed tomatoes in puree

1 cup (4 ounces) shredded mozzarella

½ cup (2 ounces) freshly grated Parmesan cheese

1. Place the eggplant in a large colander or bowl and toss with the salt. Let stand for 30 to 60 minutes to draw off some of the bitter juices. Rinse well and pat dry with paper towels.

2. Meanwhile, heat the oil in a medium saucepan over medium heat. Add the onion and cook, stirring often, until golden, about 6 minutes. Add the garlic and cook until it gives off its aroma, about 1 minute. Stir in the oregano and red pepper flakes. Stir in the crushed tomatoes and bring to a boil. Reduce the heat to low and simmer, uncovered, stirring often, until the sauce has thickened slightly, about 20 minutes. Remove from the heat and cover to keep warm.

3. Position the broiler rack about 6 inches from the source of heat and preheat the broiler. Lightly oil a large baking sheet.

4. Arrange the eggplant slices, slightly overlapping, on the baking sheet. Brush the eggplant lightly with olive oil. Broil until the eggplant is lightly browned, about 6 minutes. Turn the eggplant (no need to brush with oil again), and continue broiling to brown the other side, about 6 minutes. Set aside.

(continued)

5. Position a rack in the center of the oven and preheat to 350°F. Lightly oil an 8 x 11 1/2-inch baking dish.

6. Spread about 1/2 cup of the tomato sauce in the baking dish. Arrange half of the eggplant, overlapping the slices, over the sauce. Spread with half of the remaining sauce and sprinkle with half of the mozzarella. Repeat with the remaining eggplant, sauce, and mozzarella. Sprinkle with the Parmesan.

7. Bake until the sauce is bubbling, about 30 minutes. Let stand for 5 minutes, then serve hot.

Potato and Rosemary Frittata Under 30 minutes

For a fast supper or brunch dish, a frittata is hard to beat. Any frittata recipe is an invitation for the chef to create his or her own variations. For example, I sometimes add a cup or so of leftover pasta (including the sauce) or rice. If you wish, serve with a spoonful of your favorite salsa.

Makes 4 to 6 servings

2 tablespoons olive oil

1 pound baking potatoes, peeled and cut into $\frac{1}{8}$-inch-
    thick rounds

3 scallions, white and green parts, chopped

$1\frac{1}{2}$ teaspoons chopped fresh rosemary

$\frac{3}{4}$ teaspoon salt, divided

$\frac{1}{2}$ teaspoon freshly ground black pepper, divided

6 large eggs

1. Heat the oil in an 8-inch nonstick skillet over medium heat. Add the potatoes and cook, stirring occasionally, until they begin to soften, about 3 minutes. Cover and cook, stirring often, until the potatoes are tender and most of them are browned, about 20 minutes.

2. Meanwhile, position a broiler pan 6 inches from the source of heat and preheat the broiler.

3. Mix the scallions, rosemary, $\frac{1}{4}$ teaspoon of the salt, and $\frac{1}{4}$ teaspoon of the pepper into the potatoes, then spread the potatoes evenly in the skillet. Reduce the heat under the skillet to medium-low. Whisk the eggs and the remaining $\frac{1}{2}$ teaspoon salt, and $\frac{1}{4}$ teaspoon pepper in a medium bowl until combined. Pour the eggs into the skillet and cook until the edges begin to set. Using a rubber spatula, lift up an edge of the frittata, and tilt the skillet so the uncooked eggs run underneath the frittata. Continue cooking, occasionally lifting the frittata and tilting the skillet as described, until the top is almost set, 4 to 5 minutes.

4. Transfer the skillet to the broiler and broil the frittata until the top is puffed and lightly browned, about 1 minute. Place a plate over the top of the skillet and invert the frittata onto the plate. Cut into wedges and serve hot, or let cool to room temperature before serving.

Zucchini Pie with Polenta Crust

A vegetarian member of the deep-dish pie family, this has a cheesy polenta layer for its top crust. If you want a spicier version with a Southwestern accent, substitute cilantro for the fresh basil, and sauté a seeded and minced jalapeño with the onion mixture.

Makes 4 to 6 servings

2 tablespoons extra-virgin olive oil

2 pounds zucchini, cut into ½-inch dice

1 large onion, chopped

1 medium red bell pepper, cored, seeds and ribs removed, and cut into ½-inch dice

2 garlic cloves, minced

2 tablespoons chopped fresh basil or 2 teaspoons dried basil

One 14½-ounce can diced tomatoes in juice

Salt and freshly ground black pepper to taste

Polenta Crust

1 cup yellow cornmeal

¾ teaspoon salt

¼ teaspoon freshly ground black pepper

1½ cups (6 ounces) shredded Fontina cheese, preferably Fontina d'Aosta, divided

1. Position a rack in the center of the oven and preheat to 350°F. Lightly oil a 9½-inch deep-dish pie plate.

2. Heat the oil in a 12-inch skillet over medium-high heat. Add the zucchini, onion, red pepper, and garlic. Cook, stirring occasionally, until the zucchini is tender and lightly browned, about 15 minutes. Stir in the basil, add the tomatoes, with their juices, and bring to a boil. Reduce the heat to medium-low and simmer until the tomato juices thicken, about 5 minutes. Season with salt and pepper.

3. Meanwhile, to make the polenta crust, whisk the cornmeal with 1 cup cold water in a small bowl. Bring 1 cup water and the salt and pepper to a boil in a medium heavy-bottomed saucepan over high heat. Whisk in the cornmeal mixture and bring to a boil. Reduce the heat to medium-low and let bubble for 2 minutes. Stir in 1 cup of the cheese. Remove from the heat.   (continued)

4. Spread the zucchini mixture evenly in the pie plate. Spread the polenta over the zucchini to within 1 inch of the edges of the plate. Sprinkle the remaining ½ cup cheese on top. Place the pie plate on a baking sheet.

5. Bake until the edges of the crust are lightly browned, about 25 minutes. Let stand for 5 minutes, then serve hot.

Potato-Carrot Pancakes Under 30 minutes

Just thinking about latkes (the Yiddish word for potato pancakes), golden brown, crisp and tender at the same time, makes my mouth water. Carrots and onion give these pancakes extra flavor, elevating them above the commonplace. The secret to their lightness is the potato starch, gathered from the shredded potatoes, which holds them together without a lot of matzo meal or bread crumbs. Don't skimp on the oil, or the pancakes won't have that marvelous crunch. To round out the meal, serve with the Coleslaw with Apple–Poppy Seed Dressing (page 47).

Makes 8 pancakes

1¼ pounds baking potatoes

2 medium carrots

1 medium onion

2 large eggs, beaten

2 tablespoons matzo meal or dried bread crumbs

1 teaspoon salt

¼ teaspoon freshly ground black pepper

Vegetable oil for cooking the pancakes

Sour cream and applesauce for serving

1. Position a rack in the center of the oven and preheat to 200°F. Line a baking sheet with paper towels.

2. Peel the potatoes (*do not* place in cold water). Shred with a food processor fitted with a grating blade with large holes, or use the large holes of a box grater. Working over a small bowl, squeeze the potatoes to remove the excess liquid, and transfer the potatoes to a large bowl. Set the bowl of potato liquid aside to stand for 5 minutes.

3. Shred the carrots in the food processor (using the grating disk) and add to the bowl with the potatoes. Grate the onion with the same blade—it will be almost pureed—and add to the potato-carrot mixture, discarding any large shreds of onion. (You can also use the large holes of a box grater for the carrots and onion.)

4. Carefully pour off and discard the reddish layer that has risen to the top of the potato liquid, leaving the pastelike potato starch in the bottom of the bowl. Scrape the starch into the shredded vegetables. Add the eggs, bread crumbs, salt, and pepper and mix well. (continued)

5. Pour enough oil to make a $\frac{1}{8}$-inch-deep pool into a 12-inch skillet and heat over medium-high heat until very hot. Carefully add about $\frac{1}{3}$ cup batter for each pancake to the oil, forming four 4-inch pancakes with the edge of the measuring cup. Cook until the undersides are golden brown, about 3 minutes. Turn and brown the other sides, about 3 more minutes. Using a slotted spatula, transfer to the paper towel–lined baking sheet and keep warm in the oven while you make the remaining pancakes. If needed, add more oil to the skillet and heat before cooking the second batch.

6. Serve hot, with the sour cream and applesauce.

Double-Baked Potatoes
with Goat Cheese and Cremini Mushrooms

Originally created as a side dish for steaks, these potatoes became so popular at my house that I now serve them as a main course with a big green salad. Even though they're rich, they're so tasty that you may find yourself serving two half-potatoes per person.

Makes 3 to 6 servings

3 large (12 to 14 ounces each) baking potatoes, scrubbed but not peeled

2 tablespoons unsalted butter, divided

12 ounces cremini mushrooms, coarsely chopped

2 scallions, white and green parts, chopped

4 ounces goat cheese, at room temperature

1/3 cup heavy cream

Salt and freshly ground black pepper, to taste

3 tablespoons freshly grated Parmesan cheese

1. Position a rack in the center of the oven and preheat to 375°F.

2. Pierce each potato a few times with a fork. Place the potatoes directly on the oven rack and bake until tender, about 1 1/4 hours.

3. Meanwhile, melt 1 tablespoon of the butter in a large nonstick skillet over medium heat. Add the mushrooms and cook, stirring often, until the juices they release evaporate and the mushrooms begin to brown, about 5 minutes. Add the scallions and stir until wilted, about 2 minutes. Set aside.

4. Protecting your hands with a kitchen towel, split each potato lengthwise in half. Scoop the potato flesh into large bowl, leaving the skins intact. Add the goat cheese and heavy cream to the potato flesh and mash with a hand masher or electric mixer. Stir in the mushroom mixture and season with the salt and pepper. Mound the mashed potatoes into the potato skins. Place the potatoes on a baking sheet. Sprinkle the tops with the Parmesan cheese, and dot with the remaining 1 tablespoon butter, cut into tiny cubes.

5. Bake until the potatoes are heated through and the tops are browned, about 20 minutes. Serve hot.

Spiced Roasted Vegetables on Cilantro Couscous

There are quicker techniques for cooking vegetables, but roasting brings out their flavor like no other method. Also, the vegetables leave caramelized juices behind in the pan that can be used for a sauce. Here a mélange of roasted vegetables, seasoned in the Moroccan manner, is spooned onto a bed of herbed couscous.

Makes 4 to 6 servings

¼ cup extra-virgin olive oil

2 garlic cloves, crushed under a knife

1 medium butternut squash (1¾ pounds), peeled, seeded, and cut into 1-inch cubes (see Note)

2 large zucchini, cut into ¾-inch rounds

1 medium turnip, peeled and cut into 1-inch cubes

1 medium red bell pepper, cored, seeds and ribs removed, and cut into 1-inch squares

1 large yellow onion, unpeeled, cut into sixths

1 teaspoon ground cumin

½ teaspoon ground coriander

½ teaspoon ground ginger

1 teaspoon salt, divided

¼ teaspoon cayenne pepper

¼ teaspoon freshly ground black pepper

One 10-ounce box couscous

3 tablespoons finely chopped fresh cilantro

2 tablespoons tomato paste

1. Position a rack in the center of the oven and preheat to 400°F.

2. Heat the oil and garlic in a small saucepan over low heat until tiny bubbles surround the garlic, about 5 minutes. Remove from the heat and let the garlic infuse the oil for about 10 minutes.

3. Combine the squash, zucchini, turnip, red bell pepper, and onion in a very large roasting pan. Strain the garlic oil over the vegetables, and discard the garlic. Toss the vegetables in the oil. Roast until the vegetables are tender and tinged with brown, about 1 hour.

4. Meanwhile, combine the cumin, coriander, ginger, ½ teaspoon of the salt, and the cayenne and black pepper. During the last 5 minutes of roasting, sprinkle the spice mixture over the vegetables and mix well.

5. Meanwhile, bring 2 cups water and the remaining ½ teaspoon salt to a boil in a medium saucepan. Stir in the couscous. Remove from the heat, cover, and

let stand until the couscous is tender, about 5 minutes. Fluff the couscous with a fork, and stir in the cilantro.

6. Transfer the vegetables to a medium bowl. Place the roasting pan over two burners on high heat and heat until the pan sizzles. Add 2 cups water and the tomato paste and bring to a boil, scraping up the browned bits in the pan with a wooden spoon. Boil until the liquid reduces to $1^3/_4$ cups, about 2 minutes. Pour over the vegetables.

7. Spoon the couscous onto plates and top with the vegetables. Serve hot.

Note: Butternut squash is notoriously difficult to pare, but a number of recent developments have made that a thing of the past. I used to cut the butternut into chunks and then pare each one with a small knife. What was I thinking? Now I use a sturdy vegetable peeler to remove the peel from the entire squash, using extra pressure to dig deep enough to reach the flesh. Once peeled, the squash can be cut lengthwise in half to scoop out the seeds, and cut into chunks as required. Also, many supermarkets now carry 20-ounce packages of peeled butternut pieces. The only drawback is that the amount is somewhat on the small side, and if you buy two packages, you can be looking at leftovers. However, for most recipes, a bit more (or less) squash won't make that much difference.

Yam, Corn, and Kale Stew with Miso Broth

One of my best buddies, Skip Dye, is vegetarian . . . and a native of Tennessee. When he comes over for dinner, I like to make a dish with the Southern ingredients he loves, but without the bacon that a Southerner would naturally use for flavoring. For this stew, the answer was smoky, intensely flavored miso, the Japanese seasoning paste. To add to the depth of flavor, be sure the onion is deeply browned—not burned, just nice and golden with some dark brown edges.

Makes 6 to 8 servings

2 tablespoons extra-virgin olive oil

1 large onion, chopped

2 medium orange-fleshed yams, peeled and cut into 1-inch cubes

1 large red bell pepper, cored, seeds and ribs removed, and cut into ¹/₂-inch dice

1 jalapeño, seeded and finely chopped

4 garlic cloves, finely chopped

2 bunches kale (about 1¹/₄ pounds), well washed, stems removed, and leaves stacked and cut crosswise into ¹/₂-inch-wide strips

¹/₄ teaspoon salt, plus more to taste

1¹/₂ cups fresh or thawed frozen corn kernels

2 tablespoons white (also known as pale or sweet) miso, or more to taste

Freshly ground black pepper to taste

1. Heat the oil in a large saucepan over medium-high heat. Add the onion and cook, stirring often, until well browned, about 10 minutes.

2. Add the yams, red pepper, jalapeño, and garlic, cover, and cook, stirring occasionally, until the pepper softens, about 2 minutes. Add enough water to barely cover the vegetables and bring to a boil. A handful at a time, stir in the kale, letting each batch wilt before adding more. Stir in the salt. Cover tightly, reduce the heat to medium-low, and simmer until the yams are tender, about 30 minutes.

3. Add the corn and cook until tender, about 5 minutes. Transfer 1 cup of the stew liquid to a small bowl, add the miso, and stir to dissolve. Stir back into the stew. Taste and add more miso or salt as needed, then season with pepper. Serve hot.

Miso

In recent years, a huge variety of Asian soybean products has been sneaking into the American diet—tofu, soy sauce, and hoisin sauce were just the beginning. Miso, a savory fermented soybean paste used in Japanese cuisine, is also becoming better known here. There are three main types, white or pale (also known as sweet, made from soy and malted rice), red or dark (made from soy and malted barley and/or rice), and mame (all soybean). The white miso is probably the most versatile for Western cooks, as it can be used in soups, stews, and dressings, as well as in marinades and glazes for fish, chicken, and vegetables. Buy miso packed in small plastic tubs, as it is easiest to store. Miso sold in bags should be transferred to covered jars for storage. Tightly covered and refrigerated, it will keep almost indefinitely.

Zucchini with Sun-Dried Tomato and Ricotta Stuffing

Stuffed vegetables are fun to make and eat. Here's my most requested recipe for stuffed zucchini, filled with sun-dried tomato–flavored ricotta cheese. It shows why a supply of sun-dried tomato pesto is a good thing to have on hand. If you wish, heat store-bought marinara sauce and serve on the side.

Makes 4 servings

2 tablespoons extra-virgin olive oil, divided

1 medium onion, chopped

1 garlic clove, crushed through a press

1 cup ricotta cheese (part-skim or whole-milk)

1/3 cup plus 2 tablespoons freshly grated Parmesan cheese, divided

1 large egg, beaten

2 tablespoons Sun-Dried Tomato Pesto (recipe follows) or drained and minced sun-dried tomatoes

2 tablespoons dried bread crumbs, divided

1/4 teaspoon salt

1/8 teaspoon freshly ground black pepper

2 large zucchini (12 ounces each)

1. Position a rack in the upper third of the oven and preheat to 350°F. Lightly oil a 9 x 13-inch baking dish.

2. Heat 1 tablespoon of the oil in a medium skillet over medium heat. Add the onion and cook, stirring often, until tender, about 5 minutes. Add the garlic and cook until it gives off its fragrance, about 1 minute. Transfer to a medium bowl. Add the ricotta, 1/3 cup of the Parmesan, the egg, tomato pesto, 1 tablespoon of the bread crumbs, the salt, and pepper, and mix.

3. Cut each zucchini lengthwise in half. Using a dessert spoon, scrape out the flesh to make 1/2-inch-thick shells. Place the zucchini shells in the baking dish, and fill with the ricotta mixture. Mix the remaining 2 tablespoons Parmesan and 1 tablespoon bread crumbs in a small bowl, and sprinkle over the filling. Drizzle with the remaining 1 tablespoon oil. Cover tightly with aluminum foil.

4. Bake the zucchini for 15 minutes. Uncover and bake until the tops are lightly browned, about 20 minutes longer. Let stand for 5 minutes, then serve hot.

Sun-Dried Tomato Pesto

There is always a container of this brick-red condiment in my refrigerator. It's a snap to whip up in a food processor with standard ingredients from my kitchen—packed sun-dried tomatoes, capers, garlic, olive oil, and crushed red pepper—along with basil from the garden or market. For such little effort, you'll have a powerhouse of flavor. Use it in recipes to supply a tomato accent, but don't forget it as a pasta sauce: toss a generous spoonful of pesto with hot, freshly cooked pasta and a bit of the pasta cooking water. And when you think you have nothing to serve to guests for an appetizer, spread the pesto on toasted baguette slices for instant crostini.

Makes about 1 cup

1 garlic clove

1 cup drained and coarsely chopped oil-packed sun-dried
   tomatoes

$1/4$ cup coarsely chopped fresh basil

3 tablespoons capers, drained and rinsed

$1/4$ teaspoon crushed hot red pepper

$1/4$ cup extra-virgin olive oil, plus extra if storing the pesto

Salt to taste

1. With the machine running, drop the garlic through the feed tube into a food processor to mince. Add the sun-dried tomatoes, basil, capers, and crushed red pepper and pulse until the tomatoes are minced. With the machine running, pour in the oil to make a thick paste. Season with salt.

2. Use the pesto immediately or transfer to a small covered container and pour a thin layer of oil on top to make a seal; refrigerate for up to 1 month. After using, smooth the top of any remaining pesto and cover with additional oil before refrigerating again.

Side Dishes When I am traveling in the Deep South, I often eat at one of the family-run cafeterias that serve up great home-cooked food. All of these places give their side dishes the same attention they give their main dishes. As a matter of fact, if you like, you can order a selection of side dishes for your meal, and I often do. ¶ Yet for too many cooks, side dishes remain the underdogs of the menu. If one looks more closely at the symbiosis between main dishes and side dishes, however, it is clear that side dishes must be more than an afterthought. What is a perfect roast chicken without equally fine mashed potatoes? If those mashed potatoes are bland and watery (or, heaven forbid, prepared from a box), is the meal still saved by the chicken alone? No way.

Convenience foods have a place in everyone's cooking, but too often, side dishes are prepared from ingredients that are a bit *too* convenient for my taste. I may use frozen vegetables as a component of a dish, but I have never been known to simply boil up a block of frozen produce and toss it into a bowl. The trick is to develop a repertoire of recipes that are easy to cook, visually interesting, and, above all, delicious. In other words, if your side dishes are recipes that entice you to cook, they won't be mundane.

Looking at the list of side dishes gathered here, I am tempted to make up a Southern cafeteria–style dinner of side dishes. I'd happily eat Roasted Acorn Squash Puree, Asparagus with Gremolata Butter, and Braised Escarole for supper any day of the week. That is, if I didn't choose Baby Carrots with Apple Glaze, Crisp Oven Fries, and Radishes and Scallions in Butter Sauce. All of these dishes are so easy that I'd have time to whip up some Yogurt Drop Biscuits or Easy Yogurt Corn Bread to serve on the side of my sides. (I've included these two quick breads in this chapter because they are typically served with meals, and, lacking a breads section, this seemed the most logical place.) It's time that side dishes got some respect, and these recipes should help improve their image.

Asparagus with Gremolata Butter

Asparagus needs a gentle hand in seasoning. The trick is to use complementary flavors that enhance but don't overpower the delicious spears. Lemon zest, parsley, and garlic, the components of gremolata, which is usually used to garnish and flavor osso buco, can add spark to vegetables too. Asparagus tips are a bit more tender than the rest of the spear, so to reduce the risk of overcooking, add them to the water after the bottoms have cooked a bit.

Makes 6 servings

2 pounds asparagus

2 tablespoons unsalted butter

1 garlic clove, crushed through a press

Grated zest of 1 lemon

1 tablespoon chopped fresh parsley

2 tablespoons fresh lemon juice

Salt to taste

1. Snap off and discard the woody stems from the asparagus. Cut off the spears about 1 inch below the tips; reserve the tips. Cut the bottoms of the asparagus stalks into 1-inch lengths.

2. Bring a large skillet pan of lightly salted water to a boil over high heat. Add the asparagus stalks (not the tips) and cook for 1 1/2 minutes. Add the tips and cook until the asparagus is barely tender, about 3 minutes more. Drain. Wipe the skillet dry.

3. Melt the butter with the garlic in the skillet over medium-high heat. Add the asparagus, lemon zest, and parsley and mix gently to coat the asparagus. Remove from the heat and stir in the lemon juice. Season with salt. Transfer to a serving bowl and serve hot.

Roasted Acorn Squash Puree

Too often, acorn squash is tarted up with all kinds of sweet goop. However, its nutty flavor can stand up to more savory seasonings, such as the Parmesan and butter found here. If you wish, add a tablespoon of chopped fresh sage to the puree before serving.

Makes 4 to 6 servings

2 acorn squash (about 2 pounds each)

¼ cup freshly grated Parmesan cheese

2 tablespoons unsalted butter

Salt and freshly ground black pepper to taste

1. Position a rack in the center of the oven and preheat to 400°F. Line a rimmed baking sheet with aluminum foil and lightly oil the foil.

2. Cut each squash lengthwise in half and scoop out the seeds. Place cut side down on the baking sheet. Pour ⅓ cup water into the pan. Bake until the squash is tender enough to be pierced with the tip of a sharp knife, 45 minutes to 1 hour, depending on the size of the squash.

3. Protecting your hands with a kitchen towel, scoop out the flesh from each squash half. Puree the squash flesh with the cheese and butter in a food processor. Season with salt and pepper.

4. Transfer to a serving bowl and serve hot.

Cream of Vegetable Soup

In my kitchen, leftover mashed or pureed vegetables usually end up as a quick, creamy soup. (Like many soups made with vegetable purees, the texture is so luxurious that actual dairy cream is entirely optional.) About the only puree that won't work here is the Buttermilk Mashed Potatoes on page 269, as buttermilk will curdle when heated. But if you use a family recipe for your mashed potatoes, with regular milk, they will make a great soup; substitute the chopped pale part of a leek for the onion.

Makes 4 servings

1 tablespoon unsalted butter

⅓ cup finely chopped onion

1 cup Roasted Acorn Squash Puree (page 256) or
    Mashed Turnips with Garlic (page 273)

2 cups canned reduced-sodium chicken broth

2 tablespoons heavy cream or half-and-half, optional

Salt and freshly ground black pepper to taste

1. Melt the butter in a medium saucepan over medium-low heat. Add the onion, cover, and cook, stirring occasionally, until golden and tender, about 6 minutes. (The onion should be thoroughly cooked, as it won't simmer long in the next step.)

2. Add the mashed vegetables, then gradually stir in the broth. Bring to a simmer, uncovered, stirring often. Stir in the cream, if using. Season with salt and pepper. Serve hot.

Broccoli with Dave's East-West Butter Sauce   Under 30 minutes

My friend and colleague David Bonom gave me the recipe for this exciting way to serve familiar broccoli. The combination of butter, soy sauce, and balsamic creates a blend of sharp, smooth, and salty flavors that mingle perfectly.

Makes 4 to 6 servings

1 bunch broccoli, trimmed

2 tablespoons unsalted butter

1 tablespoon Japanese soy sauce

1 tablespoon balsamic vinegar

1/8 teaspoon freshly ground black pepper

1. Cut off the tops of the broccoli and trim into florets. Using a sharp knife, pare the broccoli stalks. Cut the stalks crosswise into 1/4-inch-thick rounds.

2. Bring a medium saucepan of lightly salted water to a boil over high heat. Add the broccoli rounds and cook for 2 minutes. Add the florets and cook until the broccoli is crisp-tender, about 5 minutes. Drain. Transfer the broccoli to a serving bowl.

3. Meanwhile, cook the butter in a small saucepan over medium heat, stirring occasionally, until it is lightly browned, about 3 minutes. Remove from the heat and stir in the soy sauce, vinegar, and pepper.

4. Pour the butter over the broccoli and mix well. Serve hot.

Israeli Couscous with Vegetables Under 30 minutes

Say couscous to most cooks, and they think of the small grains of semolina used in Moroccan cooking. Say couscous to today's chefs, and they probably think you mean Israeli couscous, which are BB-sized balls of white pasta. Both are good, but Israeli couscous is quite a conversation piece. It should be cooked with vegetables to give it flavor and color, but not so much flavor that it isn't a compatible side dish (a brief toasting also enhances the taste). If you wish, substitute canned chicken broth for up to half of the water for even more flavor, but in that case, omit the salt in the cooking water, and season the finished dish to taste.

Makes 4 servings

1 tablespoon extra-virgin olive oil

1 small onion, finely chopped

1 small red bell pepper, cored, seeds and ribs removed, and cut into $\frac{1}{4}$-inch dice

1 cup Israeli couscous

$\frac{1}{4}$ teaspoon salt, plus more to taste

Freshly ground black pepper to taste

1. Heat the oil in a medium saucepan over medium heat. Add the onion and red pepper and cook, stirring often, until the onion is tender, about 5 minutes. Add the couscous and cook, stirring often, until lightly toasted, about 2 minutes.

2. Pour in $2\frac{1}{4}$ cups water, or enough to barely cover the couscous. Stir in the salt. Bring to a boil over high heat. Cover, reduce the heat to medium-low, and cook at a brisk simmer until the couscous is barely tender and has absorbed most of the liquid, about 10 minutes. Drain in a wire strainer. Season with additional salt and pepper if necessary.

3. Transfer to a serving bowl and serve hot.

Baby Carrots with Apple Glaze Under 30 minutes

Here is my favorite way of preparing baby-cut carrots. Note that these are actually regular carrots that have been mechanically cut into smaller sizes, not mini carrots. For holidays, I search out the true baby carrots at a specialty greengrocer, but for everyday meals, I happily improve on the supermarket variety with this apple-juice-and-butter glaze.

Makes 4 to 6 servings

1 pound baby-cut carrots

1 cup apple juice

1 tablespoon unsalted butter

Salt and freshly ground black pepper to taste

1. Spread the carrots in a large skillet just big enough to hold them in a single layer. Add the apple juice and butter. Bring to a boil over high heat. Cover, reduce the heat to medium, and cook at a steady boil for 10 minutes.

2. Uncover and stir the carrots. Cook, uncovered, stirring occasionally, until the liquid is reduced to a glaze, about 10 minutes. Season with salt and pepper. Serve hot.

Asparagus with Gremolata Butter (page 255); Baby Carrots with Apple Glaze; Radishes and Scallions in Butter Sauce (page 272)

Braised Escarole   Under 30 minutes

With a milder flavor than most of its cousins, escarole is one of my favorite greens for braising. And with no thick stems to remove, it also requires less effort to clean. I think all braised greens benefit from a bit of pork, but if you prefer to omit it, substitute 1/2 cup chicken broth for the water added to the pot.

Makes 4 servings

2 medium heads escarole (1½ pounds)

⅓ cup coarsely chopped sliced (¼-inch-thick) pancetta or prosciutto

1 tablespoon extra-virgin olive oil

1 garlic clove, finely chopped

Salt and freshly ground black pepper to taste

1. Cut off the bottom of the escarole about ½ inch up from the base and discard. Cut the escarole crosswise into 1-inch-wide strips. Wash the escarole strips well in a sink or large bowl of cold water. Lift the escarole from the water, leaving the grit to sink to the bottom, and place in a large bowl.

2. Combine the pancetta and oil in a large saucepan. Cook, stirring often, over medium-high heat until the pancetta is crisp and browned, about 5 minutes. Add the garlic and cook until it gives off its aroma, about 30 seconds. Add ½ cup water to the pot and bring to a boil over high heat. A handful at a time, letting each batch wilt before adding another, add the escarole, along with any water clinging to its leaves. Cover tightly and reduce the heat to medium-low. Cook, stirring occasionally, until the escarole is very tender, about 20 minutes. Season with salt and pepper.

3. Using a slotted spoon, transfer the escarole to a serving dish and serve hot.

Southwestern Green Beans   Under 30 minutes

Plain green beans are, well . . . plain. Simmered with a fresh salsa, they take on a new dimension. If you like them crisp-tender, follow the instructions below. However, they are also great stewed: cover the skillet and simmer over medium-low heat until the beans are quite tender and have absorbed the tomato juices, about 10 minutes. Take your pick. For the quickest way to snip off the ends of the beans and cut them into lengths, use kitchen scissors.

Makes 4 to 6 servings

12 ounces green beans, trimmed and cut into 1-inch
    lengths

1 tablespoon extra-virgin olive oil

1 small onion, finely chopped

½ jalapeño, seeded and minced

1 garlic clove, minced

1 ripe medium tomato or 2 plum tomatoes, seeded and
    cut into ½-inch dice

Salt and freshly ground black pepper to taste

1. Place the green beans in a large skillet and add enough lightly salted cold water to cover. Bring to a boil over high heat and cook until the beans are barely tender, about 2 minutes. Drain well.

2. Dry the skillet. Add the oil and heat over medium heat. Add the onion, jalapeño, and garlic and cook, stirring often, until the onion is tender, about 5 minutes. Add the green beans and tomato and cook just until the tomato gives off its juices, about 1 minute. Season with salt and pepper.

3. Transfer to a serving bowl. Serve hot.

Orzo with Parmesan and Peas   Under 30 minutes

Rice-shaped orzo is one of the most versatile members of the entire pasta family—and that's saying a mouthful. Here's the way I make it most often as a side dish, brightened with Parmesan cheese, peas, and butter. When orzo is served with fish, the lemon zest is a recommended option.

Makes 4 servings

1 cup orzo

¹/₂ cup thawed frozen peas

1 tablespoon unsalted butter

¹/₃ cup freshly grated Parmesan cheese

Grated zest of ¹/₂ lemon, optional

Salt and freshly ground black pepper to taste

1. Bring a medium saucepan of lightly salted water to a boil over high heat. Add the orzo and cook until barely tender, about 9 minutes. Drain well and return to the pan.

2. Add the peas and butter and cook, stirring constantly, over low heat until the peas are heated through, about 1 minute. Remove from the heat and stir in the Parmesan and lemon zest, if using. Season with salt and pepper.

3. Transfer to a serving bowl and serve hot.

Herbed Polenta with Corn **Under 30 minutes**

A bowl of soft polenta can be a lovely culinary experience, but it has always seemed a little plain to me. With just a little extra effort, it can be turned into a side dish so tasty that you may consider it good enough to serve as a main course. Use cilantro or basil, depending on the complementary flavors in the main dish. Instant polenta, which can be found in Italian delicatessens and many supermarkets, cooks much more quickly than the traditional variety, and with the added seasonings, any slight difference in flavor and texture between it and regular polenta will never be detectable. The polenta can also be cooled and cut into squares that can be grilled or fried.

Makes 4 to 6 servings

1 tablespoon extra-virgin olive oil

1 medium onion, chopped

1 garlic clove, minced

2 cups canned reduced-sodium chicken broth

2 teaspoons salt

1 cup instant polenta

1 cup fresh or thawed frozen corn kernels

2 tablespoons chopped fresh cilantro or basil

$\frac{1}{8}$ teaspoon freshly ground black pepper

1. Heat the oil in a medium heavy-bottomed saucepan over medium heat. Add the onion and cook, stirring often, until softened, about 3 minutes. Add the garlic and cook until it gives off its aroma, about 1 minute.

2. Add the chicken broth, 2 cups water, and the salt and bring to a boil over high heat. Stirring constantly, sprinkle in the polenta. Reduce the heat to medium-low and simmer, stirring almost constantly, until the polenta pulls away from the sides of the pan, about 8 minutes. During the last minute or so of cooking, add the corn, cilantro, and pepper. Serve hot.

Grilled Polenta

Spread the hot polenta in an oiled 8-inch-square pan. Let cool completely. Unmold the polenta onto a cutting board, and cut into nine squares. Brush the squares with olive oil. Grill over a hot charcoal fire in an outdoor grill (or a gas grill on the High setting), turning once, until golden brown on both sides, about 5 minutes.

Fried Polenta

Spread the hot polenta in an oiled 8-inch-square pan. Let cool completely. Unmold the polenta onto a cutting board, and cut into nine squares. Heat 2 tablespoons olive oil in a large nonstick skillet over medium-high heat. Add the polenta squares and cook, turning once, until golden brown on both sides, about 5 minutes.

Smashed Potatoes with Pesto

If you like potatoes and butter, wait until you try potatoes with pesto. Any thin-skinned boiling potato will work well for this recipe, but Yukon Golds have a special buttery flavor that makes them my first choice.

Makes 4 to 6 servings

2 pounds small boiling potatoes, such as Yukon Gold, scrubbed but not peeled

¼ cup Pesto (recipe follows)

Salt and freshly ground black pepper to taste

2 tablespoons extra-virgin olive oil

1. Place the potatoes in a large saucepan and add enough lightly salted cold water to cover by 1 inch. Bring to a boil over high heat. Reduce the heat to medium-low and simmer until the potatoes are tender when pierced with the tip of a knife, about 20 minutes.

2. Drain the potatoes and return to the pan. Add the pesto and stir, breaking up the potatoes with the spoon, until the potatoes are smashed into large chunks and well coated with the pesto. Season with salt and pepper.

3. Transfer to a serving bowl, drizzle with the oil, and serve hot.

Seasoning Secret

Pesto

Pesto is undoubtedly one of the most indispensable ingredients in a good cook's kitchen. And now that fresh basil is available all year round, it can be made whenever the mood strikes. Basil has a tendency to darken when it comes into contact with hot food, so the additional chlorophyll provided by the parsley in this recipe comes in handy. It is fun to make pesto with one of the more exotic varieties of basil from the farmers' market, or with a bit of rosemary or thyme thrown in for good measure, or to substitute walnuts or almonds for the traditional pine nuts. In other words, it's your pesto, so make it as you wish.

Makes about 3/4 cup

2 garlic cloves, crushed under a knife

2 tablespoons pine nuts or finely chopped walnuts or
    pecans

2 cups packed fresh basil leaves

2 tablespoons chopped fresh parsley

1/3 cup freshly grated Parmesan cheese

1/3 cup extra-virgin olive oil, plus extra if storing the pesto

Salt and freshly ground black pepper to taste

1. With the machine running, drop the garlic cloves through the feed tube into a food processor to mince. Add the pine nuts and pulse until minced. Add the basil, parsley, and cheese and pulse until combined. With the machine running, pour in the oil to make a thick paste. Season with salt and pepper.

2. Use the pesto immediately, or transfer to a small covered container and pour a thin layer of oil on top to make a seal; refrigerate for up to 1 month. After using, smooth the top of any remaining pesto, and cover with additional oil before refrigerating again.

Buttermilk Mashed Potatoes

I often use buttermilk for baked goods, so I am often looking for ways to use it up by the expiration date. It has become a secret ingredient in my mashed potatoes, lending a pleasant tartness to what can be a predictable dish. Consider mashed potatoes an empty canvas, and try one of the variations on the next page when the mood strikes.

Makes 6 servings

3 pounds large baking potatoes, peeled and cut into 2-inch chunks

4 tablespoons (½ stick) unsalted butter, at room temperature

½ cup buttermilk, at room temperature

Salt and freshly ground white or black pepper to taste

1. Place the potatoes in a large pot and add enough cold salted water to cover by ½ inch. Cover and bring to a boil over high heat. Set the lid ajar, reduce the heat to medium, and cook at a steady boil until the potatoes are tender when pierced with the tip of a sharp knife, about 25 minutes.

2. Drain the potatoes, reserving about ½ cup of the cooking liquid. Return the potatoes to the pot and stir constantly over medium heat until the potatoes begin to film the bottom of the pot, about 3 minutes. (This step forces excess steam and moisture from the potatoes and encourages fluffiness.) Remove from the heat.

3. Add the butter and mash the potatoes in the pot with a handheld electric mixer on high speed or a hand masher. Gradually beat in the buttermilk. If you like softer potatoes, add some of the potato cooking liquid. Season with salt and pepper.

4. Transfer to a serving bowl and serve hot.

(continued)

Horseradish Mashed Potatoes

Add 2 tablespoons drained prepared horseradish to the mashed potatoes.

Chive Mashed Potatoes

Add 3 tablespoons chopped fresh chives to the mashed potatoes.

Parmesan Mashed Potatoes

Add 1/2 cup freshly grated Parmesan cheese to the mashed potatoes.

Perfect Potatoes

For the fluffiest mashed potatoes, use starchy baking potatoes, such as russet or Burbank—starchiness equals fluffiness. And buy big potatoes—they require less time to peel than small. The mashing utensil is controversial. I prefer a handheld mixer or old-fashioned masher because passing the hot potatoes through a ricer requires too much time and dexterity—and cools the potatoes besides. Just don't use a food processor or handheld blender, which will guarantee gluey potatoes. The mashing liquid of choice—buttermilk or milk or whatever—should be at room temperature, as chilled liquid will cool the potatoes and encourage lumping.

Buttermilk

It is rare when my refrigerator doesn't contain a carton of buttermilk—though I never drink it by the glass. While I don't appreciate its puckery taste *au naturel*, it is a fine cooking ingredient. A splash adds tang to mashed potatoes and character to creamy salad dressings. Buttermilk takes a long time to go rancid, so you don't have to worry about using it up quickly. It is available in full or lowfat versions (my market carries lowfat only), which are interchangeable. There is also a powdered version, which works best in baked goods.

Bakers know that buttermilk's acidity creates tender crumbs in baked goods. I appreciate almost everything that buttermilk has to offer, but I realize that it isn't a staple in many homes. For that reason, in some of the baked goods in the book that could have used buttermilk, I substitute a mixture of plain yogurt (which everyone seems to have in their house these days) and milk. If you wish, you can substitute an equal amount of buttermilk for the combined yogurt/milk mixture.

Crisp Oven Fries

Traditional French fries are in a class by themselves, but I don't always have the time to bother with a deep-frying setup. With this method, I can have excellent fries from the oven with a minimum of effort. Whenever I serve Hamburgers with Roast Pepper Catsup (page 82), these fries are right by their sides. A French-fry cutter, an inexpensive gadget made with strong wires attached to a metal frame, will cut the prep time considerably. Just before serving, spice up the fries, if you wish, with a sprinkle of Cajun Seasoning (page 36) or Herbes de Provence (page 165), homemade or store-bought.

Makes 4 servings

3 pounds large baking potatoes, peeled

2 tablespoons vegetable or olive oil

Salt and freshly ground black pepper to taste

1. Position a rack in the top third of the oven and preheat to 425°F. Lightly oil a large baking sheet with sides, preferably nonstick.

2. Using a large knife or a French-fry cutter, cut the potatoes lengthwise into strips about 5 inches long and 1/2 inch square. Spread on the baking sheet, drizzle with the oil, and toss to coat.

3. Bake, stirring the potatoes occasionally, until crisp and golden brown, about 40 minutes. Season with salt and pepper and serve hot.

Radishes and Scallions in Butter Sauce

You've heard of thinking outside the box, but with radishes, one should think outside the salad bowl. Sure, crunchy and peppery radishes are great raw, but when they are cooked, they lose some of their bite and acquire a mellow turnip taste. Make this in the summer with the freshest, crispest radishes at the market (look for those with perky green tops), and you'll have a new favorite side dish. This is especially tasty with grilled fish fillets, such as halibut.

Makes 4 servings

2 bunches radishes, trimmed (1 pound trimmed weight)

2 tablespoons unsalted butter, divided

2 scallions, white and green parts, chopped

Salt and freshly ground black pepper to taste

1. Place the radishes in a large bowl of cold water and scrub to remove any grit. Drain. Using the slicing disk on a food processor, thinly slice the radishes. (You should have 4 cups.)

2. Heat 1 tablespoon of the butter in a medium skillet over medium heat. Add the scallions and cook until wilted, about 2 minutes. Add the radishes and cook, stirring occasionally, until tender, about 8 minutes. Remove from the heat and stir in the remaining 1 tablespoon butter, which will create a light, creamy sauce. Season with salt and pepper.

3. Transfer to a serving bowl and serve hot.

Dilled Radishes with Scallions

Stir 1 tablespoon finely chopped fresh dill into the radishes just before serving.

Mashed Turnips with Garlic

These are a full-flavored alternative to mashed potatoes, and they're especially good with pork chops or roasts. Mellowed by potatoes and bolstered by garlic, the lowly turnip becomes a very tasty dish. Chicken broth boosts the flavor, but you can use water alone, if you wish. While you should never use a food processor to mash plain potatoes, when they are mixed with a slightly larger amount of turnips as in this recipe, you can puree in a processor without fear.

Makes 4 to 6 servings

1½ pounds turnips, peeled and cut into 1-inch chunks

1 pound baking potatoes, peeled and cut into 1-inch chunks

8 garlic cloves, crushed under a knife

1¾ cups canned reduced-sodium chicken broth

3 tablespoons heavy cream or milk

2 tablespoons unsalted butter

Salt and freshly ground black pepper to taste

Chopped fresh parsley or dill for garnish

1. Place the turnips, potatoes, and garlic in a medium saucepan. Pour in the broth and add just enough lightly salted cold water to barely cover the vegetables. Bring to a boil over high heat. Reduce the heat to medium, cover, and cook at a brisk simmer until the vegetables are tender, about 25 minutes. Drain the vegetables, reserving the cooking liquid.

2. Puree the vegetables with the cream and butter in a food processor, adding reserved cooking liquid as desired. (For a rougher texture, mash with a hand masher or electric mixer and omit the cooking water.) Season with salt and pepper.

3. Transfer to a serving bowl and sprinkle with the parsley. Serve hot.

Creamed Spinach

Most Americans know creamed spinach as a staple at steakhouses, just the thing to set off a juicy grilled steak. In Vienna, it is also the required side dish for Tafelspitz, *the traditional Austrian pot roast (see page 108). Enjoy it in either capacity, or any time you want a rich accompaniment to simply prepared meat. I have given detailed instructions here, but it is an easy recipe, and one that cooks should have in their repertoire.*

Makes 6 servings

Three 10-ounce packages spinach, tough stems removed

1 cup canned low-sodium chicken broth

¾ cup heavy cream

3 tablespoons unsalted butter

1 garlic clove, crushed through a press

3 tablespoons all-purpose flour

A few gratings of nutmeg

Salt and freshly ground black pepper to taste

1. Bring 1 cup lightly salted water to a boil in a large saucepan over high heat. In batches, add the spinach, stirring until each batch is wilted before adding the next. Cover tightly, reduce the heat to medium, and cook until the spinach is tender, about 5 minutes.

2. Drain the spinach over a bowl, reserving 1¼ cups of the cooking water. Rinse the spinach under cold water. A handful at a time, squeeze the spinach between your fingers to remove excess water and to "chop" the spinach. Transfer to a bowl.

3. In a small saucepan over medium heat, or in a heatproof glass measuring cup in a microwave, heat the reserved cooking water, the broth, and heavy cream until simmering.

4. Meanwhile, heat the butter and garlic in a medium saucepan over medium-low heat just until the butter melts. Whisk in the flour and let bubble, without browning, for 2 minutes. Whisk in the hot cream mixture and bring to a simmer. Cook, whisking often, until the sauce is thickened and no raw flour taste

remains, about 5 minutes. Stir in the spinach and heat through. Season with the nutmeg, salt, and pepper.

5. Transfer to a serving bowl and serve hot.

The "New" Spinach

Today's cooks can say good-bye to the chore of washing spinach to remove the sand and grit that can cling tenaciously to the leaves. Most prepackaged spinach, available in 10-ounce cellophane bags, either as large leaves or baby spinach, is prewashed. It can be pricey, but the time saved is usually worth the expense.

If prewashed spinach is unavailable, look for flat-leafed spinach, which is more delicate than the curly-leafed variety. Be sure to wash the spinach well in a sink of cold water. Lift the spinach out of the water, leaving the grit to fall to the bottom of the sink. Do not dry the leaves—the water will help steam and cook the spinach.

Perfect Rice   Under 30 minutes

Rice may be the ultimate side dish, but it remains a bit of a challenge to some cooks. Unfortunately, there is a lot of misinformation out there that confounds the problem. To wash or not to wash? Which rice for the fluffiest results? My list of tips on page 278 will help clear up the confusion. Armed with these suggestions, you will be on your way to a fluffy, pristine pot of white rice. There are many ways to vary cooked rice, and while plain rice is usually the ticket for Asian dishes, I often cook the French or saffron rice versions (below) when I want a bit of extra flavor.

Makes 4 to 6 servings

1½ cups long-grain white rice   ½ teaspoon salt

1. Combine 3 cups cold water, the rice, and salt in a medium heavy-bottomed saucepan. (The water should not come any higher than two thirds up the sides of the pan.) Bring to a boil over high heat. Reduce the heat to low, cover tightly, and cook at a low simmer, without stirring, until the rice is tender and has absorbed the water, about 15 minutes. Remove the pan from the heat and let stand, covered, for 5 to 10 minutes. (The rice will stay hot in the pan for up to 30 minutes.)
2. Fluff the rice with a fork and serve hot.

French Rice

Substitute canned low-sodium chicken broth for the 3 cups water. Melt 2 tablespoons unsalted butter in the saucepan over medium heat. Add ½ cup finely chopped onion or 2 tablespoons chopped shallots and cook until softened, about 3 minutes for the onion, 1 minute for the shallots. Add the rice and cook, stirring often, just until the rice turns chalky white, about 2 minutes. Add the chicken broth, bring to a boil over high heat, and proceed as directed.

Saffron Rice

Stir ½ teaspoon crumbled saffron threads into the rice before cooking.

Rice

Buying rice used to be so simple, as the choice was restricted to the long-grain variety. Now you can find black Thai rice, Bhutanese red rice, Japanese-style short-grain rice for sushi, Spanish medium-grain rice for risotto or paella, and many different kinds of brown rice, alone or mixed into blends. But as this is not a cookbook of ethnic rice recipes, I will limit my discussion to ever-popular white rice.

Whenever I make rice, I am reminded of Goldilocks and the Three Bears... too hot, too cold, too big, too small, or just right? There are a lot of variables that can affect the outcome. Here are a few tips to ensure a perfect bowl of rice every time.

Choose the right pot A heavy bottom discourages scorching, and a tight-fitting lid is a must. Raw rice triples in volume when cooked, so if you have a pot that is too small, the water will boil over. If the pot is too large or wide, the water will evaporate before the rice has time to cook until tender. Look at the pot and imagine how the cooked rice will fill it. You want the raw rice and water to fill the pot by no more than two thirds to allow for expansion. For 1$\frac{1}{2}$ cups raw rice (4$\frac{1}{2}$ cups cooked), a 2-quart pot with a relatively narrow width (about 6 inches) is ideal.

Do not rinse American rice! American white rice is processed to remove the bran, which also removes vitamins, so replacement vitamins are sprayed on (that's why the labels say "enriched"). If you wash the rice, these vitamins go down the drain. When the rice is from a foreign country with questionable harvesting practices, you can give the rice a very quick rinse in a wire sieve under cold water to wash away dirt. Soaking the rice will hydrate it, wreaking havoc with the water-to-rice balance and the cooking time.

Pick the right rice for your desired consistency Rice is divided into three categories according to length: long-, medium-, and short-grain. The shorter the grain, the more starch in the rice, and starch translates into stickiness. In some cultures, stickiness in cooked rice is considered an attribute—sticky short-grain rice is used for sushi so it will hold its shape when molded, and the starch in medium-grain Italian rice gives risotto its creaminess. So, if you in-advertently buy short- or medium-grain rice, you could be in for a surprise, texture-wise. For fluffy rice, use long-grain. For individual grains of cooked rice, use converted rice, which has been precooked to remove excess starch.

Don't rush the rice Cook the rice at a gentle simmer so it can absorb the liquid at a leisurely pace. If the flame is too high, the water will evaporate before the rice is tender and you could end up with scorched rice. Too low, and you will have soggy rice that requires draining.

Fluffy Drop Biscuits **Under 30 minutes**

My holiday table always holds a basket of warm biscuits that were cut out from a rolled dough. However, for everyday fare, I mix up a soft, sticky dough that can be dropped from a spoon to make free-form biscuits. Homemade drop biscuits are so easy that there is no reason not to serve them whenever you feel like it. You don't have to eat the entire batch at once—leftovers freeze well and can be reheated quickly in a toaster oven for breakfast or a snack. If you wish, flavor the dough with coarsely crushed peppercorns, herbs, or Parmesan cheese (see the variations following), but I must admit I love the plain ones, spread with softened butter and honey.

Makes 1 dozen biscuits

2 cups all-purpose flour

1½ teaspoons baking powder

½ teaspoon baking soda

½ teaspoon salt

8 tablespoons (1 stick) chilled unsalted butter, cut into thin slices

¾ cup plain low-fat yogurt

⅓ cup milk, or more if needed

1. Position a rack in the center of the oven and preheat to 400°F.

2. Whisk the flour, baking powder, baking soda, and salt in a medium bowl to combine. Cut in the butter with a pastry blender until the mixture resembles coarse cornmeal. Make a well in the center. Whisk the yogurt and milk in a small bowl to combine. Pour into the well and mix with a fork, adding a tablespoon or so of additional milk if needed to form a moist, sticky dough.

3. Drop 12 heaping tablespoons of the dough onto an ungreased baking sheet, spacing the biscuits about 2 inches apart. Bake until the tops are tipped with golden brown, about 20 minutes. Serve warm. (Leftover biscuits, individually wrapped in aluminum foil, can be frozen for up to 1 month. Reheat the unwrapped biscuits in a preheated 400°F oven or toaster oven until thawed and hot, about 10 minutes.)   (continued)

Peppercorn Biscuits

Mix the dough just until the dry ingredients are moistened. Add $3/4$ teaspoon coarsely crushed black peppercorns and continue mixing as directed.

Herbed Biscuits

Mix the dough just until the dry ingredients are moistened. Add 1 teaspoon dried thyme, crumbled rosemary, or rubbed sage and continue mixing as directed.

Parmesan Biscuits

Add $1/2$ cup freshly grated Parmesan cheese to the dry ingredients.

Easy Yogurt Corn Bread Under 30 minutes

Corn bread is, by nature, from the stir-and-bake family of cooking, so I really don't see the need for using a mix. Most corn bread mixes are too sweet for my taste, but of course you can add a tablespoon or more sugar to this recipe if you wish. Try this tender, moist, and golden corn bread the next time you need something to go with a Southern-style entrée.

Makes 9 servings

4 tablespoons (½ stick) unsalted butter, melted and divided

⅔ cup yellow cornmeal, preferably stone-ground

⅔ cup all-purpose flour

1 tablespoon sugar

½ teaspoon baking soda

½ teaspoon salt

¾ cup plain low-fat yogurt

¼ cup milk

1 large egg, beaten

1. Position a rack in the center of the oven and preheat to 400°F. Pour 2 tablespoons of the melted butter into an 8-inch-square baking pan. Place the pan in the oven until it is very hot, about 2 minutes: don't worry if the butter browns a bit. Remove the pan from the oven.

2. Whisk the cornmeal, flour, sugar, baking soda, and salt in a medium bowl to combine. Make a well in the center. Whisk the yogurt, milk, egg, and the remaining 2 tablespoons melted butter in another medium bowl. Pour into the well and mix with a wooden spoon just until the batter is smooth; do not overmix. Return the pan to the oven and heat for 1 minute. Remove from the oven, and spread the batter evenly in the hot pan.

3. Bake until the top is golden brown and springs back when pressed in the center, about 20 minutes. Let cool in the pan for 5 minutes.

4. Cut into squares and serve hot.

Spicy Corn Bread

Mix the batter just until the dry ingredients are moistened. Add 1 jalapeño, seeded and minced, and mix just until smooth.

Desserts *How to make friends and influence people? Bake. ¶ Nothing creates a pleasant buzz at the workplace more than the appearance of home-baked goodies. I bake just for pleasure—it's not just the taste that attracts me, but the feel of the dough, the scent of cinnamon from the oven, the sense of satisfaction when seeing the beautiful finished product. ¶ However, with only two of us in the household, I have to admit that eating an entire* cake may be a temptation but not a real option. The solution is simple: I send the surplus on to my neighbors and my partner's coworkers, and I quickly become the most popular guy in town. So, even if you aren't planning a party, go ahead and bake a whole cake (or tart or tray of blondies) and enjoy a slice or two, then pass the pleasure on to friends as a delicious surprise.

As a trained pastry chef, I know how to make intricate, time-consuming desserts, and I've even written a book about the specialties of Austro-Hungarian coffeehouses. It was in Vienna, in fact, that I observed an entire culture that believes that a great dessert is a pleasure of daily life, one that should not be reserved for special occasions. I remember interviewing the young (slim) pastry chef at a spa and remarking how odd it was that this health complex had a fabulous bakery. He said, "Well, you come to a spa to feel good, and what makes you feel better than a slice of good cake?" Amen.

But the desserts I share here are the ones I make quickly, on an impulse, when a bite of a homemade cake is the only thing that will brighten a day or add a festive note to an impromptu celebration. There's quite a range of desserts in this chapter because I love them in all their variety. Some of them, such as the Strawberry and Mascarpone Budini, Warm Blackberry Pie Sundaes, and Earl Grey Granita, require no baking at all. And for the baked recipes, I include lots of shortcuts. For example, I rarely roll out the pastry for my tarts anymore, but just simply press it into the pan. Often, when I do roll out pastry, I make free-form rounds, for an Apple and Nutmeg Custard Crostata or Pear Pandowdy with Ginger and Five Spices. When I want cookies, I may bake up a pan of Orange Shortbread Bars or Oatmeal and Chocolate Chip Blondies (my new favorites) because I don't always feel like fussing with shaping and baking separate batches. The batter for Chocolate Cake with Rocky Road Frosting, which I make for my chocolate-loving friends' birthdays (as well as my father's), is a one-bowl affair. And wait until you see the frosting, which could not be easier, thanks to a secret ingredient.

I get very discouraged when students tell me they can't bake. Anyone who can follow a recipe can make a cake or pie. But do remember that baking is chemistry that tastes good, so if you change the formula, you are asking for trouble. Also, there are certain details that are often left out of recipes that can make a difference. If a recipe calls for creaming the butter and sugar until light, there is a difference between creaming for one minute (when the mixture will look lighter than when you started but will make a coarse cake) and three minutes (when the mixture is aerated enough to improve the cake's texture).

So whether it's a slice of crumb cake for an afternoon cup of coffee, something to put in the cookie jar or lunchbox, or a treat to give the final fillip to a party, get in the kitchen and make dessert! It will make you feel good.

The Carefree Cook's Tips for Desserts

Preheat the oven   Allow at least 15 minutes to preheat the oven thoroughly to the required temperature. And many baking failures are due to an incorrectly calibrated oven, so get an oven thermometer to double-check the temperature. You may be surprised at the discrepancy between what your oven control and the thermometer say.

Know your butter   The phrase "unsalted butter, at room temperature" may need some explaining. First, professionals prefer unsalted butter because it allows the cook to add salt to the dish as needed (margarine is not an option for good bakers). The proper temperature for softened butter is indicated by touch (when it is pressed, your finger will leave an indentation, but the butter still feels malleable and a bit cool) and look (the surface shouldn't look greasy or shiny). If you forget to take the butter out of the refrigerator, don't use the microwave, which can easily melt the butter instead of softening it. Grate the chilled butter, using the large holes of a box grater, and by the time you've gathered the rest of the ingredients, it will have softened to the proper consistency.

Know your eggs   Use large Grade AA eggs for baking. Smaller or larger eggs will throw off the liquid proportions in the recipe. For the best incorporation into a batter, the eggs should be at room temperature.

Sift, don't whisk, dry ingredients   For years, I thought that whisking dry ingredients together was good enough. Then one day an undissolved glob of baking soda ruined a cake. From then on, I sifted to be sure that everything was well combined and that all baking soda or baking powder was broken up. You don't need a traditional sifter. You can use a wire sieve, as long as the mesh isn't too fine. Just sift the dry ingredients through the sieve onto a large sheet of wax paper. It's easy to lift up the paper with the dry ingredients to pour into the mixing bowl.

An electric mixer is essential I encourage people to cook without expensive tools, so I usually use a moderately priced hand mixer when testing my recipes. Standing heavy-duty mixers are terrific, but they are only necessary for large batches of batter or icing and yeast doughs, which are outside the scope of this book. If you are looking for a hand mixer, buy one with an electric capacity of 200 watts or above and with large beaters that will incorporate sufficient air into a batter. Some of the priciest mixers have tiny beaters that take forever to whip cream and perform other simple chores. The least expensive models are often the best choice because you really only need three speeds and can live without bells and whistles.

Apple and Nutmeg Custard Crostata

When you don't have the time to peel mountains of apples for a double-crusted American apple pie, make this Italian-inspired beauty. It's a free-form apple tart with a fragrant nutmeg custard. Golden Delicious apples are my favorite pie apple for their flavor and their ability to hold their shape after cooking.

Makes 6 servings

Buttery Pastry Dough (page 332)

3 tablespoons sugar, divided

3 Golden Delicious apples, peeled, cored, and cut into ¼-inch-thick slices (see page 290)

¼ cup heavy cream

1 large egg yolk

¼ teaspoon vanilla extract

¼ teaspoon freshly grated nutmeg

1. Position a rack in the bottom third of the oven and preheat to 400°F.

2. Place the dough on a lightly floured work surface and dust the top with flour. Roll out the dough (see page 306) into a 12-inch round about ⅛ inch thick. Transfer to an ungreased rimless cookie sheet (or the back of an inverted rimmed baking sheet). Sprinkle the center of the dough round with 1 table-spoon of the sugar, leaving a 1½-inch border all around. Working from the out-side in, arrange the larger apple slices in two overlapping concentric circles on the sugar, and fill in the center with the smaller slices. Sprinkle the apples with 1 tablespoon of the remaining sugar. Fold the dough border over to partially cover the outer ring of apples, loosely pleating the dough as needed, leaving the rest of the apples exposed. Brush any flour from the dough.

3. Bake for 15 minutes to set the dough. Whisk the cream, yolk, vanilla, nutmeg, and the remaining 1 tablespoon sugar until combined. Slowly pour over the ap-ples, letting the custard fill in the spaces around the slices (the crust will keep the custard from spilling out, but pour slowly and don't use all of the custard if it threatens to overflow the crust). Bake until the custard is set and the apples are tender when pierced with the tip of a sharp knife, about 20 minutes more.

4. Let cool on the baking sheet for 15 minutes, then slide the crostata onto a serving platter. Serve warm or cooled to room temperature.

Prepping Apples

Peeling, coring, and slicing apples for pie and other dishes used to be one of my least favorite kitchen chores. Then I learned an easy method from my friend Sarabeth Levine, the master cook behind Manhattan's beloved Sarabeth's bakery, restaurants, and preserves.

The idea is to slice the four quadrants off the core of the apple. Start by peeling the apple. Then stand the apple on the work surface. Using a large knife, cut off a thick slice from one side of the apple, stopping just short of the tough core. Turn the apple 90 degrees, and cut off another quadrant of the apple in the same manner. Repeat twice more, and you will have four large, evenly shaped chunks of apple and the core. Discard the core, and slice the chunks into the required thickness.

Warm Blackberry Pie Sundaes Under 30 minutes

You've probably heard of spoonbread, but what is a spoon pie? It's how I make fruit pie when I don't have the time to make fruit pie. Crumbled shortbread cookies stand in for the crust, layered in wineglasses with sautéed fruit. For warm fruit spoon pies (and who doesn't love warm pie?), use cooked fresh seasonal fruits—blackberries or other berries, as suggested here, in the summer, or apples or pears in the cool months. You'll have all the goodness of a home-baked pie with a fraction of the effort.

Makes 4 servings

2 pints fresh blackberries

Grated zest of ½ large orange

½ cup fresh orange juice

⅓ cup plus 1 tablespoon sugar

⅛ teaspoon ground cinnamon

⅔ cup coarsely crumbled shortbread-style cookies, such as Pepperidge Farm Chessmen

1 pint vanilla ice cream

1. Bring 3 cups of the blackberries, the orange zest and juice, the sugar, and cinnamon to a boil in a medium nonreactive saucepan over high heat, stirring often. Reduce the heat to low and simmer until the berries are soft and juicy, about 3 minutes. Remove from the heat. Transfer 1 cup of the berries to a food processor or blender and puree, then return to the saucepan. Stir in the remaining whole blackberries. Remove from the heat.

2. Divide the cookies among four dessert bowls. Top each with a scoop of ice cream and some of the warm berries. Serve immediately.

Blueberry-Almond Tart

Here's a fancy, show-off fresh fruit tart that rivals the best bakery pastry. Almonds in the dough enhance the flavor of the plump blueberries. Tapioca makes the best berry thickener, as their acidic juices can weaken the binding power of both cornstarch and flour. But even instant tapioca can create unappetizing globules in the filling—a dilemma that is solved by grinding the tapioca into a powder that dissolves completely and without detection.

Makes 6 to 8 servings

Almond Crust

1/3 cup sliced natural almonds

2 tablespoons sugar

1 cup all-purpose flour

1/4 teaspoon salt

8 tablespoons (1 stick) chilled, unsalted butter, very thinly sliced, plus softened butter for the pan

1 large egg yolk

1/4 teaspoon almond extract

Blueberry Filling

2 pints fresh blueberries, divided

1/2 cup sugar

Grated zest of 1 lemon

2 tablespoons fresh lemon juice

1 tablespoon instant tapioca, ground into a powder with a spice or coffee grinder or in a blender

2 tablespoons unsalted butter

1/2 cup blueberry or red currant preserves for glaze

2 tablespoons sliced natural almonds, toasted, for garnish

Confectioners' sugar for garnish, optional

1. To make the crust, lightly butter a 9-inch tart pan with a removable bottom. Process the almonds and sugar in a food processor until the almonds are ground to a powder. Add the flour and salt and pulse to combine. Add the butter and pulse until the mixture resembles coarse meal with some pea-sized pieces. Mix the egg yolk and extract in a small bowl. With the machine running, add the yolk mix through the feed tube, then pulse just until the dough begins to clump together; do not overprocess. Turn the dough out, gather it together, and press evenly into the bottom and up the sides of the pan, being sure that

the sides and bottom meet at a sharp 90-degree angle (think of how a floor meets a wall). Pierce the crust all over with a fork and cover the pan with plastic wrap. Freeze for 20 to 30 minutes.

2. Meanwhile, position a rack in the center of the oven and preheat to 375°F.

3. Unwrap the crust and line with lightly buttered aluminum foil, buttered side down. Fill the pan with pastry weights or uncooked rice. Place on a baking sheet and bake until the crust looks set, about 12 minutes. Remove the foil and weights and continue baking until the crust is golden brown, about 15 more minutes. Let cool completely on a wire rack.

4. To make the filling, bring 1 pint of the blueberries, ³/₄ cup water, the sugar, lemon zest, and juice to a boil in a medium heavy-bottomed saucepan over high heat, stirring often. Reduce the heat to medium-low and simmer until berries are soft, about 5 minutes. Add the tapioca and stir until the filling thickens. Remove from the heat and stir in the butter. Let cool until tepid but pourable.

5. Spread the filling evenly in the cooled tart shell. Arrange the remaining fresh blueberries over the filling. Bring the preserves to a boil in a small saucepan, and brush the hot preserves over the berries. Sprinkle a ring of almonds 1 inch in from the edge on the filling. Let cool completely, then cover loosely with plastic wrap and refrigerate until the filling is chilled and set, at least 2 hours. (The tart can be prepared up to 8 hours ahead.)

6. To serve, remove the sides of the pan. If desired, sprinkle the top with confectioners' sugar. Serve chilled or at room temperature.

Pie Weights

If you've never baked an empty pastry crust for a tart or pie before, you may be unfamiliar with pie weights. Made from aluminum or ceramic material, these round pellets are used to hold a dough in place while it bakes—without the weights, the dough could "melt" and slide down the sides of the pan, or the bottom could puff up and bubble. The idea is to bake the dough just until it sets, then remove the weights along with the foil. Even if you don't plan on baking a lot of pastry crusts, you still need something to weigh down the dough. Uncooked rice is an inexpensive alternative, and the rice (like the professional weights) can be used again for other crusts. Some cooks recommend dried beans, but they acquire an off smell after baking, and rice works much better.

Earl Grey Granita with Berries

Granita, related to sorbet but with a coarser texture, is easy to make in a home freezer. This icy dessert is even frostier than iced tea, and I can't think of a more re-freshing thing to serve on a hot summer afternoon. The lovely scent of citrus berg-amot, the exotic flavoring in Earl Grey tea, harmonizes perfectly with the berries.

Makes 4 to 6 servings

½ cup sugar

3 tablespoons Earl Grey tea leaves

2 cups fresh blueberries, raspberries, sliced strawberries, or a combination

1. Bring 4 cups water to a boil in a medium saucepan over high heat. Remove from the heat and add the sugar and tea. Stir to dissolve the sugar. Let the tea steep until completely cool, about 2 hours.

2. Meanwhile, put a 9 x 13-inch metal baking pan and a large metal serving spoon in the freezer to chill.

3. Strain the tea through a fine wire sieve into the chilled pan, pressing hard on the leaves to extract as much liquid as possible; discard the tea leaves. Freeze until the mixture is icy around the edges, about 1 hour, depending on the freezer temperature.

4. Using the metal spoon, mix the frozen edges into the center (leave the spoon in the pan). Continue to freeze, repeating the stirring procedure about every 30 minutes, until the mixture has a slushy consistency, 2 to 3 hours total freezing time. (The granita can be made up to 1 day ahead. If it freezes hard, coarsely chop it with a large knife and pulse in a food processor to a slushy consistency.)

5. Spoon the granita into chilled glasses and top with the berries. Serve imme-diately.

Mangoes Foster **Under 30 minutes**

Bananas Foster is a New Orleans specialty of sautéed bananas in a warm butter-scotch sauce. Mangoes have a sweet-tart edge that works well in this setting, making a dessert that can be served in record time.

Makes 4 servings

2 tablespoons unsalted butter

2 ripe mangoes, pitted, peeled, and cut into 1-inch cubes

1/3 cup packed light brown sugar

1/4 cup dark rum

1 tablespoon fresh lime juice

1 pint vanilla ice cream

1. Melt the butter in a large skillet over medium heat. Add the mangoes and cook, stirring occasionally, until they begin to give off their juices, about 2 minutes.

2. Add the brown sugar, rum, and lime juice. Cook, occasionally giving the mangoes a gentle stir, to avoid breaking them up, until the juices thicken slightly, about 2 minutes. Remove from the heat and let cool for 5 minutes. (The mango sauce can be prepared up to 2 hours ahead and set aside at room temperature. Reheat gently before serving.)

3. Scoop the ice cream into individual dessert bowls, and top with the warm mango sauce. Serve immediately.

Mangoes

A tropical fruit exported to the United States from Haiti, Mexico, and other hot-weather locales, mangoes have an exotic aroma and luscious flavor. However, the uninitiated will find them mystifying to peel and pit. Here's how to do it:

First, be sure the mango is ripe. It should have a spicy/floral aroma and a slight "give" when gently squeezed. Lay the mango on the work surface, where it will balance itself. The pit, which is about $1/2$ inch thick, runs lengthwise through the center of the fruit. Use a sharp knife to cut off the top of the fruit, going just above the top of the pit. Turn the mango over and cut off the other side. Using a large metal serving spoon, scoop the mango flesh from each portion in one piece. The peeled mango can now be chopped or sliced as required. The flesh remaining on the pit can be pared off with a small knife, or nibbled from the pit as the cook's treat.

Peach-Almond Crisp

Get out the vanilla ice cream, because you'll want a big scoop on top of this wonderful summer dessert. Almonds enhance the luscious juiciness of stone fruits, and the crumbly topping is so tasty that I make a generous amount. If possible, serve the crisp warm out of the oven, but if the topping softens, reheat the crisp in a 400°F oven for 10 minutes.

Makes 6 to 8 servings

4 pounds ripe peaches

$1/2$ cup packed light brown sugar

2 tablespoons fresh lemon juice

2 tablespoons chilled, unsalted butter, cut into small cubes

Almond Topping

$1/2$ cup sliced almonds (natural or blanched)

$1/4$ cup packed light brown sugar

$1/4$ cup granulated sugar

$1 1/2$ cups all-purpose flour

8 tablespoons (1 stick) unsalted butter, at room temperature

$1/2$ teaspoon almond extract

1. Position a rack in the center of the oven and preheat to 375°F.

2. To make the filling, peel (see Note, page 302) and pit the peaches, then cut them into 1-inch-thick wedges. (You should have about $6 1/2$ cups.) Mix the peaches, brown sugar, and lemon juice in an 8 x 11$1/2$-inch baking dish. Dot the peaches with the butter.

3. To make the topping, process the almonds, brown sugar, and granulated sugar in a food processor until the nuts are ground to a fine powder. Add the flour, butter, and almond extract and process until the mixture begins to clump together. Remove the blade and press the dough together into a mass. Crumble the topping as evenly as possible over the peaches—it will crumble into many different-sized pieces, but aim for a fair amount of $1/2$-inch chunks.

4. Bake until the topping is browned, the juices are bubbling, and the peaches in the center of the dish are tender when pierced with the tip of a sharp knife, about 50 minutes.

5. Let cool for 15 minutes and serve warm, or cool to room temperature before serving.

"Faux" Peach Tarte Tatin

The justly famous classic tarte Tatin is an upside-down tart of caramelized apples, not a dish one could call easy. I usually make this much quicker and equally impressive version with fresh peaches and brown sugar—in fact, it has become one of my Top Ten Summer Desserts. Considering the small number of ingredients, it has an amazing flavor. I have also made this with a bag of frozen peaches with great success. (Spread the peaches on paper towels to thaw and lose their ice crystals before using.)

Be sure your skillet is about 9 inches across at the top and 2 inches deep so the juices don't overflow. While the step of removing the excess peach juices from the skillet may seem unusual, it serves to prevent an overly moist tart, and the reserved juices make a fine sauce.

Makes 6 servings

4 tablespoons (½ stick) unsalted butter

⅔ cup packed light brown sugar

6 ripe medium freestone peaches, peeled, pitted, and cut
    into 8 wedges each (see Note)

Small-Batch Buttery Pastry Dough (page 332)

1. Melt the butter over medium heat in a 9-inch ovenproof nonstick skillet that is about 2 inches deep. Add the brown sugar and stir until melted and bubbling, about 2 minutes. Remove the skillet from the heat. Using kitchen tongs, carefully overlap a ring of the peach wedges in the syrup, leaving the center of the skillet empty. Place a second layer on top of the first ring of peaches, fitting them into the empty spaces. Fill in the center with a few peaches.

2. Return the pan to medium heat and cook, using a bulb baster to baste the peaches with the syrup, until the peaches begin to soften, about 5 minutes. Remove from the heat. Using the baster, siphon off most of the syrup in the skillet and transfer to a bowl; set aside at room temperature. Let the peaches cool in the skillet for 20 minutes.

(continued)

3. Meanwhile, roll out the dough (see page 306) on a lightly floured surface into a 10-inch round about $1/8$ inch thick. Pierce the dough a few times with the tines of a fork. Transfer to a baking sheet and cover loosely with plastic wrap. Refrigerate while the peaches cool.

4. Position a rack in the center of the oven and preheat to 425°F.

5. Place the round of dough over the peaches and press gently into the skillet so the peaches are completely covered. Bake until the pastry is crisp and golden brown, about 35 minutes. Let cool in the skillet on a wire cake rack until warm, 30 minutes to 1 hour.

6. To serve, whisk the reserved peach syrup to blend (the butter may have separated slightly from the juices). Run a knife around the inside of the skillet, and give the pan a shake to be sure the peaches are loosened. Place a platter over the top of the skillet, and invert them together to unmold the tart. Serve with the peach syrup as a sauce.

Note: To peel peaches, drop a few at a time into a pot of boiling water and cook just until the skin loosens, about 30 seconds. If the peaches aren't ripe enough, the skin will not loosen. Don't cook them longer than 1 minute, or the flesh will soften. Using a slotted spoon, transfer the peaches to a bowl of cold water and let them stand until cool enough to handle. Using a small paring knife, peel the peaches; the skins will slip off easily (or pare the ones with stubborn skins).

Pear Pandowdy with Ginger and Five Spices

Most bakers are familiar with cobblers and crisps, but when you mention a pandowdy, they are at a loss to describe it. Think of a deep-dish pie with the top crust basted with the fruit filling's juices, and you get the idea. Make it with a moist pear variety, such as Comice, and you are sure to have plenty of sweet juices. Serve the pandowdy warm from the oven with vanilla ice cream.

Makes 6 servings

6 ripe Comice pears, peeled, cored, and cut into 1-inch cubes (about 6 cups)

1/3 cup packed light brown sugar

1/4 cup chopped crystallized ginger

2 tablespoons fresh lemon juice

1 1/2 teaspoons Five-Spice Powder (page 147), or use store-bought

Buttery Pastry Dough (page 332)

2 tablespoons unsalted butter, melted

2 tablespoons granulated sugar

1. Position a rack in the center of the oven and preheat to 400°F.

2. Toss the pears, brown sugar, ginger, lemon juice, and five-spice powder in a medium bowl. Spread in a 10-inch deep-dish pie pan.

3. Roll out the dough (see page 306) on a lightly floured work surface into a 12-inch round about 1/8 inch thick. Place over the pears, nudging the excess dough inside and down the sides of the pan. Place the pan on a baking sheet.

4. Bake the pandowdy for 30 minutes.

5. Using a sharp knife, cut through the crust in a large crosshatch pattern. Using the back of a spoon, press the crust into the filling. Using a bulb baster, baste the crust with the juices. Drizzle the top of the pandowdy with the melted butter, then sprinkle with the granulated sugar. Bake until the top is golden brown, about 30 minutes more.

6. Let stand for 10 minutes. Spoon into dessert bowls and serve warm.

Strawberry and Mascarpone Budini   Under 30 minutes

This strawberry treat exemplifies the simple but delicious Italian approach to dessert, with Marsala, mascarpone, and amaretti cookies. (Budini means pudding in Italian.) Amaretti cookies used to only be available in tissue-wrapped pairs, but now you can buy unwrapped cookies in boxes.

Makes 4 servings

2 pints strawberries, hulled and thickly sliced plus 4 whole strawberries reserved for garnish

⅓ cup sweet Marsala wine

2 tablespoons light or dark brown sugar

One 8-ounce container mascarpone cheese, at room temperature

½ cup coarsely crumbled amaretti cookies (about 10 cookies)

1. Mix the sliced strawberries, Marsala, and sugar in a medium bowl. Cover and chill, stirring occasionally, for at least 2 and up to 4 hours.

2. For each serving, spoon one-quarter of the mascarpone into a wineglass. Top with one-quarter of the berries, with their juices, and sprinkle with 2 table-spoons amaretti crumbs. Garnish with a whole strawberry. Serve immediately.

Marsala

Originally from Sicily, although California and New York wineries now make Marsala, this fortified wine is available in sweet (dolce) and dry styles. Match the relative sweetness of the wine with the dish: for savory cooking, use dry marsala; desserts (such as the one above) are best made with sweet. If you have to choose between the two, dry Marsala is the most versatile, as more sugar can usually be added to desserts as needed.

Rolling Out Dough

Even some experienced cooks freeze up when confronted with rolling out pie dough. I used to be in the same category, always looking for shortcuts, and certainly not pleased with the greasy flavor of frozen crusts and the like. So, I either had to learn how to make homemade pie dough and roll it out, or settle for less-than-great pies. The choice was a no-brainer. I have kept dough rolling to a minimum in this book, but here are some of my tips that will help you get your pie act together when the mood strikes.

Give yourself a large work surface for rolling This means an area at least 2 feet square to allow for elbow room and easy access to the dough. You can use a smooth countertop or a cutting board. Some kitchenware shops sell portable pastry boards—a real lifesaver for pie makers with limited counter space.

Flour the work surface lightly but thoroughly The flour not only keeps the dough from sticking to the work surface, but acts as a kind of dry lubricant that helps the dough extend. Don't forget to sprinkle flour on top of the dough too, or the rolling pin will stick (flouring the rolling pin does not help a thing). If any flour clings to the dough after rolling, simply brush it off with a pastry brush, or even a paper towel.

If the kitchen is hot, refrigerate the dough to give it a quick chill One of the secrets to flaky pie dough is cold ingredients. Cold flakes of butter in the dough will give off small amounts of steam when they melt, and that gives the crust the desired light texture. Although the Buttery Pastry Dough can be used immediately after mixing, in a warm kitchen the dough can soften, interfering with the rolling-out process and making for a tough crust. If you think this might happen, wrap the disk of dough in wax paper or plastic wrap and refrigerate just until it feels chilled, about 30 minutes to 1 hour. Don't chill the dough until it is hard, or it will be difficult to roll out without cracking. (Unwrap the dough before rolling it out.)

Use a heavy rolling pin The heavier the rolling pin, the less pressure the baker has to use to roll out the dough. In other words, the pin will do a lot of the work for you. There are many styles of rolling pins, but I find that a ball-bearing pin with handles works best for novice bakers.

When rolling out dough, always work from the center outward Think of the dough as being divided into four quadrants. If you roll out each quadrant with equal pressure, rotating the dough a quarter turn after each roll, you will end up with a fairly round piece of dough. Many people make the mistake of random rolling, which almost guarantees that you will end up with a piece of dough that looks like the state of Florida.

For an evenly thick round of dough, start with a thick disk of dough on a lightly floured work surface. Dust the top of the dough with flour. Place a heavy rolling pin at the center of the dough, then use even pressure to roll out the dough about 5 inches away from the center. Note that you are stretching the dough as much as you are pressing it. Turn the dough a quarter turn, being sure that the dough isn't sticking. (If the dough sticks at any time, slide a long thin knife under it to release it, then sprinkle more flour on the work surface.) Again starting at the center of the dough, roll out the second quadrant of the dough. Repeat a third and then a fourth time, and you should have a fairly round piece of dough about 10 inches in diameter. Using lighter pressure, repeat the rolling process, one quadrant at a time, rotating the dough after each roll, to reach the desired size and thickness.

Chocolate Cake with Rocky Road Frosting

My dad is the King of Rocky Road, and he makes pounds of the candy every year as holiday gifts. So when it is his birthday, the choice of cake is clear—chocolate layer with a marshmallow-and-walnut-studded frosting. I doubt if you will ever find a better and easier chocolate cake recipe. The cake makes very tender layers, so take care when transferring and frosting them.

Makes 8 to 10 servings

4 ounces unsweetened chocolate, chopped

1 cup plain low-fat yogurt, at room temperature

1 teaspoon vanilla extract

2 cups cake flour

2 cups sugar

8 tablespoons (1 stick) unsalted butter, thinly sliced,
    at room temperature

2 large eggs, at room temperature

1 teaspoon baking soda

½ teaspoon baking powder

½ teaspoon salt

Chocolate Buttercream Frosting (page 316)

1 cup mini marshmallows

¾ cup coarsely chopped walnuts

1. Position a rack in the center of the oven and preheat to 350°F. Butter two 9 x 1½-inch round cake pans. Line the bottoms of the pans with rounds of wax paper. Dust the sides of the pans with flour and tap out the excess flour.

2. To make the cake, in the top part of a double boiler over hot, not simmering, water, melt the chocolate. Remove from the heat and let cool until tepid.

3. In a 2-cup glass measure, whisk the yogurt with enough water (about ⅔ cup) to measure 1½ cups. Add the vanilla. In a medium bowl, whisk the flour, sugar, butter, eggs, baking soda, baking powder, and salt to combine. (Because of the special mixing method, sifting the dry ingredients together is optional.) Add the yogurt mixture and the cooled chocolate. The butter will still be in pieces at this point, but it will smooth out during mixing. Using a handheld electric hand mixer, mix on low speed for 30 seconds, scraping the bowl often. Increase the speed to high and mix, scraping often, for 3 minutes to make a very smooth batter. Spread the batter evenly in the pans.

(continued)

4. Bake until a toothpick inserted in the centers of the cakes comes out clean, about 35 minutes. Transfer to wire cake racks and let cool for 10 minutes. Run a knife around the insides of the pans to release the cakes. Invert onto wire racks and remove the pans and wax paper. Turn the layers right side up and let cool completely.

5. Place a dab of the frosting in the center of a cake platter. This will help "glue" the layer onto the plate. Place one cake layer flat side up on the cake platter. Spread with about 1/2 cup frosting. Top with second cake layer, rounded side up. Spread the remaining frosting over the top and sides of the cake.

6. Mix the marshmallows and walnuts in a medium bowl. Working over a jelly-roll pan, press handfuls of the mixture onto the sides of the cake; scoop up the marshmallows and walnuts that fall onto the platter and pan to repeat the procedure until the cake is decorated. (The cake can be prepared up to 1 day ahead. Store, tightly covered in a cake holder or under an inverted bowl, at room temperature—refrigeration could soften the marshmallows.)

Grandma Perry's Plum Cake

My maternal grandmother, who was born in Liechtenstein, wasn't much of a baker—it seems that she preferred not to compete with her sisters, who were world-class pastry makers. But every autumn she would make a wonderful cake with Italian prune plums that garnered praise from the entire family. When she passed away, the plum cake recipe went with her, for, like many home cooks, she never wrote down a recipe. While I was researching Kaffeehaus, my book on Austro-Hungarian desserts, my friend Gerda Hauser made an apricot cake with a batter that was remarkably like Grandma's plum cake. I learned that this batter is one that most German-speaking cooks know by heart, and would have been Grandma's choice for her plum cake. So, when you see Italian plums in the market in the late summer, think of them not as a sign that the weather will soon be turning cool but as an excuse to make plum cake!

Makes 12 servings

1⅓ cups all-purpose flour

1½ teaspoons baking powder

¼ teaspoon salt

14 tablespoons (1¾ sticks) unsalted butter, at room temperature

1 cup plus 1 tablespoon sugar, divided

4 large eggs, at room temperature

½ teaspoon vanilla extract

12 ripe smallish Italian prune plums cut lengthwise in half, and pitted (about 12 ounces)

¼ teaspoon ground cinnamon

Confectioners' sugar for garnish

1. Position a rack in the center of the oven and preheat to 350°F. Butter and flour a 9 x 13-inch baking pan, and tap out the excess flour.

2. Sift the flour, baking powder, and salt together.

3. Beat the butter and 1 cup of the sugar in a medium bowl with a handheld electric mixer on high speed until light in color and texture, about 3 minutes. One at a time, beat in the eggs, then beat in the vanilla. On low speed, add the flour mixture in two additions and beat just until smooth, scraping down the bowl as needed. Spread the batter evenly in the pan. Arrange 4 rows of 6 plum

halves each on the batter. Combine the remaining 1 tablespoon sugar with the cinnamon, and sprinkle over the plums.

4. Bake until a toothpick inserted in the center of the cake (not into a plum) comes out clean, about 30 minutes. Let cool completely in the pan on a wire cake rack.

5. To serve, sift confectioners' sugar over the cake and cut into rectangles.

Plums

The array of plums that appears from late summer through autumn can be confusing. While all are tasty in their own way, only one variety is recommended for this cake, the dark purple Italian prune plum. These plums often have a dull blush, which is no reflection on quality. The size will vary from small (about 1 ounce each) to quite large. If your plums are larger than the ones I used to bake my plum cake, just use enough halved and pitted plums to cover the cake batter comfortably.

To pit plums, you must cut the fruit in the right place. Each plum has a vertical indentation, which indicates the placement of the pit. If you cut along the indentation, which would seem logical, the pit will not loosen. Instead, cut at right angles to the indentation: hold the plum so the center of the indentation is at 9 o'clock, and make the cut vertically from 12 to 6 o'clock, and continue around the entire circumference of the fruit. Twist the two halves apart, and the pit will be easy to remove.

Old-Fashioned Yellow Cake with Easy Orange Buttercream Frosting

Everyone deserves a home-baked cake for his or her birthday. If the guest of honor likes yellow cake with buttercream frosting, this is the cake to make. The cake has a dense texture that I love, but if you prefer a lighter cake, separate the eggs and beat the egg whites just until they form stiff peaks. Beat the yolks into the creamed butter-sugar mixture, then add the flour mixture and milk, and fold in the whites at the end.

Makes 8 to 12 servings

2 cups all-purpose flour

2 teaspoons baking powder

$1/4$ teaspoon salt

$1/2$ pound plus 4 tablespoons ($2^1/2$ sticks) unsalted butter, at room temperature

$1^1/2$ cups sugar

6 large eggs, at room temperature

$1^1/2$ teaspoons vanilla extract

$1/3$ cup milk

Orange Buttercream Frosting (page 316)

1. Position a rack in the center of the oven and preheat to 350°F. Lightly butter two 9 x $1^1/2$-inch round cake pans. Line the bottoms of the pans with rounds of wax paper. Dust the sides of the pans with flour and tap out the excess flour.

2. To make the cake, sift the flour, baking powder, and salt together.

3. Beat the butter and sugar in a medium bowl with a handheld mixer on high speed until very light and fluffy, about 5 minutes. One at a time, beat in the eggs, being sure each egg is incorporated before adding another, then add the vanilla. On low speed, add the flour, in two additions, scraping the bowl with a rubber spatula and beating just until the batter is smooth. Beat in the milk. Spread the batter evenly in the pans.

4. Bake until the cakes spring back when pressed in the centers, about 25 minutes. Let cool in the pans on a wire cake rack for 10 minutes. Invert onto a wire rack to unmold, and remove the paper. Turn the layers right side up on the rack and let cool completely.

(continued)

5. Place a dab of the frosting in the center of a serving platter. This will help "glue" the layer onto the plate. Place one cake layer, flat side up, on the platter. Spread with $1/2$ cup of the frosting. Top with the second cake layer, rounded side up. Spread the remaining frosting on the top and sides of the cake. Refrigerate until the frosting is set, about 30 minutes. Loosely cover once frosting is set. (The cake can be prepared up to 1 day ahead, and kept loosely covered with plastic wrap, refrigerated. Let stand at room temperature for 1 hour before serving.)

Frosting Cakes

Frosting a cake is an opportunity to express yourself. Are you the kind of baker who likes a smooth, slick top on your cake, or do you go in for casual but chic swirls?

A flexible metal icing spatula, preferably an offset model, is the only tool for spreading frosting efficiently—don't try to use a regular knife or rubber spatula. First, dab a couple of tablespoons of the frosting in the center of the serving platter. Center one cake layer on the platter, flat side up. The frosting will help "glue" the layer onto the plate. To protect the platter from the frosting and to give the cake a clean, finished appearance, slip three or four strips of wax paper just under the edge of the cake around its circumference.

Elevate the platter to provide a better height for frosting: passionate home bakers own a cake decorating stand, but any tall, stable object with a flat top will do. I use either a large coffee can or an overturned wide-bottomed bowl. Place the platter on the stand of your choice.

Slather about $1/2$ cup of the frosting onto the cake layer, and spread it as smooth as possible. Place the second layer on top, rounded side up. Slather a generous $1/2$ cup of frosting over the top, spreading it to the edges. Don't worry about making it perfect at this point. Using the tip of the spatula, apply large gobs of frosting to the sides of the cake, smoothing each application into a thin coat and turning the cake as needed, until the sides are frosted. Now spread the top frosting evenly to meet the sides. There will be a ridge where the top and sides meet. For a smooth look, working around the circumference of the top of the cake, use the spatula to sweep the ridge toward the top center of the cake to smooth it out. Or, for an old-fashioned look, swirl and lift the frosting into peaks. Remove the strips of wax paper.

Refrigerate the cake for at least 30 minutes to set the frosting. Always serve frosted cake at room temperature, as cold temperatures harden the butter in the cake and frosting and make for chilly, unpleasant eating.

Mrs. E's Incredible Buttercream Frosting

Instead of burying this frosting in a cake recipe, I am making it free-standing so the bakers in the group can find it and use it whenever they please. This excellent buttercream is from my friend and sous-chef Stephen Evasew's late mom, and it is absolutely ingenious. Many buttercream recipes start with a difficult Italian meringue, but Mrs. Evasew simply beat Marshmallow Fluff into creamed butter. I may never make a classic buttercream again!

Makes about 3¹/₂ cups (enough for a double-layer cake)

³/₄ pound (3 sticks) unsalted butter, at room temperature

One 7¹/₂-ounce jar Marshmallow Fluff, or use a 7-ounce
      jar of marshmallow cream (see Note)

¹/₂ teaspoon vanilla extract

Beat the butter in a medium bowl with a handheld electric mixer on high speed until completely smooth, about 1 minute. In four or five additions, gradually beat in the Fluff. Beat in the vanilla. Use immediately.

Note: While Yankee cooks swear that Fluff is in a class by itself, I have made this frosting with other brands of marshmallow cream. If your supermarket doesn't carry Marshmallow Fluff and you want to try the real thing, it can be mail-ordered from www.marshmallowfluff.com.

Chocolate Buttercream Frosting

Beat 3 ounces melted and cooled unsweetened chocolate into the frosting.

Orange Buttercream Frosting

Add the grated zest of 1 large orange to the frosting.

Lemon or Lime Buttercream Frosting

Add the zest of 1 large lemon or 2 limes to the frosting.

Banana-Blueberry Coffee Cake

For years, I searched for the perfect banana bread and was often disappointed in the quest. Finally, I came up with this for the moistest, most banana-y coffee cake around. Many recipes use shortening, and while it is easier to use than butter (no softening required), the latter wins hands-down in the flavor department. Pecans and streusel also lift the cake out of the ordinary. I sent this cake to a friend's office for a taste test, and the consensus was that it was the best banana bread they had ever eaten. The search has ended.

Makes 12 servings

Dried bread crumbs for the pan

2½ cups all-purpose flour

2 teaspoons baking soda

1 teaspoon salt

½ pound (2 sticks) unsalted butter, at room temperature, plus more for the pan

2 cups granulated sugar

4 large eggs, at room temperature

2 cups mashed bananas (about 6 large ripe bananas; see Note)

1 cup fresh or unthawed frozen blueberries

⅔ cup (about 2½ ounces) coarsely chopped pecans

Streusel

⅔ cup all-purpose flour

⅓ cup packed light brown sugar

5 tablespoons unsalted butter, at room temperature

1. Position a rack in the center of the oven and preheat to 350°F. Lightly butter a 12-cup fluted tube (Bundt) pan and coat the inside with bread crumbs, tapping out the excess crumbs.

2. Sift the flour, baking soda, and salt to combine. (If the baking soda is at all lumpy, sift the dry ingredients through a wire sieve.)

3. Beat the butter and sugar in a large mixing bowl using a handheld electric mixer on high speed until light in color and texture, about 3 minutes. One at a time, beat in the eggs. Beat in the bananas. In two additions, stir in the flour mixture and mix just until smooth. Mix in the blueberries and nuts.

4. To make the streusel, mix the flour, brown sugar, and butter in a small bowl

with your hands until combined. Spread half of the batter in the pan. Crumble half of the streusel over the batter. Spread the remaining batter in the pan, and top with the remaining streusel.

5. Bake until a toothpick inserted in the center of the cake comes out clean, 55 minutes to 1 hour. Cool on a wire cake rack for 10 minutes, then invert the cake onto the rack to cool completely.

Note: Be sure that the bananas are soft-ripe, with well-speckled skins. Do not use overripe, blackened bananas, which have an off flavor.

Perfect Fluted Tube Cakes

Mention a Bundt cake, and most Americans know just what you're talking about. Bundt is a trademark of Nordic Ware, which introduced the pans in 1950. In only a decade, the Bundt pan became the most popular cake pan in the United States. According to Nordic Ware, there are more than forty-five million Bundt pans in use at this time.

The Bundt is a domestic variation of the European *guglehupf* mold, a decorative pan with a center tube used to bake the famous yeast cake. Although today most domestic tube pans (including the Bundt) are nonstick, European ones are uncoated. Regardless of the interior surface, it is a good idea to guard against sticking with a coating of soft butter and dried bread crumbs. Crumbs work better than flour because they actually form a barrier between the batter and the pan. Use a pastry brush or paper towel to apply a very thin, even coating of soft butter to the inside of the pan. Sprinkle a couple of tablespoons of dried bread crumbs into the pan, turning to coat the buttered surfaces, then invert the pan and tap out the excess crumbs.

Heavy black nonstick cake pans absorb and retain oven heat (a shiny surface reflects the heat) and can cause the outer crust to overbake. If using one of these pans, place it in the preheated oven, then reduce the temperature by 25°F. The cake may bake to doneness in slightly less time than the recipe indicates.

Cinnamon Crumb Cake

I had never seen a crumb cake until I moved to the East Coast. But to a New Yorker, it is the ultimate coffee cake, just the thing for morning coffee or an afternoon snack. As a streusel fan myself, I fell in love immediately with the topping—a thick layer of cinnamon-scented crumbs. One day, my friend Joe Arena shared his late Aunt Margaret's recipe book with me, and there was a terrific crumb cake in her files, which I am happy to share with you.

Makes 8 servings

Cake

1¼ cups all-purpose flour

2 teaspoons baking powder

⅛ teaspoon salt

½ cup milk

½ teaspoon vanilla extract

4 tablespoons (½ stick) unsalted butter

¾ cup granulated sugar

1 large egg, at room temperature

Crumb Topping

1½ cups all-purpose flour

12 tablespoons (1½ sticks) unsalted butter, at room temperature

½ cup packed light brown sugar

¼ cup granulated sugar

2 teaspoons ground cinnamon

1. Position a rack in the center of the oven and preheat to 350°F. Lightly butter and flour a 9-inch springform pan; tap out the excess flour.

2. To make the cake, sift the flour, baking powder, and salt. Mix the milk and vanilla together in a glass measuring cup.

3. Beat the butter and sugar in a medium bowl with a handheld electric mixer at high speed until the mixture is light in color (it will look gritty, not fluffy), about 3 minutes. Beat in the egg until it is completely incorporated. In three additions, add the flour mixture, alternating with two equal additions of the milk mixture, beating after each addition until the batter is smooth. Scrape the batter into the pan and smooth the top.

4. To make the crumb topping, combine the flour, butter, brown sugar, granulated sugar, and cinnamon in a medium bowl. Using your hands, squeeze the

ingredients together until they form a soft dough. Crumble the dough in pea-size chunks evenly over the batter.

5. Bake until the topping is firm and a toothpick inserted in the center of the cake comes out clean, about 40 minutes. Cool the cake in the pan on a wire cake rack.

6. To serve, remove the sides of the pan and slice into wedges.

Dulce de Leche Ice Cream Pie with Mocha Fudge Sauce

Dulce de leche, condensed milk cooked until the natural sugars caramelize, is usually served by Latin American cooks as a sweet sauce. A few years ago, as yet another example of the globalization of cuisines, it became an all-American ice cream flavor. This ice cream pie uses it to great effect, layered in a vanilla crumb crust with the same fudge sauce used for serving. This recipe has more steps than others in the book, but it is very easy and the results are great.

Makes 8 servings

Crust

1/3 cup chopped pecans

2 tablespoons granulated sugar

2/3 cup vanilla wafer crumbs

1/2 teaspoon ground cinnamon

2 tablespoons unsalted butter, melted

Fudge Sauce

1 cup granulated sugar

2 tablespoons unsweetened cocoa powder

1 cup heavy cream

1/4 cup light corn syrup

1 tablespoon instant espresso powder, dissolved in 2
   tablespoons boiling water

2 ounces unsweetened chocolate, finely chopped

2 tablespoons unsalted butter

1 teaspoon vanilla extract

Filling

2 pints dulce de leche caramel or caramel-swirl ice cream,
   divided

1/2 cup heavy cream

1 tablespoon confectioners' sugar

1/2 teaspoon vanilla extract

2 tablespoons finely chopped pecans, for garnish

1. Position a rack in the center of the oven and preheat to 350°F. Lightly butter a 9-inch pie pan.

2. To make the crust, process the pecans and sugar in a food processor until the pecans are ground into a powder. Add the crumbs and cinnamon and pulse to combine. Add the butter and process until the mixture is evenly moistened. Press evenly into the pie pan.

3. Bake until the crust looks set and the crumbs are very lightly toasted, about 10 minutes. Let cool completely.

4. To make the sauce, whisk the sugar and cocoa together in a medium heavy-bottomed saucepan. Whisk in the cream, syrup, and dissolved espresso. Add the chocolate and butter. Bring to a boil over high heat, stirring constantly. Reduce the heat to medium and cook, stirring occasionally, until lightly thickened, about 4 minutes. Stir in the vanilla. Transfer to a bowl and let cool until tepid but pourable, about 30 minutes.

5. Soften 1 pint of the ice cream at room temperature, and spread evenly in the cooled shell. Drizzle 3 tablespoons of the sauce over the ice cream. Freeze until the sauce sets, about 10 minutes.

6. Soften the remaining 1 pint ice cream. Spread evenly in the pie shell and drizzle with 3 tablespoons of the sauce. Freeze the pie, uncovered, until the ice cream is firm, about 10 minutes, then cover with plastic wrap and freeze until solid, at least 4 hours, or overnight. Cover and refrigerate the remaining sauce. (The pie and sauce can be made up to 1 day ahead.)

7. When ready to serve, reheat the sauce in a small saucepan over low heat, stirring often; keep warm. Whip the cream, confectioners' sugar, and vanilla in a chilled medium bowl with an electric mixer until stiff. If you have a pastry bag, fit it with a 1/2-inch open star tip, fill with the whipped cream, and pipe rosettes around the edge of the pie; sprinkle with the pecans. Lacking a bag, spread the whipped cream over the top of the pie, and sprinkle with the nuts. Cut the pie into wedges and serve with the warm sauce.

Instant Espresso Powder

To add a dark-roasted coffee jolt to desserts, use instant espresso powder dissolved in a small amount of boiling water. This intensely flavored powder (which isn't very useful as a beverage) can be found at Italian delicatessens and many supermarkets. It keeps forever in a cool, dark cupboard. In a pinch, use regular instant coffee.

Peanut Butter and Jelly Pie

Here's a dessert that celebrates one of the happiest culinary marriages in history, peanut butter and jelly. It is a towering pie that will make you think back to your childhood—not just because of the flavors, but to recall a time when calories were of no concern. Actually, fruit-sweetened spread, thicker and less sweet than sugar-sweetened jam or preserves, works best here. But Peanut Butter and Fruit-Sweetened Fruit Spread Pie sounds a little clinical, and I hope you'll forgive the discrepancy. Once you taste this dessert, you'll forgive me anything.

Makes 8 servings

Crust

1 cup graham cracker crumbs (crushed in a food
processor or blender)

$1/4$ cup granulated sugar

4 tablespoons ($1/2$ stick) unsalted butter, melted

One 10-ounce jar ($3/4$ cup) fruit-sweetened raspberry or
strawberry fruit spread

Peanut Butter Filling

$3/4$ cup plus 2 tablespoons heavy cream, divided

12 ounces cream cheese, at room temperature

$3/4$ cup plus 2 tablespoons creamy peanut butter

1 cup confectioners' sugar

$1/4$ cup finely chopped unsalted peanuts, for garnish

1. Position a rack in the center of the oven and preheat to 350°F.

2. To make the crust, mix the crumbs, sugar, and butter in a medium bowl until well combined. Press firmly and evenly into an ungreased 9-inch pie pan. Bake until the crust is set and barely beginning to brown, 10 to 12 minutes. Let cool completely on a wire cake rack.

3. Spread the preserves over the bottom of the crust. Freeze until the preserves are a bit firmer, about 20 minutes.

4. To make the filling, whip $3/4$ cup of the heavy cream in a chilled medium bowl with a handheld electric mixer on high speed until stiff. Beat the cream cheese, peanut butter, and the remaining 2 tablespoons heavy cream in a large bowl with the mixer on medium speed until smooth and fluffy. On low speed, gradually beat in the confectioners' sugar. Fold in the whipped cream with a rubber spatula.

5. Spoon the filling into the crust, using the spatula to smooth the filling into a dome. Refrigerate, uncovered, until the filling is chilled and set, at least 3 hours. (The pie can be made up to 1 day ahead; once the filling is set, loosely cover the pie with plastic wrap, and keep refrigerated.)

6. Just before serving, press the chopped peanuts onto the filling around the edge of the pie. Serve chilled.

Oatmeal and Chocolate Chip Blondies

I like thick and chewy butterscotch blondies even better than brownies. And these have oatmeal and chocolate chips in them, giving another couple of old favorites, oatmeal and chocolate chip cookies, a run for their money. To avoid having to dig the blondies out of the pan, use my technique for lining the pan with foil—then the cookies can be lifted out in one piece and cut without waste. For a simple icing, sprinkle 1 cup chocolate or butterscotch chips over the hot blondies when they come out of the oven. Let stand for 5 minutes, then spread the melted chips in a thin layer. When cooled, the chips will harden into an icing.

Makes 12 blondies

2¹/₂ cups all-purpose flour

1 cup old-fashioned or quick-cooking (not instant) rolled
   oats, divided

1 teaspoon baking powder

¹/₂ teaspoon salt

¹/₂ pound (2 sticks) unsalted butter, at room temperature

1³/₄ cups packed light brown sugar

2 large eggs, at room temperature

2 teaspoons vanilla extract

1 cup (6 ounces) semisweet chocolate chips

1 cup (4 ounces) coarsely chopped pecans

1. Position a rack in the center of the oven and preheat the oven to 350°F. Line the bottom of a 11 x 8¹/₂-inch baking pan with a 14-inch length of aluminum foil (nonstick or regular), pleating the foil lengthwise to make an 8-inch-wide strip. Fold the foil hanging over the two ends to make "handles."

2. Combine the flour and ¹/₂ cup of the oats in a food processor and process the oats into a powder. Add the baking powder and salt and pulse to combine. Remove the blade and stir in the remaining ¹/₂ cup oats.

3. Beat the butter in a large bowl with a handheld electric mixer on high speed until smooth, about 1 minute. Add the brown sugar and beat until the mixture is light in color and texture, scraping down the bowl often, about 3 minutes. One at a time, beat in the eggs until thoroughly incorporated, then beat in the vanilla.

Stir in the flour mixture just until combined. Stir in the chocolate chips and pecans. Spread the batter evenly in the pan.

4. Bake the blondies until the top is golden brown and a wooden toothpick inserted in the center comes out clean, about 40 minutes. Transfer to a wire cake rack and let cool completely.

5. Lift up the foil handles to remove the blondies from the pan in one piece. Peel off and discard the foil. Cut into 12 bars. (The blondies can be stored airtight at room temperature for up to 3 days.)

Orange Shortbread Bars

Lemon bars are sneaking up on chocolate chip as America's favorite cookie. Many recipes for lemon bars require making a nerve-racking lemon curd (cook for one second too long, and you have scrambled lemon curd), and I prefer recipes with a simple baked-in filling. These orange-flavored bars are a welcome change from the lemon version. Lining the pan with aluminum foil helps you remove the cookies without crumbling, but even when well-buttered, the foil can be stubborn when it comes time to remove it. I strongly recommend nonstick aluminum foil, a new product that has many uses but seems to have been invented specifically to take care of culinary dilemmas like this one.

Makes 9 bars

Crust

1 cup all-purpose flour

8 tablespoons (1 stick) unsalted butter, at room
    temperature

1/4 cup confectioners' sugar

Orange Filling

3 large eggs, at room temperature

1 cup granulated sugar

1/3 cup thawed frozen orange juice concentrate

Grated zest of 1 large orange or 1/2 teaspoon orange oil
    (see Note)

3/4 teaspoon baking powder

1/4 teaspoon salt

Confectioners' sugar for garnish

1. Position a rack in the center of the oven and preheat to 350°F. Lightly butter an 8-inch-square baking pan. Pleat a 14-inch-long piece of nonstick aluminum foil (or use regular aluminum foil) lengthwise to make an 8-inch-wide strip. Fit into the pan, letting the excess hang over the ends to act as "handles." If using regular foil, butter it well. Dust the buttered sides of the pan with flour and tap out the excess flour.

2. To make the crust, combine the flour, butter, and confectioners' sugar in a medium bowl, and beat with a handheld electric mixer on low speed until the dough is well combined and starts to clump together. Pour into the pan. Press the dough firmly and evenly into the bottom and about 1/4 inch up the sides of

the pan. Bake until the dough is set and lightly browned around the edges, about 18 minutes.

3. To make the filling, whisk the eggs, sugar, orange juice concentrate, orange zest, baking powder, and salt in a medium bowl until well combined. Pour into the hot crust, return to the oven, and bake until the filling is evenly risen and deep golden brown, about 25 minutes. Let cool completely in the pan on a wire cake rack.

4. Sift confectioners' sugar over the top of the pastry. Run a sharp knife along the two sides of the pastry touching the sides of the pan to release it. Lift up the foil handles to remove the pastry in one piece. Using a sharp knife dipped into hot water, cut the pastry into 9 bars. (The bars can be stored in an airtight container, refrigerated, for up to 3 days.)

Note: Orange oil, made especially for cooking, has a much more aromatic flavor than orange extract. It is available at specialty markets.

Chocolate Orange Bars

Substitute 1/4 cup unsweetened cocoa powder for 1/4 cup of the flour.

Black Forest Chocolate Pudding

If there is such a thing as chocolate pudding for grown-ups, this is it. When I go to a chocolate shop, I never agonize over my choice, I just go right for the chocolate-covered cherries. So it was a pleasure to create this recipe with the same flavors. This is one of my favorite ways to use a high-cacao-content (70 percent) bittersweet chocolate—the nuances of the chocolate can be appreciated in such an uncluttered setting. For a kid-friendly version, omit the soaked cherries and their kirsch, and substitute semisweet chocolate for the bittersweet. And if you happen to like pudding "skin," don't cover the puddings during chilling.

Makes 4 servings

1/3 cup dried sweet cherries

3 tablespoons kirsch, brandy, or cognac

2 cups milk, divided

1/2 cup sugar

2 tablespoons cornstarch

2 large egg yolks

4 ounces bittersweet chocolate, finely chopped

2 tablespoons unsalted butter, cut into bits

1 teaspoon vanilla extract

Sweetened whipped cream (see Note) for serving

1. Heat the cherries and kirsch in a small saucepan over low heat just to warm the kirsch. (Or combine in a small bowl, cover with plastic wrap, and microwave on High for 20 seconds.) Let cool.

2. Pour 1 1/2 cups of the milk into a medium heavy-bottomed saucepan and add the sugar. Sprinkle the cornstarch over the remaining 1/2 cup milk in a small bowl and whisk to dissolve. Whisk into the saucepan. Bring the milk to a boil over medium heat, whisking constantly.

3. Meanwhile, whisk the yolks in a medium bowl. Whisk in about half of the thickened milk mixture, then return the yolk mixture to the saucepan. Bring to a boil, whisking constantly, then reduce the heat to low and cook at a low boil for 30 seconds. Remove from the heat. Add the chocolate, the cherries and kirsch, the butter, and vanilla and let stand for 1 minute, then whisk to melt the chocolate.

4. Transfer the pudding to four 6-ounce ramekins or custard cups. Cover with

plastic wrap, pressing the wrap directly onto the surface of the puddings. Using the tip of a sharp knife, poke a few holes in each piece of wrap. Let cool for 1 hour, then refrigerate until chilled, at least 4 hours. (The puddings can be made up to 1 day ahead.)

5. Serve chilled, with a dollop of whipped cream on each pudding.

Note: To whip cream, place 1 cup chilled heavy cream in a chilled medium bowl, preferably stainless steel. Add 2 tablespoons confectioners' sugar and $1/2$ teaspoon vanilla extract. Using a handheld electric mixer on high speed, whip the cream until it forms soft peaks. Cover and refrigerate until ready to serve.

The New Chocolate

Life was so simple when the only chocolates available to the baker were unsweetened and semisweet. Now a trip to the chocolate section of an upscale supermarket reveals a confusing array of bars from exotic tropical places with equally odd numbers indicating the cacao-content percentage. While it is fun to know the origin of the chocolate bar and the variety of bean used, most of this information only serves to disorient the average consumer. But it is very helpful, if not imperative, to know what those numbers mean.

Cacao means the unsweetened cacao bean. All of the ingredients listed on any chocolate bar label, of course, add up to 100 percent, so a high percentage of ground cacao beans means less sugar has been added. Thus, the higher the cacao content, the stronger the true chocolate flavor. Most popular supermarket brands, such as Lindt Excellence, Baker's Bittersweet, and Callebaut Bittersweet, average 55 to 60 percent cacao, and they are what I usually use. In some cases, in fact, if a high cacao-content chocolate is substituted, a recipe may not work. This is especially true of ganache, the combination of heavy cream and melted chocolate used as a frosting and truffle filling, and in many baked goods. So unbaked recipes, such as Black Forest Chocolate Pudding (above), are a good way to show off the flavor of a high-cacao chocolate with minimal risk.

Just keep all of this in mind the next time you are faced with a huge selection of chocolate. A higher price may mean a richer chocolate flavor, but not necessarily a successful dessert. And if the chocolate comes with a list of instructions on how to adjust your recipes, follow the suggestions.

Buttery Pastry Dough

I learned this exceptional all-purpose pastry dough from my friend Carolyn Beth Weil when we worked together on a baking book with recipes from the best bakers in California. The high proportion of butter to flour creates a buttery, flaky crust that is as versatile as it is delicious. I also appreciate this dough for its easy-to-remember proportions: 1 cup flour, 1 stick butter, 2 tablespoons sugar, a bit of salt, and some ice water equals a great pie or tart crust. Better yet, when used for a tart, it doesn't have to be rolled out—it can just be pressed into the pan. Finally, unlike pastry doughs that require a chilling period before use, this one can be used immediately after making. Do you need any more recommendations?

Makes enough for a 9- to 10-inch single pie or tart crust

1 cup unbleached all-purpose flour

2 tablespoons sugar

½ teaspoon salt

8 tablespoons (1 stick) chilled unsalted butter, cut into very thin slices

3 tablespoons ice water, or as needed

1. Pulse the flour, sugar, and salt in a food processor to combine. Add the butter and pulse until the mixture resembles coarse cornmeal with some lentil-size pieces. Transfer to a medium bowl. (Or mix the flour, sugar, and salt in a medium bowl. Using a pastry blender, cut the butter in.) Gradually stir in enough of the water so the dough clumps together. Gather up the dough and press it into a thick disk. You can use the dough immediately. (If desired, wrap the dough in plastic wrap and refrigerate for up to 1 day. Let the chilled dough stand at room temperature to soften slightly before rolling out.)

Small-Batch Buttery Pastry Dough

Use ¾ cup flour, 1 tablespoon sugar, ¼ teaspoon salt, 6 tablespoons (¾ stick) butter, and about 2 tablespoons ice water.

Index

Acorn squash. *See* Squash

Aïoli, chive, potato and pea salad with, 58

Almonds
blueberry-almond tart, 292–94
peach-almond crisp, 299

Apple(s)
glaze, baby carrots with, 260
-horseradish sauce, Viennese pot roast with, 108–9
and nutmeg custard crostata, 289
–poppy seed dressing, coleslaw with, 47
veal scaloppine with cider-balsamic vinegar sauce and, 130–31

Apricots, spiced, lamb chops with garbanzos and, 128

Arugula
arugula, grapefruit, and peanut salad with honey-yogurt dressing, 44
farfalle with sausage, garlic, and, 196–97
flank steak and, with warm balsamic vinaigrette, 94–95

Asian pears, spinach salad with goat cheese and, 60

Asparagus
crab Louis with sun-dried tomato dressing, 51
fettuccine with ricotta and, 198–99
with gremolata butter, 255
and potato salad, 58

Avocado
black bean salad with red pepper and, 46

chipotle guacamole and bacon sandwich, 76

Bacon
and chipotle guacamole sandwich, 76
grilled Cheddar, tomato, and bacon sandwich, 78

Balsamic vinaigrette, warm, flank steak and arugula with, 94–95

Balsamic vinegar, 11
–cider sauce, veal scaloppine with apples and, 130–31

Banana-blueberry coffee cake, 317–18

Basil
basil ricotta, wide noodles with meat sauce and, 200
Italian fried rice, with shrimp, pancetta, and, 221–22
pesto, 268

Bass, porcini-crusted, on spinach and cremini, 178–79

Beans, 64. *See also* Garbanzo(s)
black: and chorizo soup, sherried, 25; salad with avocado and red pepper, 46
and escarole soup, Tuscan, 26
green: salad with grape tomatoes and olive vinaigrette, 56; Southwestern, 263
pink, vegetable chili with corn and, 232, 232–34

Beef, 92–110
brisket, with beer-smothered onions, 110

hamburgers with roast pepper catsup, 82–83
short ribs: borscht with dilled sour cream, 23–24; pasta sauce, 107; Provençale, 104–6
soups: Chinese beef, bok choy, and noodle, 20–21; Korean beef and root vegetable, 22
steak: bistro skirt steak sandwich on sourdough toast, 86–87; filet mignon au poivre with bourbon-shallot sauce, 92–93; flank steak and arugula with warm balsamic vinaigrette, 94–95; porterhouse with vermouth-glazed onions, 96–98
and vegetables: Italian stir-fry, 99–100; roast, with Moroccan spices, 102–3
Viennese pot roast with apple-horseradish sauce, 108–9

Beer
-smothered onions, beef brisket with, 110
turkey and beer gumbo, 34–35

Beets, short ribs borscht with dilled sour cream, 23–24

Berries, Earl Grey granita with, 296

Biscuits, fluffy drop, 280–82

Black beans. *See* Beans

Blackberry pie sundaes, warm, 291

Black Forest chocolate pudding, 330–31